GENIUS DENIED

THE LIFE AND DEATH OF MAX EWING

Wallace K. Ewing, Ph.D.

First published under the title *From Pioneer to Fame and Back: The Selected Correspondence of Max Ewing.*

Expanded and retitled in 2012.

Published by Wallace K. Ewing
Grand Haven, Michigan
Copyright January 2003
Revised and reprinted July 2012

No part of this book may be reproduced in any manner whatsoever, without written permission from the author, except in the case of brief quotations embedded in critical articles and reviews.

ISBN-9781-4675-3444-4

Table of Contents

Foreword 7
Author's Note 11
1. Pioneer 13
2. Europe 25
3. New York 34
4. Hollywood 171
5. Home Again 258
Appendix A: Fragments of Undated Correspondence 327
Appendix B: Allusions to People, Places, and Miscellaneous Items ..345
Appendix C: Yale University Max Ewing Collection 387

Max and I share ancestors whose remarkable lives created family legends that shaped our lives. We were fortunate to be bound by characters wise and adventuresome, people to reflect upon and learn from. For me, that includes Max.

Foreword

Max Ewing spent his first 17 years in Pioneer, Ohio, and he spent his last months in the same small town. His life was brief, and some would say tragic. At 31 he committed suicide by walking into a river in Binghamton, New York, leaving his clothes neatly folded on the bank. Pioneer, Ohio formed the parentheses of Max Ewing's life.

In the years between, Max traveled in a wide world that included New York, Paris, and Los Angeles. More important than the geographical places was Max's social nexus.

It is remarkable that Max knew so many people. He didn't have much money, beyond what his parents sent him. His apartment was small but big enough to host a Thursday salon. He was not a social climber in the usual sense of the expression. But in his brief life, Max managed to meet many of the most important people of High Bohemia.

His meetings and friendships say a great deal about the period, as well as Max's zeal for meeting people and encapsulating them in photographs, sculptures, and a novel.

Reading the diaries of his friend, Carl Van Vechten, for example, you understand that there were many social meetings every day: a lunch, a drink (during Prohibition time, a dinner, an after dinner gathering, a going up to Harlem, often ending at four a.m.). It was Carl Van Vechten who initiated Max's social connections.

From Max's letters to his parents, the reader sees his insatiable sociability. Max's letters were filled with people that were important at that time, some of them important now. Max liked to drop names in his letters, whether or not his parents would recognize them. Nevertheless, he did, and decades later we are grateful. Grateful that his mother saved them, grateful that his cousin, Doris Ewing, saved them, and that Carl Van Vechten arranged to put them at the Beinecke Library at Yale, so they could be read by succeeding generations. History is formed in odd ways.

Max Ewing knew an illustrious crowd of people of the Twenties and early Thirties. His friends included Carl Van Vechten, Muriel Draper, Alelia Walker, Adrian, Margaret Anderson, Jane Heap, Paul Robeson, e.e. cummings, and George Antheil. The list could on and on.

There were two "significant others" in his life. Both were women a generation older. One was his mother, Clara, and the other was Muriel Draper.

Van Vechten wrote to Muriel Draper: "In a strange way he was obviously in LOVE with you. All he wanted from you, however, was ALL your time, ALL your attention. I guess he would have given you as much in return, but never his inside, nor even the extremes of his outside."

"Muriel Draper is without any doubt the most stunning woman in America. She is in fact the only woman in the world who could wear what she does for the street. Muriel Draper is always at least five years in advance of everything. Poirier designed a gown for her five years ago, which she wore in Paris, and in next month's *Harpers Bazaar* it is going to be shown as the most advanced one ever encountered. To talk with her is to experience explosion. She has a mind that flies faster than lightning. What it takes most people ten years to know about you, she knows after an hour's conversation. She has the kind of a mind that could attend a 60-ring circus, and not miss a move of any muscle of any performer in all 60 rings. Nothing escapes her. Nothing will ever escape her. Muriel is magnificent because of what she drives other people to do. Well, she met us at the Ritz. The Queen of Sheba, the Shulamite, Marie Antoinette and the Empress Josephine would look like dishwashers beside her. It is only a woman like Draper, who has done everything, lived everywhere, known everyone, felt everything, seen, heard, studied, smelled, touched, faced, conquered everything, and still . . . ."

Max ardently played the notorious avant-garde piece, *Ballet Mechanique*, in its American premiere at Carnegie Hall in April, 1927, Max played with nine other pianos, eight xylophones, electric bells and an airplane propeller. Max played so hard that he damaged a nerve in his hand, ending the hope for a music career at the age of 24, and his finger was in pain.

After 1927, Max developed a writing and visual career. It was always connected to his social connections, which began with Carl Van Vechten and Muriel Draper, and then moved to Harlem and beyond.

What Max Ewing produced is not widely recognized now, although it had a brief moment of acclaim.

Max wrote a novel, *Going Somewhere*, published by the acclaimed Alfred Knopf. A roman à clef, it featured Muriel Draper as Aurora Overhaul and many others. It was widely and positively reviewed, but during one of the low points of the Depression the frivolity of the Twenties was no longer admired, and the book did not sell many copies.

Max Ewing exhibited "A Gallery of Extraordinary Portraits" in his large clothes closet. The gallery is a gay man's pantheon from the 1920s. It was modest—one cannot be grand in a clothes closet. For his Christmas gift, he asked his parents to pay for a small printed catalogue on good paper. They agreed. Henry McBride briefly reviewed "The Gallery of Extraordinary Portraits" in *The New York Sun*.

Max photographed his friends for "Carnival in Venice." He devised a project in which each of his friends appeared in front of a backdrop curtain of Venice, which he bought from Muriel Draper. Everyone appeared in costume—or lack of costume, for some appeared nude—as if they were at the Carnival of Venice. Max provided a few props, and the subjects enacted their personas. His photographs were shown in 1933 at the Julien Levy Gallery, widely known as the introducer of Surrealist painters, and one of the few galleries that exhibited photography. One could say "Carnival in Venice" was a forerunner of Andy Warhol's "Screen Tests" three decades later; that would be pretentious, but not entirely wrong. Max's photos allowed people to appear in their own fantasy, indifferently lighted and shot from the same perspective. What matters to us now is who those people who were captured by the camera: e.e. cummings, Paul Robeson, Taylor Gordon, Berenice Abbott, Lincoln Kirstein, George Platt Lynes, Julien Levy, Muriel Draper, Joe Gould, and, of course, Max Ewing. "Carnival in Venice" was also shown at the Waldorf-Astoria, and Max tried very hard to convince Clara, his mother, to come to New York, but without success.

The author of *Genius Denied* has collected dozens of the socially-populated letters that Max wrote to his parents, especially his mother. The letters and the author's accompanying narrative describe the High Bohemia of the 1920s in infinite detail. The letters also provide insight into Max's creativity, his bouts of euphoria and depression, and his friendship with Jack Pollock, the boxer.

Steven Watson
June 2012

[*Steve Watson is a cultural historian whose works include* The Harlem Renaissance, Strange Bedfellows, Prepare for Saints, The Birth of the Beat Generation, *and* Factory Made: Warhol and the Sixties. *Especially helpful in providing background for Max's life in New York City were* Harlem Renaissance *and* Prepare for Saints.]

Author's Note

Maxwell Anderson Ewing was the subject of whispered family conversation since at least 1934, and probably earlier. Usually his accomplishments as a pianist, composer, novelist, poet, sculptor, and photographer were overshadowed by his homosexuality and his unlikely friendship with a prize fighter named Jack Pollock. Max's suicide in 1934, just after celebrating his 31st birthday, adds drama and sadness to this remarkable man's mostly happy but short life. In his brief life span, Max mingled with dozens of artists, authors, composers, musicians, politicians, stage and movie stars, and wealthy families in Europe, New York, and Hollywood and he left at least a small mark on the literary and musical scenes in America. His only published novel, *Going Somewhere,* can be read today with the same quiet amusement and recognition of society's foibles as it was 80 years ago.

Max's artistic skills blossomed when he was still a young man, but a series of tragedies snipped the flower before it could fully mature. First came the death of his father, John Caleb Ewing, at the age of 65. Two years later, in 1934, his mother, Clara Barto Ewing, became mentally and emotionally unstable, and soon she passed on. Congruent with both these losses was the Great Depression, which caused financial difficulties for the family, aggravated Clara's decline, cut short the sales of Max's novel, and created a job shortage for almost everyone in the country, including Max. Like the protagonist in a Greek drama, he seemed immobilized by this series of events, unable to recover from the shocks, too stunned to act. At the same time he was eerily aware of his lethargy. Ironically, Max spent the last few months of his life in his small hometown of Pioneer, Ohio, the community he saw as provincial, meddling, and stifling. On June 16, 1934, two months after his mother's death, he drowned by walking into the Susquehanna River in Binghamton, New York.

Max's best moments and his worst moments—and much in between—are clearly revealed in his letters, written primarily between 1926 and 1934. Few of the letters are dated, although many of them include the day of the week in which they were written, and in a very few cases the envelopes—with postmarks—have survived. Where necessary, I used content to determine at least an approximate date of origin. Jack Pollock's letters to Max were especially difficult to place in chronological order.

Almost all of Max's letters and many of Jack's contain references to people and places that may be unfamiliar to today's readers. A list of these references, with a line or two of biographical data or explanatory material, is located in Appendix B. Unfortunately, no information was uncovered regarding a few of the people and they remain merely names.

The Yale University Beinecke Rare Book and Manuscript Library has a substantial collection of Max's correspondence and many of his manuscripts, typescripts, and diaries. His cousin, Doris Ewing, and a friend, Carl Van Vechten, started the collection and contributed most of the material. A list of the library's holdings can be found in Appendix C. I also am indebted to Steven Watson for sharing the results of his research about the era in general and Max in particular. His work has helped complete this sketch of Max's life.

Brackets [ ] show my insertions. Parentheses ( ) are retained when they appeared in the original correspondence. Also, I have made some format changes to the letters in order to enhance readability and consistency. For instance, each letter begins with a date, regardless of where it appeared in the original letter.

We are fortunate that Max's letters allow us to view his brief but fascinating life decades after that life came to an end.

       Wallace K. Ewing, Ph.D.
       July, 2012

1. Pioneer

On Friday, June 15, 1934 a family friend wrote the following letter to A.E. Ewing, Max Ewing's uncle and an attorney in Grand Rapids, Michigan. By the time A.E. received the letter, it was too late to act.

Dear Mr. Ewing:

I feel today, especially, that I would like to report to you—the nearest of kin—something of the situation in Pioneer. Really Mr. Ewing, Max is in very serious condition and it troubles me greatly that there is no one, vitally interested, to be near him to guide things a little. I appreciate how very difficult it all sounds, having been thru the experience, but nevertheless, I think it should be done now and could be.

I assume that you are familiar with the present arrangement, that his friend Jack the Prizefighter is here again, and that he and Max are in the house alone.

The friend seems like a kindly fellow, very, and I think honestly wants to be of help to Max but—there are objections to the plan and I would be greatly relieved if you, whose interests are at stake as well, could look the situation over.

I have hesitated to write you, for I so well remember the commotion of a few months ago when everyone seemed to be writing someone, but today I felt compelled to write. The whole situation is so pitiful. And I might add serious.

I shall not mention the fact that I have written to any one, and I am sure you will not, but I would be "eased" if at least some of the reins were in your hands.

I shall continue my interest in the case just as I have been doing, and will continue to do anything that I possibly can for Max, but he so pitifully needs a strong hand now for every reason.

Trusting that I have not overstepped the bounds in writing to you, and assuring you again of my "honest to goodness" interest and loyalty to all, I am

            Sincerely,
            Clara H. Sweet

That evening, about 5:30, Jack Pollock, "the Prizefighter," loaded Max and some luggage into the Ewings' 1926 Studebaker Big Six Custom Brougham and headed east on U.S. 20 bound for New York City. Their departure increased Clara Sweet's anxiety, and she decided to call A.E. that night rather than wait for him to get her letter. "He's in no condition to go anywhere," Clara told Max's uncle, "but Jack forced him to go. I know there's nothing you can do, but I just felt it important for you to know." Clara was a former resident of Pioneer, Ohio, and a close friend of Max Ewing's parents She now worked and lived in Toledo, but maintained her friendship through letters and occasional visits to her hometown.

Clara Barto Ewing, undated.

John Caleb Ewing married Clara Bartoe [Barto] in Pioneer on May 27, 1901. Clara was a few months short of her 30th birthday and John was 34. Two years later, on April 7, 1903, Max was born in Pioneer. Their only child, Max was given almost every advantage available to a young man in the early 20th century. The family lived in a large "four-square" two-story frame home and by 1910 were owners of that technological marvel called the automobile. By the 1920s they also maintained a summer cottage on Clear Lake in northeast Indiana. Clara's mother, Doddy Barto Gonter, owned a home in Pioneer, and some of John's relatives, including his parents, still lived just over the state line in nearby Hillsdale County, Michigan, where John, A.E., and a third brother, Frank, spent their childhoods. Frank owned a hardware store in Grand rapids, Michigan, where A.E. had opened his lawyer's office in the mid-1890s.

Max and Clara.

Max and his father, dated April, 1904.

Max with his violin and little red wagon.

John, Clara, and Max at their Clear Lake Cottage in Indiana.

Pioneer, Ohio, was a small farming community of about 800 inhabitants located in the far northwest corner of Ohio. The town was served by the Toledo & Western Railway, but a growing number of automobiles used U.S. 20, an east-west highway that preceded I-80/90 and ran just south of Pioneer. The highway provided a convenient route west to Chicago or east to Toledo and points beyond.

Not long after their marriage in 1901, John and Clara purchased a retail business owned by Albert C. Marshall on Main Street in Pioneer. Martin T. Hodson's store occupied the other half of the building. Clara Barto had taught school for one year before becoming a clerk at a dry goods store owned by Tom Hall and George Solier, while John was working for Jesse F. Hadley. Hadley operated a rival retail outlet in the farming community. J.C. Ewing & Co. in its early years carried dry goods, carpeting, shoes, and millinery. Later the owners added men's and women's ready-to-wear. When John and Clara saw the need to expand their business, they bought a building across the street from their original site and moved there. They worked at their store together for nearly thirty years, until John died of prostate cancer on April 23, 1932. J.C. Ewing & Co. was a financial success. Both Clara and John were hard workers and capable money managers who invested their funds well. Unfortunately their hard work and investing wisdom did not protect them from the impact of the Great Depression, an impact that sent Clara and Max into depression, as well.

The J.C. Ewing store in Pioneer in its first location.

A view of the Ewing store in its later location.

Both of Max's parents had a love for music, a predisposition they passed on to their son, who as a child demonstrated an aptitude for the art. When he was two and a half, Max posed for the camera with a miniature violin cradled in his short arms. By the age of three he was playing the piano, and not long after that he stroked a real violin. The piano, however, became his favored instrument.

By his early teens Max was composing music with lyrics, albeit nonsense verse with a touch of youthful humor. In a July 31, 1916 letter he told his cousin Doris Ewing, A.E.'s daughter, "You know you liked 'Soup Song' so well. Well I have another one which is much funnier. I took the words from a [Rube] Goldberg Cartoon & have a real cute time for them. If I come up [to visit Doris in Grand Rapids] I shall teach it to you—Here are some of the words:

> 'The nightingale sings sweet & low
> My tailor's middle name is Moe,
> O' Bumble bee where is thy sting?
> The front door bell goes ding a ling
> All nature vibrates to the thrill
> I'll meet myself down by the mill
> A gentle sigh—then all is still
> My name is Joe, so call me Phil.
> Ah! Life is like a soup tureen
> Yet no one knows just what I mean.'"

Max interspersed his verse with musical notes. His parents continued to encourage Max's innate love of music by taking him to concerts and operas. In February, 1916 the family drove to Toledo to attend an Ignace Paderewski piano concert. "He was just <u>grand</u>," Max noted in his diary. Some months later Max mentioned another trip that had a musical purpose.

Oct. 7 or 8 (I don't know which), 1916

THE WALDORF
Toledo,

Dearest Doris, Ohio

As you see by the top of this sheet, I am <u>here</u>. I came so unexpectedly that I have to pinch myself to see if it's really true. We drove down this P.M. and are going home tomorrow.

Papa and I are coming down again next week to hear "Carmen" Monday night and "Il Trovatore" Tuesday night. Geraldine Farrar will sing in "Carmen" and Emmy Destinn and Louise Homer in "Il Trovatore." Won't that be fine? I can hardly wait.

School is fine. We haven't had to write any themes yet on such quite <u>toady</u> subjects as you. What on Earth did you write about a cow smoking a cigarette?

Isn't this great weather?

I got your letter and am glad Walkley [Doris's brother] got along O.K.

Papa may be here by now so I must go to our room. Don't know what we'll do tonight. Answer this right away. I'll be in Pie-on-ear.

Macques.

Geraldine Farrar's performance, sponsored by the Toledo Civic Music League, took place in Terminal Auditorium, which apparently was part of the Toledo railroad station. He also enjoyed the movies and noted in his diaries the silent films he attended, such as Theda Bara in The Serpent *and Francis X. Bushman in* Romeo and Juliet.

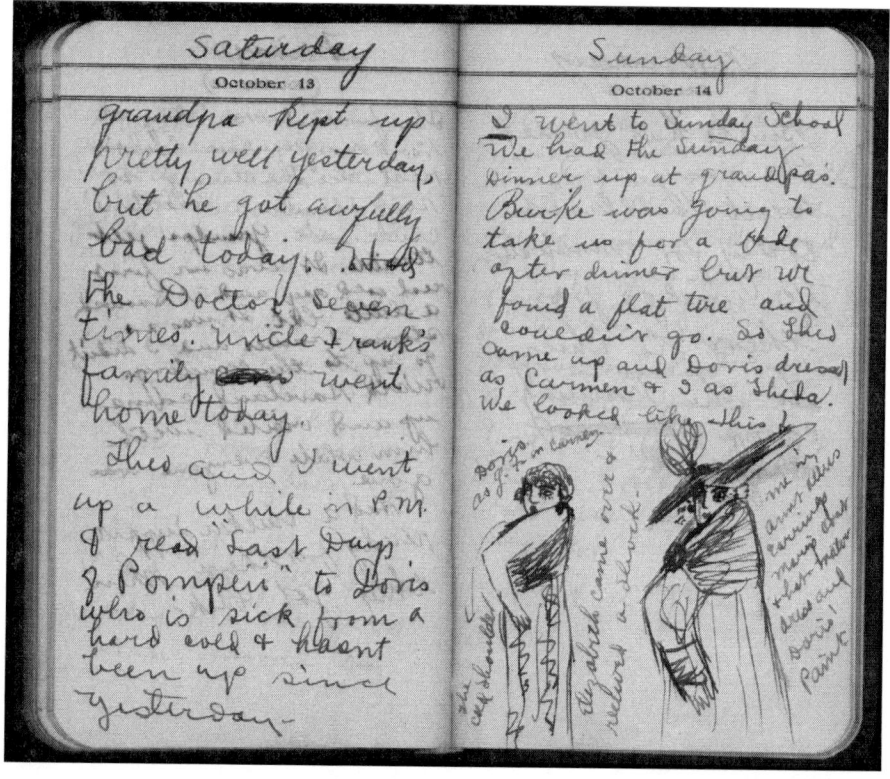

Max's entry for October 13 and 14, 1917. [Image courtesy of Beinecke Rare Book and Manuscript Library, Yale University.]

An October 14, 1917 entry in Max's diary read, "Doris dressed as Carmen and I as Theda. . . . Elizabeth [a young neighbor] came over and received a shock." Accompanying the entry were pencil drawings of two females in elaborate gowns. Presumably they represented Max and Doris. In the summer of 1918 Max picked up the Carmen theme again in his diary: "We are planning a big 'July-May Festival' next month when Doris comes. 2 nights—Concert 1st & Carmen 2nd. Cast Carmen Max & Theo; Jose Max & Theo; Escamillo Doris, Max; Migalla Elizabeth, Frasquinta Theo; Morales Doris." He drew a cartoon of himself as Carmen.

A few months earlier Max and "Papa" had again visited Toledo, this time to hear Jascha Heifitz.

Max attended Pioneer public schools. After finishing high school in 1920, he enrolled in the School of Music at the University of Michigan with the goal of becoming a concert pianist. On Friday afternoon, April 28, 1922, he gave a recital at St. Cecelia in Grand Rapids. An article in the Grand Rapids Press the next day praised his performance, noting in the headline that "Pianist Shows Insight, Avidity for Modern Idiom in Music." The reporter continued, "Max Ewing, a lad of 19, from the University of Michigan School of Music, is endowed with very unusual musical talent. His tone has depth and rich musical quality. The rising generation he represents turns with avidity to the modern school, indication that its new idiom is contributing something enduring." Among the pieces that Max performed were "Romance" by Sibelius, "At the Convent" by Borodin, "Enigme" by Scriabin ("pure impressionism") and three compositions by "the young Russian composer, Prokofieff."

Max also showed skill with the written word. As a sophomore he became music critic for the Ann Arbor Times-News. The next year he was named music editor of a publication called The Sunday Magazine, which was part of the University of Michigan Daily. Sunday Magazine caught the attention of H L. Mencken, who praised it, and University officials, who suppressed it. The last issue of the magazine included Max's critique of the early books of Carl Van Vechten. The two had met in the fall of 1921 during Max's sophomore year. Max absorbed as much of Carl's works as he could. The two corresponded, and Max began to reflect the author's taste, attitudes, and aesthetics. He wrote to his parents on October 25, 1922, "My heart beats faster every time I think of the kind of writing he does. To be his successor would be my idea of an accomplishment. Van Vechten recalled, "I remember seeing

Max Ewing around the campus of the University of Michigan in 1921. Everyone stopped to look at him. He was too tall for a student: tall and thin as a Russian wolfhound. And his hair was too long. No student lacking funds for a haircut ever dared to let his hair grow so long as that. Yet his hair was always perfectly kept. He carried his head well up, as though it had been put there to be looked at. Stare as hard as you would, the eyes never dropped, the face never flinched. Students looked upon him as though they thought the whole thing was a pose, as though he might be a fellow made up and in costume. They wanted to catch him, sometime, out of character, but the chance never came." [Quotation included in email correspondence with Steven Watson, December 20, 2004.]

Within a few years Max and Carl were close friends. After Max moved to New York City, he spent the evening of October 9, 1923 with Carl, who inscribed in a book "To Max Ewing, who may write a play or . . . qui sait [who knows]?" Max, in turn, ecstatically exclaimed in a letter to his parents, "He likes me. He can introduce me to anyone I want to know." [Quotations included in email correspondence with Steven Watson, December 20, 2004.]

While at the university, Max dated Helen Lynch, who later became a star of the silent movies. On February 25, 1922 she wrote of Max, "He bores me, therefore, I must tell him to leave me undisturbed from now on." She described Max as a "girlish boy." A week later she wrote she did like him as an artist: "He is a brilliant person in every phase of art." They disagreed on many things. "I like him, though we disagree fiercely (artistic temperament is often catty) he admits very frankly that the only woman he has ever loved is Geraldine Farrar." ["Going Nowhere: A Study of Max Anderson Ewing," 1951 unpublished paper.] Max made many enduring friendships with fellow students, including Lawrence and Roberta Conrad, Albert Lockwood, and Thomas E.

Dewey. Another friend, Donald Coney, wrote of Max in June, 1923, "Max is not a queer boy like people think. He lives in another idiom." Coney added, "People thought he was affected. It was his Eastern accent." [Quotation included in email correspondence from Steven Watson, December 20, 2004.]

On October 22, 1922 Max wrote to his parents explaining a club he and others had formed. Called Indipohdi, it met on Saturday nights. "[It] started," he wrote, "with the loftiest of philosophical aims, and at the meeting, nothing less than the seat of the soul was discussed at first. Then I appeared with my demoralizing influence and read my book of insane verse [probably "Sonnets from the Paranomasian"], and it has become the fad among the whole crowd. "

2. Europe

Max either failed to return to the university for his senior year or left the campus within a few days of arrival. [Lewis H. Stoneman, in the same class as Max, years later wrote Carl Van Vechten that Max was never interested in pursuing a degree. A university official noted that "Max did take several music courses and was a good student here."] On Tuesday, September, 18, 1923 Max wrote that he planned to move to New York City the following Monday. He occupied an apartment at 152 East 22nd Street, "Gotham." His apartment, he noted, was "Very cold—a sweater and two coats—could not practice—fingers numb." Despite the cold and other difficulties, he had decided by the end of October that he could "never live anywhere else in America again." That turned out to be an accurate prediction.

Not long after moving to "Gotham" he wrote to Ed Ailes, "I am studying, as you probably know, with Siloti. I have my first real 'lesson' Wednesday—but have played for him & talked with him, of course, before. I like him enormously, and know I'm going to do much with him. He teaches only in French, which . . . may be disadvantageous." He added, "Going to see Van Vechten tonight." During the winter season Max attended numerous operas and symphonies. In reference to a performance of "Beethoven variations," he exclaimed, "I loathe variations as a musical form." Interestingly he wrote on May 26, 1924, ". . . I have been granted a diploma from the School of Variations, which I attended this winter, and am playing Bach's C minor fantasy in octaves, and a whole galaxy of Chopin etudes."

For two years Max studied under Siloti, who in turn had studied under Franz Liszt. "A most encouraging hour with Siloti yesterday. After my first effort, 'Ce n'est pas mal!' Later on, 'Enfin, ca me plait!' and all kinds of such rare (for him) comments. And we went down town together in the subway, so help us both, he discussing on how talented

25

but frivolous Arthur Rubenstein was, how inconsequential a <u>pianist</u> Stravinsky was, & how tiresome a <u>composer</u> Medtner was."

In the summer of 1924 he attended the Grand Street Follies: "The news from Grand Street last week was that people were still standing up to see the spectacle there. But that Gertrude Lawrence, Walter Hampden, and Reggie Vanderbilt were among recent amused sitters down." The Follies became an important of his musical life the following summers.

On a Friday in September, 1924, Max wrote, "In the <u>biography</u>, the beginning season 1924-25 will probably appear uneventful, if collected <u>letters</u> are to form the material! The conclusion will be a false one. On the contrary, the season is so jammed that I write nothing, for lack of the thing called time. I fully expect to get into trouble for neglecting to sign or date my checks with the haste I write even them with." Presumably, he is trusting that someday someone will write his life story and be hard pressed to find letters from 1923 to 1925 to fill in the details of his life. Again, he would be correct.

Max had a knack for getting into the homes and lives of famous people. Towards the end of November, 1924, he recorded that he spent "an evening chez Joseph Stella, his wife, Madame Stella, and his dog, Fat-Darling Stella. The dog was even particularly a nonentity. Mme. Stella is primarily the-wife-of-the-great-man, a bright and amiable lady, but a subordinate. Joseph Stella is a very big man and a very great artist, a delightful colossal child." The next month Max and Stella attended a Stravinsky concert at Carnegie Hall.

In 1924 Max published a book of poems that he called "Sonnets from the Paranomasian." The small paper-bound book contained 26 sonnets "From the Paronomasian And Other Languages Beginning with P." "Paronomasia" comes from Greek and Latin words meaning word play, or punning. Max noted that the poetry was "Conceived With a bow to Mrs. Browning and salaams to Donald Evans." It was printed in New York. He starts the book with three quotations: "Nothing is perplexing if there is an island." [Gertrude Stein] "Je voudrais avoir un nouvel ami/pour dire des choses incomprehensible." ["I want to have a new friend to whom I can say incomprehensible things." [Francis Picabia] "But it excels in this, that as the fruit/Of love, it is a book too mad to read/Before one merely reads to pass the time." [Wallace Stevens] Each sonnet was titled and dedicated to different individuals. For instance the first poem is called "Alchemy in Fairfax Arms, Sonnet from the Paronomasian, For Carl Van Vechten:"

> "He sat, Scheherazade by his side,
> A furry carytatid bearing high,
> Like megapodes against a tired sky,
> The standards of the feathers that had died.
> And, mixing with unmeasured ginger beer
> Mad memories of rapids, cedar-fanned,
> He conjured forth with pale and polished hand,
> A paragon of impious atmosphere:
>
> "A tattoed countess, tinged in nicotine,
> Held close by ink-stained pages, lithe and thin,
> Between the covers of her folding bed,—
> A phoenix on the middle western scene.
> The alchemist sensed her rare penchant for sin;
> 'She'll go to the borzoi dogs at once,' he said."

On December 10 1924 he wrote to Ed Ailes, "You mention a possible piece of publicity in the Daily about the 'Sonnets from the Paronnomasian.' Tant mieux. How shall it be managed? When you get your copy (probably late next week) do you simply want to look it over, and draw your own conclusions, and announce them in the paper?

Or shall I go through the official business of sending a copy to the Literary Editor (who is it?) for reviewing purposes? The only other editor I intend to treat so royally is Jane Heap of the Little Review." Near the end of the month he asked Ed, *"Can you let me know, as soon as possible, in what issue of the Daily your review of the sonnets will appear? I will want to have some copies sent to the book-stores up there, in time to meet the great demand for books which your article will precipitate! I took a copy of the book to the Van Vechtens one night last week, and Carl's comment was that it was TOO DIVINE!"*

The jarring rhythm and abundance of consonants echo Igor Stravinsky's works. There's no record how many copies were printed, but the book is now a rare item.

On October 29, 1925 Virginia Tryon of the University of Michigan shared news with her readers: *"Music and Drama Hosannah! The first of a series of monthly articles by Max Ewing on the New York theater and its personalities will appear in the Music and Drama page of the Second Section—they call it chimes—this Sunday, November 1 [1925]. Max Ewing was formerly music editor of the Sunday Magazine at its prime, is now studying in New York with Silotti, and is quite patently Michigan's off-chance to genius. The first article is on Noel Coward and his comedies, and with all modesty is the finest piece of writing since the halcyon days of the unmentionables."*

The year before, in 1926, Max made his second trip abroad, an excursion that took him to most of the major European tourist sites. In Paris he spent a short time studying with Marcelle Meyer, a well-known interpreter of Igor Stravinsky's piano music. Max wrote to his cousin Doris of preparations for the trip.

April 8, 1926

181 Madison Avenue [New York]

    Hail, sweet Squirrel, and Farewell, for a while. I'm off next Thursday, April 15, on the de Grasse, to Paris, London, Monte Carlo, Villefranche, Venice, Florence, Rome, and points up and down. Max getting himself packed and stored and out of one apartment, and getting himself off to another continent is a spectacle of no efficiency whatever, you may well imagine. Most of my luggage is composed of stacks of letters of introduction to armies of people: Gertrude Stein, Jean Cocteau, the Sitwells, Marcel Duchamp, Diaghilef, Lady Colfax, Lady Rathemere, your friend Norman Douglas, and so on. Sileti [Alexander Siloti] is having the Pleyel Piano Company provide me with a piano for my stay in Paris, so everything looms pleasant and more. If you are feeling particularly charitable and prompt to write you can address me by April 15 here, or on ship, de Grasse, Cabin 422, Pier 57, foot West 15th street. My Paris address will be care of the Guaranty Trust Company, 3 Rue des Italiens, in case you are feeling charitable but not prompt. Bearing in mind your correspondence of last summer, I am looking forward with considerable embarrassment to the sight of all those people without panties whom you found so disturbingly in evidence last summer. I shall compare notes and inform you if conditions have in any way improved—one way or the other.

    Best to you always, sweet Toad; we are rotten correspondents, but awfully good cousins, I feel.

                Max.

The "points up and down" that Max visited included Milan, Turin, and Switzerland. In Venice he shared a gondola with Cole Porter and Elsa Maxwell. Max continued to correspond with Doris and his parents, keeping the family up to date on his Grand Tour and its musical interludes. The following letter is addressed to Doris.

May 12 [1926]
Paris

My dear delirious pet—Always thanks for your so well-worded well-wishings which reached me but today—at a time when indeed I did need them more than at time of sailing—for this morning I was already late for an appointment with George Copeland (Isadore Duncan's one time pianist) when I saw that my bank was going to close both today & tomorrow in celebration of Christ's ascension. I flew to it before it could close at noon, & bought some francs & found your letter. By that time it was pouring rain, & once I got a taxi the driver was getting so wet he had to stop to put his half of the top up which took him some time. And after this delay he promptly drove me across the river to the wrong street. So my only consolation during this none too happy trip was your letter—your letters!

If you had arrived at the epoch of Gentlemen Prefer Blonds, and were not (as you say you are) in the dark era of Little French Girl, I would say that, as to Paris, Lorelei Lee was right. Her word for it is divine. Divine it is, and much too hospitable to keep any sort of equilibrium in. It is one party after another. And last night I had to cancel one party engagement in order to go to two others! One at the house of the Sculptress Mills who had George Antheil and George Copeland and Virgie Thompson there to play—and Ray de Mare and Noel Murphy etc to listen. Noel and I went on then to a late party at Mme. Durand's in honor of the Countess de Noailles. Amusing and exhausting!

Gertrude Stein, sweet, insane, wise, ingratiating old dynamo, had a tea for me, & asked the people I wanted most to meet—from Rene Crevel to Pavel Tchelietchoff. I have spent two evenings at her house since and I adore her. What a head she has!

I have been seeing a lot too of Gilbert Seldes and his wife; met Heifetz the other night after his concert at the opera, and am seeing him again soon with Sarah King and her sister Julia Hoyt; have arranged to have Georgette Leblanc (Mme. Maeterlinck) sing some of my jazz songs in Monte Carlo in July & here in October; have had the daily use of three grand pianos offered to me—so how can I complain of Paris? In fact there are so many amusing & promising opportunities here I may not go to London at all. I'm living at the Hotel Foyot which looks out on the Luxembourg Gardens which are too beautiful just now. Nothing costs anything. A taxi would go to Nice for a dollar! Why didn't you come this year? Write again. The shows are terrible compared to New York. Concerts are fair—but the Ballets Russes are coming! Max

c/o Guaranty Trust—3 Rue des Italiens

Thursday, July 1 [1926]

Hotel-Restaurant
De La Tour Eiffel

1 Percy Street,
Tottenham Court Road.
Londres, W.1.

Dears—London, socially, is just as brilliant & incessant and exciting as Paris. Last night it was with the Goosens. They gave a dinner party at the fashionable London Ivy Restaurant for Mr. and Mrs. Knopf from N.Y. (the publishers for Carl V. V. [Van Vechten] etc.) and Nikola Romanoff, the Russian ambassador to England, and me. After dinner we went to His Majesty's Theater to see the ballets, [Eugene] Goosens conducting. Douglas Fairbanks, very brown, and Mary [Pickford], very white, were in the 3rd row & made it a good night at the theater! After it, we all went to the Goosens apartment to a grand party, & everyone in London came—Noel Coward, Iris Tree, Tallulah Bankhead, Lady Jean-

Paul, Diaghilev, dozens of others, including Oscar's niece, Dorothy [Dolly] Wilde. Also that marvelous French girl pianist Marcelle Meyer. It is wonderful to get to know the Goosens so well. For a few months each winter Goosens conducts the Rochester Symphony with guest appearances with the [Walter] Damrosch N.Y. Symphony. I told him I wanted to play the Stravinsky Concerto one time with his Rochester orchestra & he said he would talk that over seriously soon. I think that the way to artistic success has to be via social success. Everybody plays well these days & there are hundred & hundreds of fine pianists over here. You've got to be something more. You've got to cut a big figure and be spectacular & know everyone and do everything and go everywhere, and not give anyone a chance to overlook you! Anyway I'm cutting a swell figure with this new cape & high silk hat I bought in Regent Street!

  Monday night I went to Queen's Hall & heard d'Alvarez. I found myself sitting next to Eva Gauthier, who was alone & wearing a vast hat of waving red ribbons. She & I went back & paid our respects to Marguerite [d'Alvarez]. Eva was a little jealous of her success! They adore d'Alvarez here in the same way N.Y. adored Farrar. I walked home with Gauthier thru Picadilly [Piccadilly] Circus and we had a pleasant visit. Tuesday night I heard the [Edith] Sitwell performance of "Façade."

  Tuesday afternoon I went in to attend a performance of old English church music in Westminster Abbey, and someone poked me in the knee with an umbrella to make me move along in the pew. I was most indignant & glared up at the offender—& saw it was Frederic Sanchez from Ann Arbor! and his Spanish wife Nina. They arrived in England only a few days ago en route to Spain, & we too had a pleasant visit, the more so because so unexpected. They asked me to go with them out to Canterbury tomorrow to see the town & Cathedral, & I probably shall—

unless something better turns up! I think you met Sanchez at Michigan. He lived with W. [Warren] Bower.

London was not as immediately ingratiating as Paris, but it seems better each day. It is terribly dusty & grim and big, almost as many people as New York, but whereas N.Y. puts its business into 40 storey buildings & gets it over with, London puts it into 4 storeys, so it has to stretch for miles farther.

All traffic turns to the left, a great nuisance. And there are practically no street signs with names of streets. You just have to imagine whether you're in Pall Mall or Leicester Square, but I have a good imagination about those things.

Buckingham Palace is impressive, but in no way charming like French palaces.

The paintings in the National Gallery are superb.

There are almost no restaurants! Blocks & blocks and no place to eat. I don't know what people do. Perhaps they eat at home. But people in Paris & N.Y. do not. It is a marvelous restaurant attached to this hotel. Michael Arlen & the Prince himself dine here at times.

A letter from Mother—June 14—was forwarded from Paris. Stop worrying about the present. It wasn't much. But I'll send no more. I'll wait & bring some things. It will be safer that way, even if I do have to pay some duty.

Love Max.

Max sent a picture postcard to Muriel in early August, 1926: "Muriel—the summer surpasses belief. I fled from the Riviera. I was in Rapello. The next minute I was unexpectedly in a motor with Esther [Murphy] and Miss [Natalie] Barney moving toward Gardone to see d'Annunzio. Romaine Brooks drove here from Venice. All is remarkable. And all is real. Gardone, August 6 Max" By September 26, Max had returned to his New York City apartment.

3. New York

Except for his trip to Europe in 1926 and occasional visits with his mother in Pioneer, Max spent most of the years between 1924 and 1933 in Manhattan. Among his other activities, Max participated in a variety of exhibits, revues, and musical extravaganzas. In 1927, 1928, and 1929, he was part of a team that composed the music and lyrics for "The Grand Street Follies." He was credited with composing the complete score for the 1927 revue. The following year the Follies opened at the Neighborhood Playhouse on May 19 and at the end of the month moved to the Little Theater on 44th Street. The revue ran for 148 performances. J. Brooks Atkinson, theater critic for the New York Times *wrote, "Like most of those annual topical revues, which used to keep the Summer gay on the east side, the new lampoon does not escape dullness in perhaps half its scenes. Even so, it is the best of these semiprofessional potpourris in years." Max is cited only in the credits. An anonymous reviewer ["P. De R."] gave Max a line or two: "One song, 'Just a Little Love Song,' credited to Max Ewing, may be heard from again. The rest of the music is fully acceptable, but not especially brilliant." James Cagney and the other dancers also elicited faint praise: " . . . their dancing brought nothing new to Broadway, the tap and step capital of the world."*

March 30, 1927

Rehearsals go on. Only three or four of the original pianists selected are still at it. Everyone save Carol Robinson, Aaron Copeland, Colin McFee and myself gave up in despair, and it has been a problem to find substitutes, since every day was a day later, and every day the problem was increased.

When Helen Scoville gave up, I sent for Sascha [Gorodnitzki] who came down and looked at the score, and said he would not attempt it.

Then I sent frantic messages to Stephanie, who accepted, and is learning it. She and I play adjoining pianos. She is terribly enthusiastic, and always a dependable musician, and I am glad both that she is playing with me, and that I was able to get her this thing to do. Naturally it never occurred to me to back out, once I had decided to play it. Everything is progressing famously. Vast black and silver backdrops are being painted for the back of the Carnegie Hall stage, which was never done there before. News reels of the thing will be shown all over the country. Roxy [Rothafel] is so excited, he offered George [Anthiel] and [Donald?] Friede $40,000.00 (forty thousand dollars) to play it at the Roxy Theater for a week. But Friede won't allow it in a common movie house if it is the biggest and gaudiest on earth. Carnegie Hall is already so nearly sold out for the night of the tenth, that is now likely that the whole thing will be repeated the following Sunday night, the 17th. It is the greatest nonsense that you don't come. And of course the first performance would be twice as amusing and brilliant as the second, which would accommodate only the overflow.

    George's father from Trenton New Jersey, sits at the rehearsals in a bewilderment that is remarkable. He has not seen George for six years, and then to suddenly hear these unprecedented sounds which George has put together surprises him to death. He told Stephanie and me a rather sweet story about how George, when a small boy, had been crazy about a hill on the Delaware River near Trenton and had said he would like a house there. So two or three years ago he wrote George that he had bought him that hill. And George who naturally was no longer interested in possessing hills in New Jersey, sent back word that he didn't want it, so Mr Antheil sold it again last summer, all of which is both amusing and pathetic.

    Dorothy Crawford visited her there last week and had a bad time, because she said Alice kept four black crabs and three lizards in the house along with her grey mice, and they crawl over the floor and the beds day and night. Last year Miss de la Mar took pelicans with her. They were put in the baggage car but got loose and chased the conductor through the Pullmans, and rather upsetting the passengers. So things go on. Many people are behaving oddly, but they are all up and at it just now.

April 7, 1927

Another birthday today, and much the busiest one of the twenty-four! I was up and early at Twelfth Avenue rehearsing the Ballet Mecanique. Everything rehearsed today, all the pianos, all the wind-machines, propellers, and engines, and it is surprising that anyone at all can stay in the same neighborhood while we are at it all day. Goossens is conducting the rehearsals now, and even he is having a time. He says it is the most difficult score he ever conducted. But it will be a good performance by Sunday night, after two more days work. Only the drummers and the xylophonists are sometimes bad now. We go to the warehouse in the forenoons and take an hour off for lunch. And it is so far to any real restaurant, that we take food along, and then all go into an old boxcar where they sell coffee and rolls to the longshoremen, and eat with them, including Goossens himself and Antheil and Friede, etc. It is all very odd and a lot of fun, as well as a history-making event, and great experience.

The second Antheil Concert in Carnegie Hall, will be Wednesday night, April 20. An exact repetition of this one. The place is sold out to the last inch for Sunday night. It is all amazing. Muriel meant to have a party for George after it Sunday night. But so many people had to be asked, since it was an affair of world-wide importance, that no one person could entertain them, so Friede has taken over the Club Deauville for the night, and after the concert the performers and as many hundreds in the audience as he decides to invite, will go on to it.

On April 10 Max performed in the American premiere of George Antheil's Ballet Mécanique at Carnegie Hall. The dust jacket on Max's later novel described the performance this way: "Under the direction of Eugene Goosens and along with ten other pianists, including the composer, and to the roaring accompaniment of drums, tympani, gongs, bells, and whirring airplane propellers, [Max] played the piano score, which was intended to be played by electrical pianolas [player pianos]." Max performed with such vigor that he injured a nerve in one of his fingers and was forced to play with the remaining nine digits for the next three years. The injury also precluded pursuing a career as a concert pianist.

Tuesday, April 3, 1928

Finishing up learning the Bach Concerto Italien. Muriel has been shutting herself up for the last week finishing the book. It is coming out in September, and these articles in Harpers are excerpts from it. She will be out and about again by tomorrow. George Antheil is not coming over after all. Latest word from him is that he is going off to Spain to spend the spring in the Pyrenees, because he has incipient tuberculosis, and is forbidden to live in Paris.

[Albert] Carroll was very blue, and talking alarmingly about suicide. He was terribly affected by the suicide of Emily Stevens this winter, who was one of his best friends. None of the newspapers called it suicide. They reported that she was simply found dead in bed. But her friends knew that she just was too bored to live, and so stopped it. Carroll and I telephoned Marion Morehouse and she came down here for a while looking very handsome, and dressed in a gold tea gown trimmed in black, which made her look very beautiful on the black and gold sofa, as if she were part of the interior decoration and ought to stay put there.

No, Esther Murphy doesn't know Florence Louchheim. They all live in Park Avenue, but the Louchheims are obviously lately-rich. The Murphys are authentic American aristocracy, in so far as we have any.

I have made two trips to Europe, first as a more or less sight-seeing investigation, and second with my interest and attention primarily devoted to personalities over there. When I go the third time it will be with a quite different purpose: not in order to investigate what other people are doing, but to exhibit a product of my own for other people to attend to. I shall not go until this product is satisfying to my own mind. But after working this winter as I have very largely on Marcelle Meyer's technical equipment, and next winter on a definite number or compositions, I can go to Europe a year from this summer, no longer as a young man of promise, but as someone with a tangible accomplishment. And I will arrange some appearances over there. These things have to be done socially to be done well. I know I can interest the Princess Polignac in Paris and Baroness d'Erlanger in London. These things I am determined to do, and nothing can stop it.

I enclose a clipping about the Antheil thing. When he found out Muriel was ill, he went straight to Trenton, New Jersey to spend two days with his family which he has not seen for six years, and is coming back to New York tomorrow, and is going straight from the station to Muriel's, so that he can say that she was the first person he went to see in New York. He insists that anything he ever writes or does in his life will have been due to her stimulus.

I am sorry you do not want to come on for the concert, and I hope you will still change your minds, and both come. Your excuse that you "can't spare the extra money" is tiresome nonsense, and as for your time, it is your own to do with what you most want. And I may add that if I can stand it to appear on the platform without "diamonds and furs," you ought to be able to do as much in the eighth row.

Max in Venice in 1927.

    According to one of Max's letters, the inspiration for writing Going Somewhere *came from the novelist Lloyd Morris. Max wrote in May, 1927, "He wants me to write an amusing story of contemporary New York literary life, insisting that I know more people in it than anyone else does, and have a more detached slant on the whole thing. Who knows, I may do it." [From Steve Watson's email message of December 20, 2004.]*

    In June, 1927 Max returned to Paris. Regarding a party given by Marchesa Casati, Max wrote on July 3, 1927: "that fantastic Italian woman who has given the most marvelous parties in France for the past fifteen years." The Marchesa *"greeted her guests standing on a leopard skin rug on a dais. She was dressed in golden trousers with a train of gold cloth yards long, a bodice made of ropes of pearls woven together, a high white wig, silver roses on her shoulder, a gold mask across her eyes, and she carried a large knife inlaid with diamonds."* On this journey Max added Venice, Vienna, and Berlin to his European itinerary.

The next few letters were directed to Max's uncle, A.E. Ewing.

August 22 1928

19 West 31rst Street
New York City

Dear Uncle,

Thanks for both your notes. The second arrived this morning and I found it surprising that anyone should think I was living in 131st Street, since that is the heart of the Negro metropolis, Harlem! I go up there quite a bit, but I haven't taken to living there yet. I have not heard from Doris at all, but no doubt I shall when she arrives in town. And I will see that she receives any mail sent to her or Aunt Lotta in my care. One letter has already arrived from one Helen Tag of Adrian Michigan. She enclosed a letter for Doris, and in an accompanying explanatory note to me she asks pardon for addressing me without ever having met me, but goes on to add that my sister Doris has spoken of me so often she feels she knows me anyway. How careless of Doris to thus confuse our relationship.

It seems that Burke and Marjorie went to see the Grand Street Follies, and left word backstage that they had called, and were hurrying on to New England or thereabouts. Please tell them that I was sorry to have missed them and to come again.

Mother is arriving the end of this week for a short visit, and I think it is about your turn next. When you come let me know and we will plan something gala. Meanwhile best to all the Grand Rapids family, most of which has gone into a silence which is only as abysmal as my own!
Always,
Max

September 5 [1928]

19 West 31st street
New York City

Dear Uncle,

Your two letters addressed to Aunt Lotta have arrived here, and I am holding them for her arrival, letters keep coming from points west for Doris, too, from friends whom she has apparently instructed to reach her in my care. But myself, I have no word from her since she left, so all I know of her peregrinations to the Far East has reached me from the Middle West.

I have to attend a wedding in Larchmont [New York] Saturday noon, returning to New York Saturday afternoon, and I can meet the ship unless it happens to dock within those six or eight hours when I am incapacitated. And providing, too, I learn which ship it is! Many thanks for the five dollars, a gracious though unnecessary contribution. I shall use it in transporting the Prodigals one place or another:

More news later.
    As always,
        Max

[September 11, 1928]

Dear Uncle,

My apologies today for my bad temper of yesterday. A letter from Aunt Lotta in Naples arrived this morning, telling of Doris' unfortunate sickness, and saying that they are delayed, and will sail on the Colombo, arriving here about the 17th. She also asks that I meet them and have two tickets to Grand Rapids ready for them in advance so that they can go straight through. This I will do, though, I cannot engage tickets long in advance because, as I said before, one is never certain exactly which day the boat will dock until the last minute. But be sure that I will do what I can to make their progress easy. I read some weeks ago about the fever epidemic in Athens and wondered at the time whether Doris would escape it, for I knew she planned to be there at about that time. If you receive any further news please let me share it.

Yours,

Max

Doris recovered fully. The Colombo *arrived in New York just before noon on September 17, culminating a 12-day trans-Atlantic voyage. Max was there to greet his cousin and aunt and to entertain them for a few hours before their train departed for Michigan.*

Max felt at home in New York City, but he was well aware of its frenetic pace: "[New York] is supposed to be the speediest city on earth, but its cumbersome machinery for speed slows everything up, because it is in its own way! Everyone is here, but so is everyone else; everyone can be got hold of, but everyone else is trying to get ahold of everyone. And to merely reach anyone by telephone takes endless time. To cross the street takes still longer."

Ten days later, on November 29, 1928, he made his Christmas list: "I'll tell you what I want for Christmas—a small financial sum to cover the printing charges on a small printed catalog of the pictures in my gallery. It has become a really amazing room, containing some of the most rare and remarkable photographs of prominent people in the world. It is really important as a collector's collection, but I like it simply because it amuses me so much. A printed list of its contents will make everyone in New York want to come and see it . . ." Apparently he got his wish, because the following January 10 Max wrote, "George Lynes writes that the [photography] catalog caused high commotion in Paris, and that the chief topic of discussion at Gertrude Stein's is the absence of Muriel from its pages." Among those he photographed were Anthony Sansone, an Italian-American body builder. Max noted that Anthony had reached "the peak of physical perfection, [and] is the most renowned of sculptor's models. He is very anxious to come and see his likeness in my gallery."

On April 21, 1929 Max was one of many guests at a party hosted at the Dark Tower by A'lelia Walker. Of one of her parties Max wrote, "You have never seen such clothes as millionaire Negroes get into. They are more gorgeous than a Ziegfield finale. They do not stop at fur coats made of merely one kind of fur. They add collars of ermine to gray fur, or black fur collars to ermine. Ropes of jewels and trailing silks of all bright colors." Max attended the last party at Dark Tower in November, 1929. Taylor Gordon sang. A'Lelia subsequently sold the house.

In October, 1929 Max had a deformed nasal passage removed. Despite the operation, Max continued to suffer from frequent nasal infections.

Steven Watson noted that Max was one of "a dozen potentially influential guests invited to a party held at Carl Van Vechten's flat to hear Virgil Thompson play and sing an opera in the making." Virgil Thompson composed the music for the opera, titled **Four Saints in Three Acts**, and Gertrude Stein wrote the libretto. On February 16, 1929, the day after the gathering, Max wrote to his mother, "Carl [Van Vechten] is trying to interest someone to perform [the opera]. I doubt anyone will, it is so mad." [Prepare for Saints, p. 68.] Max was wrong. The opera did receive the necessary financial support and publicity to open at Hartford's Athenaeum on February 7, 1934, and before long it appeared on Broadway. In 1931 he was still residing at 19 West 31st Street in Manhattan.

In early 1930, after attending the Beaux Art Ball in Manhattan, Max joined the Stettheimer sisters for dinner. He arrived, Max wrote on January 29, to find that "Carl VanVechten and Eddie Wasserman and Mrs. Knopf and ten or twelve others have been dining. . . . [The] three Stettheimer sisters, dressed for a quiet evening at home, looked dressed for a ball, themselves. Florine had on white satin trousers underneath a trailing affair of spangled net. Ettie had on a black lace creation and was wearing a red wig. I was startled because I thought she had suddenly dyed her hair, but she maintained she was wearing a wig. The third sister Carrie, wore a golden crown, a golden throat band, a gold dress, and over it a cape of black lace." He wrote of Muriel at the ball: "Muriel simply wore one of her Poiret evening dresses. Her evening dresses are always so extraordinary that people think she is dressed for a costume ball every time, so that when a costume ball is at hand she never needs to make an effort!" At the end of the next month he noted, "Ettie Stenheimer is going to introduce me to her nephew Walter Wanger, a millionaire magnate of Paramount Films, and I may get some music placed this spring."

On March 11, 1930, Max began giving a series of "Mondays," as he called them. On March 11 he wrote in his diary, "My 'Mondays' are becoming quite a regular in established events." Among his guests were Lloyd Wescott, Marguerite D'Alvarez, John Mosher, Donald Angus, Eugene MacCown, George Davis.

February 21, 1930

    Here is another note being written with great discomfort on the bench, because the desk is full of another statue the fifth so far and the biggest and the best. It is a lamp, this new one, entitled Muriel Enlightening the World. I started with the Statue of Liberty Enlightening the World as my model, but I departed quite a bit from this original! This statue developed out of a criticism of my last one which was entitled Muriel More So. You may recall in her book there is a chapter devoted to her visit to Mabel Dodge's in Florence, when Carl V.V. [Van Vechten] and Robert Edmond Jones were there, and Jones, who was painting her said, "Muriel, everything about you should be more so, your aigrettes in your turban should be higher, your earrings should be longer, EVERYTHING about you ought to be MORE SO." So I made this statue just about as more so as it could be. One startling feature of it was that it had electric flash light bulbs for breasts. Everyone looked at these in amazement, and then said "Do they light?" It was very annoying to be asked this, because they did not light and I felt that was asking too much. But I decided to show them I could make something that would light. So I bought the framework for a desk lamp, left nothing but the standard and the bulb, and then built the clay up around it, with the wiring inside, and the effect is magnificent. It does not look like a lamp covered with clay, but like a statue with wire inside! The figure of Muriel painted black and red stands beside the column which is gold, and when it is lighted up it lights the whole room. For two years I have been going to buy a desk lamp, but now I made one far better than anyone could buy! She is holding a red battle axe in her right hand, the light in her left, and a miniature loud-speaker and two red plumes are coming out of her head.

    Muriel says these statues will be the greatest record of and comment on her life when she is dead!

My finger is a little better and I am working on the program I hope to play in Ann Arbor.

Although the salutation is missing, the following letter was clearly intended for Jack Pollock.

[about September, 1930]

It may have been wrong of me not to buy steaks Wednesday but I didn't. The market was open only three hours and everybody predicted the most awful crashes for the rest of the week. Even Eddie became alarmed on Wednesday. He had a big party Wednesday night and everyone talked finance. Banks were said to be on the verge of closing up, and Carl Van Vechten said that he would even have to write a book soon to make some money, but that the trouble with that would be that no one would have enough money to buy a book with! The only person who did not seem worried about the market at Eddie's party was the Rajne of Padakuta, an English woman who married one of the richest Rajahs of India, and acquired her remarkable name, and whose Rajah husband then died, so she has come to New York, very large, very blonde, very beautiful, and so rich it is TOO BAD. She was hung, strung and bestrewn with diamonds in every conceivable place where diamonds could be put. She came to the party with Cecil Beaton, the English artist who has just arrived back. All kinds of people were there including Emily Vanderbilt who looks more dead than alive. The Rajne of Podakuta met A'Lelia Walker there, and A'Lelia was hung and strung with all her trophies too, beads and pins and diamond arrows across her chest, and the pair of them was a weird sight. No more weird than the sight of Fania Marinoff and Marguerite D'Alvarez at lunch at the Crillon yesterday. The season is on with a vengeance. Carl gave this luncheon party yesterday to celebrate the return of d'Alvarez to this continent. D'Alvarez has been in Germany, singing and becoming remarkably slim. And acquiring jewelry to put your eyes out. Three ropes of huge gold objects hung about her neck, and large gold objects hung about her neck, and large gold objects hung in her ears, and large lumps of solid gold set into rings were on her fingers. And a large gold object was pinned to her hat. Fania Marinoff, not to be outdone, wore a gold hat and had golden fish attached to her ears. The rest of the party consisted of Carl, myself, and TR Smith, and Jean Carr, a young English pianist who has just arrived over here. She wasn't quite as heavily bowed down in gold as the other two ladies. I can assure you that the whole Crillon restaurant stopped eating when we came in. And traffic almost stopped in Park Avenue when we went out. As if one such meal was not enough for one day, I was invited to Bob Candler's [Chanler's] to dinner at night. I took Lloyd Wescott to meet Bob, and Clem Randolph was there and Anthony Wrynn and a great many other people who always fill Bob's house. Bob himself having nearly died all summer long has pulled himself together again and seems quite well. He nearly exploded with pleasure when I told him Muriel was out lecturing. He beat his fists on the table and roared with laughter until I was afraid he might die then and there.

This Thursday Pollack could you come back here with me and see the shell pink bathroom and all the new phenomena? I have a big poster of the film Freaks, showing the banquet scene, with KooKoo the bird girl dancing on the table. People can thus be photographed with her as background if they insist. You should insist it would be a good picture to send to England as a poetess.

In 1931 Doris returned to Europe to take a teaching position with Roberts College for Women in Istanbul, Turkey. She arrived in New York towards the end of August to board ship and set sail for her new assignment. Once again her mother accompanied her, but this time only as far as New York. With them was a "gentleman friend" from

Oklahoma. Doris's departure from New York was neither smooth nor easy. Max described the situation in a letter to his parents.

Friday [August 25, 1931]

Dear family,

    I enclose some clippings that may interest you about the death—and life—of A'Leia [A'Lelia Walker]. The funeral finally took place yesterday after nearly a week of conferences pro and con. Nobody seemed to know what to do, since she left no relatives at all except an adopted daughter in Chicago. The funeral which I went to with Muriel [Draper] and Dorothy Sheldon was quite a terrific event. Police were in the streets lined up to keep the mob in control, and only people who had cards of invitation were admitted to the chapel. The most surprising part of the service was that waltz song of Noel Cowards was sung in place of a hymn! And then there was a parade of floral tributes that was like the entrance of Caesar into Egypt. It was impressive, but all very racking.

    Beatrice Locher and I meant to get started for Massachusetts today but her car is out of order and is in a garage being repaired. We may get off tomorrow or possibly not until Tuesday. She put the car into the garage for a thorough overhauling before taking the trip, and the mechanics have made the car worse than it was before, and now it won't go at all! It is promised for tomorrow however. For me it is a rather fortunate delay, because Natalie Hammond is in New York for a few days. She came down to supervise the construction of some stage sets she has designed for a new play of Anita Loos'. I dined with her last night before going to the Rody Halls' farewell party. They leave for Japan tonight. If I arrive at Gloucester before Natalie does I am to spend a few days with Beatrice at Marsden Hartley's. Bobby Locher is coming up too for over next Sunday. All this probably sounds very complicated, and as a matter of fact it is. I am quite excited over going somewhere new. It is surprising to think that I have not been in a new place in this country since our trip to Boston about ten years ago. Since then it has been only New York, Pioneer, and Michigan for me—except Europe, of course. But a place like Gloucester seems as remote and more foreign than Absynnia [Abyssinia].

    Mother, if she likes, may skip the following paragraph which is going to be about Doris. It, also, is complicated. Doris arrived Thursday to sail on the Saturnia on Friday. The old gent from Oklahoma [Perry Maxwell] motored her here. He drove from Oklahoma to Grand Rapids to get her and then drove her on to New York. Aunt Lotta also came along again for the trip. Doris put her luggage, trunks, etc. on board the ship, all her new wardrobe for three years in Turkey, and everything was shipshape until the school authorities saw her passport and learned that she had been divorced, and at that they said she could not go to Turkey because they could not employ divorced teachers. Did you ever hear of anything more idiotic? They accused her of not having told them she was divorced. And she replied that they had never asked, and that it wasn't her business to go about announcing that she had been married unless they asked her. They said it was an absolutely basic rule of the school that no one could teach there who had been divorced. And Doris maintained that if it was such a basic fundamental rule they ought to inquire first of all whether a candidate was divorced or not, and she is quite right. They interviewed her for more than five hours when she was here before, and the question of marriage and divorce never came up at all. They chose Doris out of four or five other applicants because her credentials and recommendations were the best. And then they refused to accept her because she had been divorced years ago. Of course she had a signed contract which was legal and valid, and she could force the issue if she wanted to, or probably even win out in a law suit. But she hated so the idea of going half way around the earth in to a strange school community which would probably be hostile to her when she got there, and she hated to work for an institution which was asking her to resign. Well, you can imagine what a commotion all this was. Of course Aunt Lotta was rather relieved, because she never wanted her to go, but only thought she should for the sake of the money. And of course the old gent from out west was delighted since he thought she would now marry him in despair of getting anything to do. Well, there were more conferences and discussions and debates and interviews, and the whole question was finally put off until Tuesday when the high authority of the school will be back in town. He is now on his vacation. If he says Doris can go, she will sail on Tuesday on another boat and still get there in time. Otherwise they will send her home and pay her a financial settlement of some kind to cover the expense of her trip here and her clothes and her mental anguish, etc. I have an idea they will let her go, since it is so late to get anyone else. At least they may send her for one year instead of three, which would please her still more. Anyway it is a mess. Over Sunday since they could do nothing until Tuesday they have gone to Boston to show Aunt Lotta the sights. They left yesterday and will probably return tomorrow. Possibly Beatrice and I will pass them on the road. I do hope Doris goes to Turkey. I think it is very enterprising and admirable of her to undertake such a thing, and it would be such a help out of their muddle. The whole financial situation in Grand Rapids seems to be extremely critical all around with no money in sight anywhere. Just to add a touch of confusion to all the events of the week, Riford Worth seems to have become practically engaged to the daughter of the Oklahoma gent! He can't marry her because he is married and he can't get a divorce because he can't find his wife. Aunt Lotta seeks to maintain a balance of power between her daughter and her daughter's suitor and her daughter's suitor's daughter and her daughter's suitor's daughter, and she feels quite swamped. I have not been involved in any of these activities, as they have all been living at the Prince George hotel. I had dinner with them once at the Oklahoma gent's invitation—at Alice Foote MacDougalls of all places!

Dinner at the Stettheimers was dramatic Wednesday night. Such a storm came up as you can't imagine, and we were caught in a cloudburst on Riverside Drive where all cars were stalled for an hour because all the motors were flooded. Helen Westley, the Theater Guild actor was at the dinner and she and I had a long talk about sex menace.

John Glenn and his friend negotiated a loan from a man named Furness who controls the Furness steamship lines to Bermuda. So they are on their feet for a while, and they are going to take care of Elektra while I am away.

Hope you enjoy the weekend at Hastings, and that it will be as eventful as things are here.

Max

Using a mixture of firmness and tact, Doris was able to salvage her job, and after a short delay she set sail for Istanbul. She spent the next four years teaching at Roberts College, leaving Max free to pursue his interests in New York and Florida. During his vacation, he made a side trip to the Bahamas.

Late Thursday afternoon [March 17, 1932]

The Miamian
New York-Palm Beach-Miami
Pennsylvania Railroad
Richmond Fredrickburg & Potomac R.R.
Atlantic Coast Line Railroad
Florida East Coast Railway

Dear Mother,

Here I am on the train en route to Palm Beach—and it's all very simple after you've made up your mind. I am feeling much better today with the excitement of a change.

I left the most awful weather in N.Y. There was even a hail storm last night, and this morning it was pouring rain through fog. This sort of weather kept up until after Baltimore. But since getting south of Washington it is bright and sunny. And tomorrow morning I'll wake up among the palm trees! There is nothing like a change of surroundings to change your state of mind.

Last news before leaving N.Y. was that Muriel [Draper] was sick in bed too. She fainted dead away on her door step on her way from writing at the Shelton. She has been working so hard and has worn herself out. I hope she will rest up now and eat. Carl [Van Vechten] was delighted that I was going south & said he might fly down and join me. He said he would give me letters to friends in Richmond & Baltimore if I cared to stop over on my way north. I may do this. My ticket permits it. And it would be just as cheap to stop in a new city as to pay for Pullman.

It all depends on if I am crazy about staying in Palm Beach [within] my time limit. Am very happy to be going. Take the letter to Dad.
    Max

Max returned to Pioneer after his father died on April 23, 1932. People noted his death: "Pioneer loses esteemed citizen . . . . With his passing not only the village but the entire community loses a man of sterling worth–a character beyond reproach; a man of excellent habits, mild of temperament and candid."

"May 1901 he married Miss Clara Bartoe. To this union there was born one son, Max Ewing. He was an active member of the Civic Organization, the League of Public Welfare. He was an honored

member of the Masonic fraternity and a trustee of the local lodge. He became a member of the Pioneer Methodist Episcopal Church this last Easter, March 27, signed the register and received the Easter Communion, and thus he has left final confession of faith in Christ and acknowledged his allegiance to the church. He was true to his family, loyal to his community, sincere in his Masonry, and in his final decision at Easter for Christ and the Church we found the real Christian."

August 16, 1932

We breakfasted at Muriel's, and sat in her budding grove, our name for her back yard.

Esther and Emily and I had tea together yesterday, Sunday, and congratulated ourselves long and thoroughly on having given the one big party so far in 1928 where no one was violently insulted and where there were no casualties. People on the whole were amiable. Everyone came who was invited except the Fitzgeralds in Delaware who couldn't make it. And not very many came who were not invited. I was terribly pleased to have the thing here, because it made this apartment familiar to many people who probably would not have to go here otherwise. Esther and Emily spent about two hundred dollars on the evening,—not much of an effort for their combined purses, but certainly more than I can do for one nights entertainment. Taylor Gordon sang and though he is no longer a novelty everyone adores him and he does sing superbly. There were many odd features of the evening. Bob Chanler came and behaved very sweetly, and he who has lived for years in Paris, and was one of the last great friends of Isadora [Duncan]. Bob brought him over this winter to live with him, and Louise is terribly mad about it. Both Walter and Louise stayed in a corner and were comparatively subdued all night. Louise was magnificently got up in a diamond necklace and a flowered dress that was very long and full, about fifteen yards around the bottom, which hung in a loose billows all around her. Bob took Esther aside and thanked her effusively for letting him bring Louise because he said he wanted people to give her a chance to show she could behave! The room was a strange sight, because although dozens of people were in it, the whole place looked black and white. All women by some coincidence dressed in either black or white. Only two wore color: Mildred Whitall who was dressed in pink spangles, and Mercedes de Acosta who wore red velvet trimmed with gold flowers. Sarah Marsh and Jimmy Leopold stayed in different ends of the room, and neither precipitated a scene. Larsson proved to be a great surprise, for most people didn't know he was in the country. Jacques Rigaut, a French poet, and a friend of Muriel's was supposed to be taking Madame Eyre de Lanux out Saturday night, but when he received the telegram asking him to this party he refused to see Mme de Lanux and came here. Unfortunately his wife was giving a party in her Park Avenue apartment the same night. She was formerly Mrs Barbour, a millionaire widow whom Rigaut married about two years ago for some reason or other. Anyway he came to the party, and later on in some mysterious way she showed up too with a French painter named Sakier. Neither she nor I had ever seen her, and Esther knew her very slightly. Esther offered her every hospitality, but she only stood by the door and refused to remove her wrap, and kept repeating, "Pray pay no attention to me, I must go at once, please do not concern yourself over me, I have guests at home, I must go." So she stayed about half an hour and then went, as strangely as she had arrived, like a phantom. And after that things went on as before. The party stayed here until four o'clock, and then moved on. Many people went to the Jungle Club to dance. I went with Emily Vanderbilt to Douglas Parmentier's to breakfast with six or eight others. By that time Bellstrom had "behaved" as long as was humanly possible for her, and she commenced at breakfast to insist that Bob had to marry her within two weeks. At that he commences to rave about Lina Cavlieri, and say he won't ever marry. And they go on like that. Emily and I discovered in the course of the evening that we were the same age, and the two youngest people in the party. Everyone always thinks that we are both much older than we are.

Last night I got around to see Alfred Lunt and Helen Westley in Volpone at the Guild Theater, and afterward Adlai Harbeck and I dropped in to see the Dance Marathon for half an hour. This is the very limit, the very extremist topmost summit of insanity to be found in this city which is more and more insane all the time. It is a dance endurance race in Madison Square Garden, doubtless you have been reading about it. The dancers, more than a hundred couples, started dancing a week ago last Sunday. Last night about twenty couples were still going, some about passing out, but most of this week! It is simply incredible. The men have grown beards, and the girls can scarcely drag one foot after the other. They have 15 minute intermissions occasionally, but they are not allowed to sleep even then. Some of them have gone to sleep dancing, and have been sent home. A Red Cross hospital is in the center of the floor to take care of people who faint or almost die. One girl lost her reason completely and was found dancing in the subway with her mouth filled with newspapers. The winning couple will win $5000.00, but I'm sure the doctor bills that follow such a performance must eat up the profit! Even if they win, what have they won? as Louise Hellstrom would say. Well, that was that, and an experience different from any other I have ever had.

The important thing however seems to me to live the full and civilized life. But I realize that you consider the money-making an important function in itself. And that is why I try to make it, in order that you may think me a "success" in terms of your own values. But every time I try to invade any business citadel, it is just like beating my head against a stone wall, and becomes an absolute nightmare. I may get over it. Give me time.

My "Mondays" are becoming quite a regular and established event. Yesterday being Monday, the great and the near great collected here. The great was represented by Marguerite D'Alvarez, who came for the first time. She was in magnificent form, and for two hours poured out the kind of extravagance with which she is famous for. She was particularly in her element because, with the exception of Dorothy Sheldon, D'Alvarez was the only woman here.

Much of the rest of this week is being given over to a repetition of what he called last year the Murphy Marathon. Esther sails Friday evening, a large gap in the life of the city. Sunday night the Whitalls gave a dinner for her which thirty people attended, and which was very agreeable. Tomorrow night Esther is giving a large farewell party for herself at home, with thirty for dinner and more coming later. Thursday night Muriel is having a sendoff for her, and Friday she gets off.

Here is an end of the week chronicle–this being Saturday. This moment at having finished my masterpiece of sculpture—a full length figure of Muriel in gold costume and covered and flowering with all kinds of Woolworth jewelry. It is a scream, and I am secretly very proud of it. The other heads I made ten days ago have enjoyed great success, but they were merely heads, while this is everything and greatly improved in technique and is likely to provoke a panic.

He was extravagant in his praise of my music, my lyrics, my apartment, my gallery, my statues of Muriel whom he knows, my furniture, my curtains, mirror, my all.

He left saying, "you will be a rich man, you will be a rich man." So god help us all.

There is not a single letter in the lot that there is any reason for sealing. I will send these to Yale as soon as I hear from you.

What money I make in my life I shall make solely to gratify YOU, and make you see some return for your efforts; to give you some more tangible proof of my worth than I can give you by simply voicing it. I want to do this, because to you, I know, "money talks." To me it doesn't. I mean itself. I have luxurious and extravagant tastes of course which I would love to satisfy,—but not at the expense of what I hold still more valuable, which is my intellectual leisure as fed by my curiosity. Certainly it is a difficult attitude to explain to those parents of whom by some extraordinary chemical and biological miracle I am the child! What I mean is—all my life has been devoted to developing myself as a hot-house product, and always about three times removed from reality, 0 and so you must not be surprised when faced with the fact that it isn't a garden variety after all. People get what they want if they want hard enough.

People cut their own direction unless they are physically disabled. That I CHOOSE to follow a path of glory through misty region some eyes can't penetrate is my problem. Let him have his house and his dollars. The last time I saw him his eyes were sad.

Going Somewhere, *Max's only published novel, came out in late 1932. Dedicated to one of his closest friends, Muriel Draper, the book offered a humorous and satiric look at contemporary society, especially as he had experienced it in New York City. A letter to his mother provides some helpful insights about the novel's characters.*

The front cover of *Going Somewhere*, designed by Robert E. Locher.

December 20, 1932

Mother

    Greetings on Tuesday. Still cold but not SO cold. I hope things with you are not so bad. People have been calling up all evening, people who have just received the Knopf winter catalog. Most surprising of all,

Mrs. Sol Guggenheim rang up and asked me to come to tea right away today at the Hotel Plaza. So I will go. Last night Alice De La Mar, back from her first trip to Palm Beach, and like the angel she is, took me to the Metropolitan Opera to hear Elektra, a new production there this season which is a sensation, and one of the greatest since Salome. Gertrude Kappel is the star, and it was very thrilling. Alice and I had excellent seats downstairs, quite a treat for me, as I always stand up when I go there, because I can't afford eight dollars a seat and I get dizzy sitting upstairs. Her mother was there in a box with Eva Gauthier, but she and Alice paid no attention to each other. We ran into Helen Westley in the intermission and she introduced me to the man she was with, saying, "Meet Sex Menace." She can never remember my name but, she always remembers that I first told her about Sex Menace! After the opera we went to a little party at Jo Meilziner's. He is a scenic designer who is designing the sets for the Metropolitan's production of The Emperor Jones, with Lawrence Tibbett next month.

I sent you and Doddy copies of the book, and I hope you will consider it a great event when you open it. I think it is a grand job of book-making, and I have a hunch it will sell. Time will tell. I am impatient to read some reviews of it. I hope the reviewers will get what I am driving at. The tone of the book is flippant, and often farcical, but underneath the surface flippancy it is quite serious and solid. The underlying theme of it, in case people feel called upon to ask you about it, is that people nowa-days all have a mania to go somewhere, anywhere to get away from where they are, and that when they get there they generally find that life is no more admirable one place than another. In the book, I bring a French Princess and a group of English people to America in search of a change. An American sculptress goes to South America. A lady elocution teacher goes all the way around the world. And a character named Aurora Overhaul (who is Muriel [Draper] in disguise) finally gives it all up and leaves the earth entirely, hoping that things may be better regulated on one of the other planets! She finds life as it is lived today undistinguished and tawdry and can see nothing to do about it except carrying going somewhere to the very limit, and going off into space. So the book ends. Some of the characters are portraits. The Princesse de Villefranche is the Princess.Murat; Lenore Lanslide is Louise Hellstrom as she was in the old Chanler-19th Street days; Nioba Why is more or less like Lorna Lindsley. And Napier is an idealized Derek Patmore. Send your comments at once. I think it is the best Christmas present I ever sent you, and I hope you won't be at sixes and sevens too much to enjoy it.

    Much Love.   Max

January 1, 1933

Dear Mother,

    Happy New Year. There is some satisfaction in waking up on the first day of a <u>new year</u> and finding myself plastered over the newspapers of the nation as a <u>new American novelist</u>. I enclose a big type announcement from today's N.Y. Times, in which I head the list in a pleasant way. Also a review from today's Herald-Tribune, which calls me a "worthy disciple" of Carl Van Vechten and Ronald Firbank, which is music to my ears—or eyes. I will send you more from time to time, and I want you to show them to our friends, and save them all.

    As further music for YOUR ears and eyes I enclose a column about Florida, also from today's Tribune. New Year's Eve came and went and was very full. At five o'clock I went to the Stettheimers. They had a big assembly of all sorts of people including a Scottish Chief in kilts and sword. At six o'clock I went to a party at Kay Mills. At seven o'clock I hurried home and got into tails and top hat ("so off he went in his opawee hat, whevver his muvver would let him or no . . . ") and went to Alice De La Mar's. We waited for Esther [Murphy] and the Rogers, and then the five of us went to Nancy Bryant's place to dinner. She tried again to tell my fortune, and she insisted that she saw me going to England or something to do with a movie scenario. She said that a year ago things were very low for me, but that now I was going up and up and that all sorts of good things were on the way. She was like that about me. But she was absolutely amazing about Esther, whom she had never seen or heard of. She told Esther she was upset and lonely in New York, that she saw two important deaths in her family over the past year, that she had been married and living in England, but that the marriage was ending in a divorce, and that Esther was living in a N.Y. hotel in the meantime. She also said that on Xmas eve Esther had given away a valuable piece of jewelry to someone on the spur of the moment, and that she had felt quite relieved ever since This was practically hair-raising, for on Xmas Eve Esther <u>had</u> given her wedding ring away to the small daughter of Gilbert Seldes. And practically no one at all knew this. Well, after these revelations from Nancy Bryant (who was dressed for the gala night with a red bandanna on her head, and also a gilded tiara from which rose a tall aigrette of white tissue paper!) we went on to Rita Romilly's and. picked up her and Carl [Van Vechten] and Fania [Marinoff], and all arrived at Muriel's about the stroke of twelve. There was a big crowd, but smaller than on other years. Muriel had only invited thirty-five people, so there were only about a hundred there. She used to invite two hundred and four or five hundred would come. When I left the party Dudley Murphy was just arriving. He had flown in an aeroplane in snow storms from Hollywood to get there for Muriel's party!

    Alice De La Mar leaves for Florida again tomorrow. She plans to fly to Mexico for a while in February, but says she would love to have me come to Palm Beach again in March. We will see what the winter brings forth before making any definite plans. Anyway, I am now a new American novelist. In another year or two I hope to be a new American playwright. And after that we will be all set, and you may GO ANYWHERE you like.

Max

Among the reviews of his novel that Max set aside were these: "To many his sequined and scintillating chronicle of Manhattan will be the most amusing of the year."

"Mr. Ewing's mood, it must be admitted, is a yesteryear mood, harking back to the most glorious days of Van Vechten and Firbank. It survives in Evelyn Waugh, but bitterly."

"It is really then a mood of remembrance of things past, for though the motions continue we have lost the mood, with the last lost generation. To regain and retain that is a merit in Mr. Ewing, so long as he does it with style and humor and is not taken in by it."

"Everything succeeds by excess and mounts to a fantastic climax. It manages to be as expansive as a circus and as smart as an intimate revue."

"It seems very much like a comic novel. In fact it is a novel and on first reading parts of it seems very funny, other parts seem funny enough and the rest of it sounds so familiar that the wry smile of recognition on our lips hasn't much chance of breaking into a laugh."

"Going Somewhere has an irritating and deceptive quality of appearing like a frivolous book. It is frivolous like a bit of arsenic left by mistake on purpose in somebody's liquor glass, or frivolous like a broken plate glass window which betrays the tires of a Rolls Royce."

"In a hundred year's time Going Somewhere will be republished with careful notes and comment to explain all the contemporary allusions."

"If the depression still has you in its grip there is a balm in "Going Somewhere."

"Our grandmothers would not have touched the book with a poker, but—what percentage of our novels to-day would they have found to be 'really nice.'" He did not specify the source of the reviews, although the last one came from the London Times.

In 1926 in New York City Max purchased a pull-down window blind. He wrote to his parents, "It is painted, showing the Piazza in Venice. When it is pulled half way down you see only water with a gondola. When pulled down all the way you see all the Piazza and the whole thing serves as a full length panel as well as a blind." In late 1932 and in January the following year, he invited friends to have their pictures taken posing in front of the blind and dressed as if they were at the Carnival of Venice. Among the many who agreed to pose were Agnes de Mille, John Becker, Isamu Noguchi, Louise Hellstrom, Berenice Abbott, Miguel Covarrubias, Eva Casanova, and Lou Telegen. The resulting photographs formed the exhibition he refers to in the next letter. The exhibit would be held at the Julien Levy Gallery later in January. [Reference to the blind and the photo shoots are included in email correspondence with Steven Watson, December 20, 2004.]

January 3 1933

Dear Mother,

I enclose some evidence that today I am headline news in New York, along with the death of Jack Pickford, and the confession of Larry Gay's killer. The reviews enclosed are from today's N.Y. World Telegram and the N.Y. Evening Sun. They are both excellent reviews, winning more space and more praise than I ever expected. I am sending you two copies of the Sun review, in case you want to give it away. I am also sending a copy of each to Uncle A.E. who seems vastly interested and pleased. If you are either one, or in any way gratified, I wish you would make some little sign to show it . . .

In spite of being news today, I have worked all day at Eddie Moeller's, in the dark room, getting enlarged prints ready for my exhibition. Then this evening I looked in at the Seldeses. It was Gilbert's birthday. We're having warm weather again, and everything is pretty nice.

Yours,
Max

Monday, January 9 [1933]

Dear Mother,

Just got your note. If the previous book reviews made you feel "overwhelmed," then this enclosed one from the Philadelphia Public Ledger will just knock you out entirely. It is by far the best one so far, and I am very happy over it. The other one by Gilbert Seldes is good too, and doubly valuable because his column is syndicated like McIntyres in various papers across the country. Certainly I cannot complain of the press reception of the book, and if it doesn't sell well it will not be the fault of the writer, the publisher, or the reviewers. It will be only the fault of the hard times which keep people from buying what they would like to buy. In any case, it is a great satisfaction to me to have this project work out so well. Others of my projects have fallen through, and it has sometimes seemed like a long hard pull. But whenever one project has gone wrong, I have tried another, and now in this one I have accomplished a real substantial success. The book has added immeasurably to my prestige, and has made me more or less well known across the whole country. And whatever I try to do in the future ought to be easier to put over on account of it. I am of course terribly disappointed that the book was delayed too long for Dad to enjoy our satisfaction. But from every other point of view it was a godsend that it was held up until Knopfs took it. They have handled it far better than any of the publishers would have who rejected it. Especially Joe Brewer whose firm has given up the ghost completely. Muriel takes bitter pleasure in reading the enthusiastic reviews to Joe and watching his discomfiture! The ten per cent royalty on the first printings is standard fee for writers. The enormous expense of publication, manufacture, advertising, etc. has to be made back by the publishers first. If the book sells above a certain number of copies then the writer's royalty increases proportionately. I think Dr. Bready is right to want the book in the Church. At bottom it is a very MORAL book. Some of the people in it behave in a disreputable way, but because I write about it, that does not mean that I endorse it. Quite the contrary. In the end I make it clear. Aurora, the one entirely admirable character, finds the whole scene so wrong and so empty that she packs up and leaves the whole planet in disgust. The Philadelphia review is superb in the way it points out my serious attacks under all the froth on top. You did not enclose the Bryan [Ohio] clipping as you wrote you were doing. When some of the reviews come in, you should clip excerpts—I don't mean really CLIP—I mean select excerpts and have them appear in a column in the Alliance. The most flattering excerpts, of course!

More soon. Probably tomorrow.

Max

Thursday [January 12, 1933]

Dear Mother,

I have been so busy lately I have been letting the clippings about me speak for me. But here I am again in person. The days have been very full. Esther [Murphy] is AT LAST really sailing on Saturday this week. And. all her friends have been giving her farewell parties. When she left to be married in England there were a lot of parties which we called the Murphy Marathon. This has been almost like it, only this time she is leaving to get a divorce.

Can't say yet about book sales, but there have been good reports from small shops. A place called the Folio Bookshop in East 54th St. sent for me to come and sign copies the other day. I signed a dozen copies which had all been ordered in advance, all by people I never heard of. The woman said I would have to come back and sign more copies this week. Lewis Galantiere who works down in the Wall Street section tried to get the book in a shop in the Equitable Building the other day, and the clerk said she had sold all her copies and Lewis would have to wait till she got more. She said so many people were reading it. And Sallie Marsh (Sarah King) trying to save money, went to rent it at a library, and the woman told her the copies were all out, and she would have to leave her name on a waiting list. So all that sounds good. Of course most of my friends have got it, but that doesn't count for much in the long run. Everyone is enthusiastic except a stupid reviewer on the Times. I'll send you his or her review when I get an extra copy. I had a copy sent to Geraldine Farrar, and had a very sweet note from her. Mrs. Tellegan (current one) is coming to be photographed next Wednesday.

I also had a letter—and an order—from Fred Elder, who had seen an announcement and a picture of me in the Cleveland papers last week. I've not been sent it yet.

Sorry about the coupons. What do we do—just wait?

I trust Doddy is progressing steadily. Do give her my love and tell her I will write to her especially again soon.

Howard Rothschild, a very rich young man, took me to lunch today. Tonight I dine at Rita Romilly's, after a party at Douglas Parmentier's, which is of course for Esther.

Tuesday the Stettheimers had me for luncheon with Francis Lederer the new Czech actor who is a sensation this year in N.Y. after winning over London last year. You must have read about him in the play "Autumn Crocus" if you follow theater news at all this year. He is charming and delightful, and said he would let me take his picture for my show. If he does it will be a triumph, for he is the most sought after young man in the city, and all the ladies are at his feet swooning row on row—practically.

The Whitalls gave a party last Saturday for Harold Nicholson [Nicolson] and Vita Sackville-West. I enclose an article about them. As they live in an English castle with 365 rooms, perhaps they are going to give me one of the rooms and thus fulfill my fortuneteller's predictions!

Will write again soon. Lots of love, best love, and I hope you are holding up well under the strain of being the mother of a highly publicized young man! I think that of the younger generation of Ohioans, Libby Holman and I are doing well in getting attention this season!

Max

Friday [about January 13, 1933]

Dear Mother,

Your letter came today—with coupons & check. Many thanks. Next July when I receive my semi-annual royalty check from Knopfs you won't have to send any money. Too bad, isn't it, because you collect a lot of coupons in July!

I enclose some elegant proof that my recognition is not exclusively in literary circles this month. The big exhibition of <u>New York Beauty</u> opened at Bergdorf-Goodman last night, & contained 3 of my photographs, as you can see in the list. The Russian Grand Duchess Marie was there, & all the best Bergdorf-Goodman public. They made a movie tone of it for the News Reels, with Muriel as the announcer (unseen—only her voice being heard).

Am anxious to see the Chicago Tribune review. Fanny Butcher is Chicago's most influential book critic, & her praise will sell a lot of copies.

Love, Max.

Saturday—Jan. 14th [1933]

Dear Mother—

Here's a lot more material for your scrap book. If you haven't got a scrap book already, let me know and I'll send you one—big sized one to hold big clippings. Good reviews keep pouring in—also good reports from book shops. And frankly I too am surprised.

I wish I could make you accept the advice of the Philadelphia Record which tells its readers

"Drop whatever you are doing

Meet the pyrotechnic Ewing!"

Thanks for the check in place of the coupons. It arrived yesterday.

I'm glad things in Pioneer are calmer. Don't let me hear of you feeling down again.

Max.

Sunday [about January 15, 1933]

Dear Mother,

Here is a big article from the Boston American. It is Lincoln Kirstein's column, and it is syndicated in all the Hearst papers in New England. I begin to feel almost IMMODEST, sending you so many flowery tributes to myself. But I get them all from my clipping bureau, and whenever I can get duplicates I want you to have them. What with the West Coast (San Diego) saying that hundreds of young men would give ten years of their lives to have written my book, and the East Coast (Boston) saying the book will be revived in a hundred years with explanatory notes, I feel as if all the ground had been covered, and that my head should perhaps begin to be turned!

My week has been filled with my Exhibition. Some weeks ago I gave the editors of <u>Vogue</u> a look at the pictures to see if they would reproduce any of them. They did not realize what a to-do the pictures were to cause, and they turned them down. Then I took them to their rival, <u>Town and Country</u>. Town and Country accepted to do a page about me, and it is all set for the February issue. Then after the exhibition Vogue came around again and wanted a choice of the pictures, and found that Town and Country had got in ahead of them, and had the pick of the best social figures, like Mrs. Saportas, and the Princess Chachavadze, who is the sister of Mrs. Leeds, the former Princess Zenia [Xenia]. So it goes.

Dudley Murphy is coming in tomorrow, before he leaves for Hollywood. I want to have a long talk with him. I've got a real Hollywood bug for this summer.

Not much news today. I'm spending the day in, catching up with lots of odd jobs, and correspondence. I almost need a secretary! I wrote a letter to that Cleveland editor and told him that since he seemed to so strongly resent the photograph Berenice Abbott made of me that perhaps he would feel more charitable toward the photograph I had made of Berenice Abbott. I enclosed the list of the Carnival of Venice. He wrote back that he had only been trying to be amusing!

Everyone made a great effort to attend the Carnival. The Winslows came in to New York from Fieldston. Peter Jack came in from Staten Island. John McAndrew even came down from Poughkeepsie where he is teaching at Vassar. I'm sorry there was no delegation from just north of U.S. road #20.

Beginning today, Muriel is installing herself in Alice De La Mar's apartment, to finish the book. No one is to know she is there, except three or four intimate friends. She is telling everyone else she is going to the country.

More soon.
Max

Monday [about January 16, 1933]

Dear Mother

    Here's a copy of the London Times review which just arrived from Edgar Ailes in Detroit. Quite a lot of ground has been covered by this clipping by the time it arrives in Ohio!

    I also had a note from Nellie Gilpin today. She said you were feeling better on the day she wrote but that you looked tired out. I am so afraid that in spite of your condition you are going ahead and doing things you shouldn't. Who, for instance, is building those damnable store fires? If your trouble is overwrought nerves and a weak heart then the prescription must include rest and relaxation. And if in spite of this you are still trying to do a man's job, then you are just deliberately counting disaster of a sort you know will make me unhappier than anything possible could. Maybe you are NOT building the fires. But if you are I insist you stop immediately. You owe it to yourself, and you owe it to me, and furthermore you owe it to some wretched man who needs the job, and who would do it for little or nothing. You can't say there are no men out of work, and can't say you can't afford to have him. The only reason for saving money is that you will have it a later time when you need it. And that time is now. Use good sense. Furthermore, if you are on a diet you can't generate as much energy as you could on full meals.

    One comfort about the bank situation for you as far as Toledo is concerned is that Toledo has been on a bank moratorium for years already! It's nothing new there.

I still take Ovaltine in a pint of milk at night. Why don't you do that if you are allowed milk? It is very restful and sends you to sleep.

You ask about Stephanie. She lives with Mrs. Walton and I almost never see her. She leads a drab life, playing accompaniments when she can. Someone with money always has to pay for a musician's expenses these days. It is Frank's good fortune that he has a rich, socially prominent, crazy woman paying for his. It is Stephanie's bad fortune that she has an obscure, dullish woman like Mrs. W. paying for her. That is the difference. Frank leads an amusing life Stephanie does not.

You can stay here at my apartment any time you will come to N.Y. I can always sleep in a bed downstairs somewhere while you are here. There are two new tenants in the building this week and the landlord is joyous.

I saw Muriel last night. We went to the movies surreptitiously. Everyone thinks she is in the country, but she is really secluded in Alice De La Mar's apartment. She hadn't been out for five days till last night and she said if she sat still any longer she might begin to forget how to use her legs.

More soon. And REMEMBER–
               Max

Tuesday [January 17 1933]

Dear Mother,

This is to acknowledge receipt of the coupons once again. Am sure it will be ok this time. Will apply on next month's allowance, as you suggest. My bank is part of the Federal Bank system, and is safe as any can be if you ever care to send money for safe-keeping. Hope you are not being carried away by the antics of Howard Scott and Technocracy! Howard Scott is its founder and its prophet. Muriel is having him to lunch with Mr. Certauld [Courtauld] tomorrow. Probably hair will fly when the wildest of the American Reds and the stolidest of the British millionaires sit down at the same table.

Douglas Parmentier is not interested in Esther. She has sailed at last, thank God. We were all about exhausted by farewell parties for her. She has been about to sail since June.

I don't think Sarah Marsh has to economize very drastically. But everyone pretends to these days whether they have to or not. That's half the trouble, I'm sure.

Yes, Aunt Alice wrote me a nice letter about the book. So did Aunt Lotta, as well as Uncle A.E. Have your nose looked at and attended to AT ONCE. You probably banged it.

Louise Hellstrom came in the other day and let me take her picture in Venice for the exhibitions. She looked fine in furs and white satin but she complained of being broke. Said she was leaving for Mexico in the Spring. She hadn't read my book yet but said everyone had told her it was swell. I showed her the reviews, and she will like it, I'm sure. Carl put her into Parties, and made her much MORE SO than I did, and she loved it.

I guess this answers all your questions!

Over the weekend I went to tea at Mrs. Floretta Guggenheim's (not Mrs. Irene Guggenheims. I know them all now!) and to parties at Zelma Brandt's and Lawrence Langner's and Donald Angus'. Donald's party was given in honor of Carl's snake. It is black and six feet long. We all had to hold it and pet it and it was quite enjoyable once you got over your first reluctance. It lives at Donald's because [Fania] Marinoff is petrified of it.

Lou Tellegen is coming to be photographed tomorrow and then that completes my series. Gilbert Seldes says that I must take all my Venice pictures to the Italian Lines Travel Bureau and tell the people there that I have given Venice more publicity than it has had in years, and that furthermore, as the author of a successful book on Going Somewhere, that I want free passage or more or less free passage on the Italian Lines, and will probably get it. Gilbert went to Sweden last year for less than half the price because as a writer with a public name he wrote little things for the travel magazines which they use as publicity. All travel lines make enormous concessions to writers who will write for their passage. The trouble is I don't particularly want to go to Venice this season! But whenever I do want to go you will have to go too, and it will cost us next to nothing if I work things right with the steamship lines. We won't dare mention this to Aunt Lotta or she will want me to take her to Turkey almost any minute! The trouble with that is that I don't want to go to Turkey just now either. Alice De La Mar writes me that she has room for me at Palm Beach whenever I want to come. But I'm staying right here until the end of February anyway. After that anything may happen. Wishing luck to us all.

[after January 17, 1933]

Your letter came this morning. I should think you would be happier in our own house. There is bound to be a feeling of loss no matter which house you are in. And certainly our own house must have far pleasanter associations for you. And there are more places in it to escape into, if you know what I mean!

I realize, of course, that a lot of friends will rent or borrow the book instead of buying it. It isn't their fault. I'm sure they would like to buy it. If it makes good money I'll be pleased. If it doesn't I will not be surprised, and I'll be pleased anyway. If it didn't make a cent I would still count it a great feather in my cap. For the press recognition of its worth and mine has been extremely gratifying, and is like a public justification of myself and my way of life. I never felt the need of any justification of anything I did. I always knew I was good. So did you and Dad, I'm sure. But it is a great satisfaction to have such a complete and. widespread recognition of the fact. I'm sure that money will come from it, indirectly at least, if not from the book itself. I re-read my contract the other day and found that I receive a statement of my royalties next summer, but do not receive the actual money until late fall. So I hope this brief delay won't upset you too much!

    I had a very sweet letter from Clara Sweet yesterday expressing her pride and pleasure in my acquaintance!

    I wrote Carl [Van Vechten] and told him it seemed to be definitely established that I was one of his "disciples," and that if it were all the same to him I would like to be Saint Peter. He wrote back that I could be both Saint Peter and Saint Paul, but that he hoped. I would never be Judas! He and Donald have finally given theirs to the zoo because it wouldn't eat.

    I have written to Alice to ask more definitely about her dates and plans. If I go down there I'll not get a return date this time. I'm sure she wouldn't care how long I stayed. She has lots of room and she likes people with her whom she is fond of, for she doesn't go in for the Palm Beach crowds. I could probably spend several weeks there if I enjoyed it. Anyway, no plans until I hear from her. Marion Saportas said Sunday night that she was going to California in June to stay with Lilyan Tashman at her Malibu Beach house, and that she was sure Lilyan would like me to stay there too! This sounds improbable to me. But Marion is sending Lilyan my book, and you can't tell what may develop. I'm very glad the investments are holding out so well, and looking up. And I hope you can get your taxes readjusted. I think we have good times ahead in spite of the bad times. Will write again soon about the exhibition.

                              Max

Wednesday [January 18, 1933]

Dear Mother,

    Here's something from today's World Telegram. It seems to be news if I just stop in at a book shop! Lou Tellegen & his wife were just here to be photographed. Lou didn't look very Venetian, so I dressed him in my cape and top hat and he looked better! His wife wore something elaborate of black lace. Dorothy Sheldon was here too with the Duke de Arcos & his dog, & it was pretty odd for half an hour. Hope Doddy is behaving and you are improving your nose.

                      Max

Friday [about January 20, 1933]

Dear Mother,

    Here are two clippings which you may have seen already. If you have them then you can give these away. Or keep them anyway. The Detroit review is extremely good. Mr. Elrick Davis of the Cleveland Press seems to be quite het up over the fact that I was born in Pioneer. It apparently makes him very cross and resentful. This is *just too bad.* However, I suppose that all the young men who do not escape (as he puts it) from Ohio are a little bit resentful of those who do. So we will let him make his fun and enjoy his resentment all he likes, and be glad for the nice amount of space he gives me anyways!

    I have gone at last to the Radio City Music Hall. It's a marvelous theater but a rotten show. Roxy is a halfwit and he ought to be deported. The show is just like the shows always were at the old Roxy, only worse. We're having warm balmy summer weather. Very nice. No need to go to Florida this week, but you can't tell what it will be like next. I wish I could decide what to do about going down to Alice's and when I think I'll go. Even including carfare or boat fare it's cheaper than staying here, and it is so pleasant and bracing and luxurious down there! Last year when I went in the middle of March the "season" there was practically over. I would like to see it once in full sway in February. Alice writes me to come any time, but says she may go flying to Mexico or Yucatan late in February. I'll have to communicate with her further and learn more about dates. I could write on my play down there— try to at least. I'm going to return to working on it just as soon as my exhibition at Julien Levy's is over next week. I'm not going to rest on the book laurels. There's going to be no let up from now on. I'm off to a good start now, and I'm going to go on and on. So pull up your shoulders and be ready to come along too. We've got to go somewhere now.

      Max

Monday, January 23 [1933]

Dear Mother,

  Here are two announcements of the exhibition of my Carnival of Venice. It goes on all day Thursday for the general public. The more special public, including all the people whom I have photographed, are invited to a party for the opening Wednesday night. The people are invited to come to the party in the costumes in which they are photographed, so it promises to be pretty miscellaneous! It is stirring up a lot of interest and commotion, and the people who are not invited are absolutely furious. But we have to limit the invitation list somewhere, because with seventy-five people, each bringing someone, it makes a hundred fifty to begin with!

  The weekend has been very pleasant. Marion Tiffany Saportas took me to dinner at Spivy's Saturday night, and she had other guests a Swede named Holmsen, and Mrs. William Randolph Hearst, junior. Edith Hoffenstein joined us later. Then yesterday the Hoffensteins and Dick Clemmer and I went to Mrs. Saporta's suite at the Elysee at tea time. We were sitting around trying to decide what to do about dinner. Someone rang up Tallulah Bankhead who lives upstairs, but she was sound asleep. Then the telephone rang and someone downstairs said Madame Claire was calling. We thought it was a joke and Mrs. Saportas told the man to send "Madame Claire" up. So up she came and it was Ina Claire! Everyone was quite surprised, as she was not expected. But she said she had been at tea at Frieda Hempel's, and had been so bored she fled as soon as she could to come and join some people she could laugh with. She was looking smarter than anyone alive, and she looks twenty years old in the brightest light. I don't see how she does it. She was very vivacious and amusing, and said she had gone to the Opera to Scotti's farewell performance on Friday, and that in his dressing room afterward, Geraldine Farrar swept herself up and flung herself into his arms, but that Scotti put her gently and firmly aside and turned to Ina, and said "Ina, when I see you next?", and that Geraldine was left standing very much annoyed and perplexed! How they do go on—these girls! Well we all got off to dinner at last about nine o'clock. We went to Spivy's again. There are two pianos there. Spivy and I played both of them for a while. I played "Come with me, come to the ball" from The Quaker Girl, in deference to Ina Claire, and it was all very festive.

I'm very sorry you cannot attend the exhibition, but whenever you do come to N.Y. I promise you some good events. Everything goes on at the most hectic rate, and if there is a Depression it seems to be around the corner.

Max

On January 26 Max presented at the Julien Levy Gallery on Madison Avenue an exhibit of 76 photographs of many of the notables of the day, as well as his friend Jack Pollock. All of the black and white photos were taken at his New York studio-apartment with the Venetian blind as a backdrop. In his introduction to the exhibit, Gilbert Seldes wrote of Max: ". . . I discovered something totally unexpected and disarming about him: he always tells the truth. The more highly colored, the more removed from the ordinary his accounts of things may be, the more certain they are to be literally true, to the smallest detail. He chooses that smallest detail rather well."

Among those attending the Wednesday night opening party was Henry McBride, art critic for the New York Sun. The headline to McBride's ensuing article was "Max Ewing as a Camera Man: Strange Qualities Are Revealed in Novelist's Photography." The article started, "Max Ewing, poet, novelist, composer, pianist, photographer, and man-about-town, was given a one-night exhibition of his photographs and a party to accompany them . . . . It was a gay party. I had scarcely entered when two young things, with tears of pleasure in their eyes . . . buttonholed me with 'Wouldn't you call it brilliant?'. . . And all this, mind you, for photography! . . . And with it all, Mr Ewing, I fear, is not to be named among the ranking ten of the world's photographers. . . . I should scarcely call him a photographer at all were it not for the indisputable fact that he does take photographs. However, he has other merits. It was not for lack of technique that he was given a one-night stand . . . . Not at all. He has merits. He is very subtle in choosing sitters and still more subtle in encouraging them to psychoanalyze themselves while posing. Each print on the walls could have been handed in to a doctor who could thereupon indicate the exact medicine necessary to that particular case. It was because of the intimacy of revelation that the one-night stand was decided upon. It was thought better not to puzzle the general public with too much psychoanalysis. Some of the gentlemen sitters, for instance, were but lightly attired. Looking at these prints, Miss [Lorna] Lindsey, though just from Paris, remarked that the exhibition was giving her renewed confidence in the innate modesty of her own sex, for it was only the *gentlemen who felt the urge to strip for the camera. . . . His main object, as Mr Seldes insists, was to entertain, and that he succeeds in admirably."*

Writing on Levy Gallery letterhead, Max shared the opening night with his mother.

Thursday [about January 27, 1933]

602 Madison Avenue New York City
Julien Levy Gallery
Paintings—Photographs—Drawing—Books

Just a note to tell you that the Preview party last night was a tremendous success! In spite of a windy blustery night nearly two hundred people came out to see the photographs. Some had been at the Opera first, others at Madison Square Garden, others at Noel Coward's new play with the Lunts, but they all got to the Levy Gallery eventually, and by half past twelve I felt quite a lot like President Hoover after shaking hands and being cordial for three hours and a half without sitting down or stopping. Today I am going back for we expect throngs this afternoon. Copies of the announcement slip which I sent you were mailed out to hundreds of people, and it will be excellent tonic for the book . . . It was really a great night. I've been at lots of big parties in New York, but never at such an enormous one where the one and only attraction was myself and my handiwork. Eve Casanova and Lou Tellegen were the first to arrive, and they stayed for hours. As more and more people in ermine and top hats came pouring in until there was hardly any standing room. Eve said, "My dear, what drawing powers! What is your secret?" I told her I would tell her next week! The gallery had to close at twelve-thirty, and after that people dispersed to other places. Eddie and Mrs. Hearst Junior and the Princess Chavchavadze went off to the Wrightners. I looked in at Spivy's for half an hour but after that I was too tired to go to Harlem where a lot of others went.

Frank Bishop plays tonight in Town Hall for the first time. He went to bed last night and did not come to the exhibition at all, but his wife came, and said Frank had been sleepless for weeks dreading the critics tonight. I said I found it much more comfortable to WRITE and hear from the critics later. Muriel is having Frank and Claire and a few others come in after his concert. It is a good week and I wish you were here.

Max

Friday [about January 27, 1933]

Dear Mother,

Here are some clippings and things that may interest you—not about me, for a change.

The resume of Mrs. Belmont's life is interesting. "She never let her memories get her down" is an admirable statement to be made about any of us.

The red and silver bit is an invitation to be part of Cobina Wright's Saturday Night Club at the Waldorf-Astoria. As I am not spending $7.50 a night for supper this season I am sending it on to you to use as you see fit.

I spent yesterday at the Levy Gallery shaking hands with the overflow people who were not invited to the big night–people like Warren Bowers, Elaine Freeman, etc. The Levys are delighted with the result of the exhibition and so am I.

I went to hear Frank Bishop play last night. He played very well indeed. He had a moderately good audience, though not at all a distinguished one. I sat with the Sheldons and Rogers.

Thank Doddy for her letter which just came. I am very glad indeed that she is better.

I miss writing Dad a birthday note this week. I always did it. And I wish I always might. He deserved Happy Birthdays if anyone ever did.

Will write more soon.

Max

Sat. Jan 28 [1933]

602 Madison Avenue New York City
Julien Levy Gallery
Paintings—Photographs—Drawing—Books

Dear Mother,

Here's a small enlargement of Lou Tellegen and Eve [Eva] Casanova. Also an article about the party by Henry McBride from today's N.Y. Sun. You can see it was quite an event. Last night I went to the Capitol Theater to hear Mary Garden – her first appearance in a movie theater. I came home and wrote a column about it for Gilbert Seldes' use. He is leaving for vacation in Bermuda, and I was glad to help him out. The column will probably appear next week. Don't think you won't receive a copy!

Max

Monday, Jan. 31 [1933]

Dear Mother,

Your letter came this morning. It is quite a shock about Norman Riste, and I feel so sorry for Josie and the girls. I will write her a note today. Last week I sent her an announcement of the Carnival of Venice. I am so sorry too that you have had to be sick with a cold. Almost nobody I know has escaped it, but I have so far. I have been taking extraordinary precautions to avoid it—gargling every time before I leave the house and all that sort of thing. I know I just had to be well during this January and February. The excitement alone of the past weeks has been something of a strain on the nervous system, but I've been fine otherwise. I usually run down around the end of February or March, and that is why I think Florida would be a good idea again.

You must take care of yourself, and get a lot of rest. Your well-being is the most important thing in the world to me. Whatever success or distinction I win is pleasurable to me half on my own account, and half to you. If you were not there to enjoy them, even at a distance, half the kick would be gone for me. So pull yourself together fast and be ready to enjoy more successes, for they are just starting, I am sure. Please, please engage more help, and don't do strenuous odd jobs, yourself. What is the sense in it, when workers are so cheap. Why tire yourself out and be worried with little jobs that anyone can learn to do? From now on, wherever you go, people will say "That is Max Ewing's mother." And you must keep yourself FIT. The Levy exhibition was chiefly for the glory—mutually. They were glad for the glory I brought them. And I was glad for the glory of a show under such smart auspices. It was a very expensive party to give on Wednesday night. So we charged admission, and made back the expenses on the printing, the refreshments, the servants, and all that. People wanted to pay. In fact they were fighting for the privilege of paying. We had Maud Massey—Muriel's old Maud, in a black uniform to take money!

I enclose my article about Mary Garden from today's N.Y. Journal. I hope she likes it. She ought to. Last night I stood up to see Design For Living—Noel Coward's new play with himself and the Lunts in it. Seats are out of the question as they cost five dollars apiece, and the whole theater is sold out for weeks in advance. Which goes to show that people will pay anything to see what they want to see, if it's good. Between the acts I ran into Lloyd Morris for the first time in a year. We were very polite and cordial. I also ran into my former pupil, Nick

Putnam, who was there alone. After the show we went to Childs and had coffee and a talk. He is not as flush or as wild as he was in the old days, but I was glad to see him again.

Tonight I am being taken to see Eva Le Gallienne's production of Alice in Wonderland–with Muriel and the Marshes. I was supposed to be dining at Elsie Arden's, but Elsie let me out when this other thing came up, and is having me dine on Thursday instead.

Write me right away that you are feeling better—if you are.
      Max

Thursday [about February 2 1933]

Dear Mother,

I thought you might like to see this picture of Mrs. Julien Levy, who was responsible for much of the social success of the exhibition. She is seen holding my Christmas tree of white tissue. She is quite a beauty, as you can see. I still get letters every day from people who did not get to come to the exhibition—people I do not know—who hope to see it somewhere eventually.

I enclose a letter from Mr. Edward Paul England III, one of the social high moguls of the Waldorf-Astoria, who sent for me to come and meet him, which I did today, and found him very charming. You can see from his stationery that he is quite an elegant young man. He said the whole boat was hilarious on the way to Bermuda on account of Going Somewhere.

Today's mail also brought a lovely letter from Mary Garden, thanking me warmly for my article about her, and asking me to come see her next week. She is singing at a soiree at the White House in Washington next Friday night, but asks me to set my own time otherwise.

Also a note from Helen Morris enclosing the News Bee write-up.

Dined at Elsie's tonight in a quiet way and am now going gratefully to bed.

        Yours,
        Max

Feb. 2, 1933

Dear Uncle,

Thanks for your note. Also for the note last week about Dad's birthday. I wrote one to Mother at about the same time, saying almost the same thing.

If you are trying to keep in any way a thorough going Max Ewing file you should get a copy of the magazine called <u>Town and Country</u>, the issue of February 1st. It contains my greatest glorifications to date. There are reproductions of several of my Venetian photographs—one of a Romanoff Princess telephoning in Venice, one of Lois Moran holding a statue of my head in Venice, one of me looking haughty in Venice, and more than a page of facts about me and Romanoffs and Pioneer and Paris and pianos and Going Somewhere—as well as Venice. I hope you can get it in G.R. Doubtless the Pantlind news stand would have it. It is not on the street newsstands even in N.Y., as it is a very swank sheet.

Yes, I saw the Detroit News review. I get all of them from my very efficient clipping bureau. They are mounting up into quite a staggering volume.

Now that the preliminary excitement of the book is over, and the photograph exhibition is over, and things are showing signs of calming down a little, I am getting back to work on my play. More of that anon.

    Love,
        Max

Max's reputation continued to grow, boosted certainly by the mostly positive reviews of his novel. A celebration of his new fame was to be held at the Waldorf-Astoria in mid-February, and would include an exhibition of his photographs. He badly wanted Clara to join him at the fete, and in addition to his own pleading, asked his uncle to use whatever persuasive skills he could muster to achieve the same end. Both failed in their endeavor, nor did A.E. and his wife make the trip. Lotta told her husband, "The only thing more difficult than not going is going." Not going prevailed.

Saturday [February 4, 1933]

The Waldorf-Astoria
New York

Dear Mother,

On Saturday February 18th—the Waldorf-Astoria Hotel is giving a large tea and dance in my honour in the Empire Ballroom. Will you consider coming? Close the store for a few days if necessary—and do your spring buying here. You will do twice as much business if you go & come with that publicity! The whole staff of the hotel is bringing all its pressure to bear on this occasion. There will be widespread publicity—and it is a great honor to me. Elaborate engraved invitations are being printed. You will receive one. Please accept & R.S.V.P.

Max

Page 2

Saturday night [February 4, 1933]

Dear Mother,

This morning I wrote you a letter, the first part of which I attach on a separate page. The end of the letter was to the effect that the Waldorf-Astoria might be giving a party for me. But when I wrote this morning it had not been settled. This afternoon it was settled and the date was set for February 18th,—two weeks from today. The social directors of the Waldorf-Astoria have decided that it would add prestige to the hotel to give a party in my honour. So a big tea and dance is going to be given. In addition they are going to show my photographs on silver screens on the terrace to accommodate all the people who did not see them at Levy's. A list of patronesses for the event is being drawn up, including Mrs. Whitney, Mrs. Morgan, Princess Chavchavadze, Mrs. Tiffany Saportas, and Mary Garden, if she will be here by that time. Elaborate engraved invitations on gold tissue are being sent out, with a decoration of a Venetian lady in black lace and a gold mask. I went to the Waldorf-Astoria today and talked over the plans for the event. I wrote you a note from the hotel just so you could believe it! The management is all worked up over it. The letter from Mr. England which I received some days ago and sent on to you was a feeler.

  I am writing now, in desperation, to ask you one more time if you will make a superhuman effort and come for this event, and share a little bit of the rewards which you deserve. Close the store, engage a nurse for Doddy, and be here. And don't say it cannot be done. You can sell a bond if you have to. What if it does reduce your capital a little. Everybody has reduced his capital. I am on my way to big money now. There is no doubt about it. I will never miss it if I have a few hundred dollars less in 1953. I will feel deprived forever though if you do not come and see me now. Is there anything under the stars and moon and sun that would bring you to see me, if the whole Waldorf-Astoria being turned over to us to do me honour does not bring you? For years you have considered the Waldorf-Astoria as the pinnacle of earthly glory. You used to like to go and just sit in its lobby, and write a note on its stationery to your friends. Now the whole place is bringing all its staff to do me honour, because to have me there does them honour. I have accomplished this through your efforts, and you ought to come even if it cost you a thousand dollars. As a matter of fact it would cost very little. And if you still have the shrewd business sense which you have always had, you will realize that to come will bring you business in the end. You can send notices to the papers in the neighboring towns that you are going to New York to a party the Waldorf-Astoria is giving in my honor. And that you will do more spring buying, and will have the new goods at a certain time. It will be good advertising copy for you and people will come from miles around to touch the hem of your garment.

So once again, make a big effort. Indulge me just once in this, and I won't ask anything else of you for another blue moon. This will be something you will enjoy. And you will enjoy the memory of it when it is over. And I will always enjoy the memory of it when it is over. If you don't do it I will always feel disappointed. You denied yourself many things for a long time. You have thrown so much effort and ambition into producing me and launching me. Please come if only for those three hours and reap a little reward of these last thirty years.

All you need is a new hat and gloves. Wear your black lace dress and your fur coat. Try and get here Friday the 17th. Then we will have Sunday together, and the first of the week you can do your buying. If you can go to Chicago and spend two nights you can come here. And I will say just this, that if you DO go to Chicago and don't come here, when coming here means so few extra hours and so few extra dollars, then I will know that you are not as proud of me as I always hoped you would be.

The first plan was to have the party on the 11th. I was against that because I thought it would be too short notice for you. But having it the 18th gives you two weeks, and plenty of time. Mary would take charge of the store that Saturday. And there are half a dozen other people who would help her.

I might even be able to negotiate to get you free rates at the Waldorf-Astoria,—though perhaps this would be asking too much. At any rate, you could live downstairs here for next to nothing. I would see to that. So—very seriously, I hope you will come. I have an idea that if I were being inaugurated as President of the United States you would stretch a point and come. But in my scale of values this is just as important. I am not interested in politics. And I will never be a guest of honor at the White House. But short of that there is no more distinguished place to be a guest of honor than the Waldorf-Astoria in New York. There are some things in life that demand some recognition as symbols. There are some ceremonies that are important on the way of living and dying. Obviously, it is not worth your while to cross three states only for the sake of tea. But this tea stands for something, can't you see? It is more than just another tea. It is formal recognition on mine—and therefore your—achievement under the most distinguished auspices this country's social life affords. So will you please come, because you are my mother, and because I have no other?
        Max

Sunday [February 5, 1933]

Dear Uncle,

    This is in a way a business letter—almost a legal letter—a letter in which I hope to test your powers of persuasion as a legal advisor!

    Here is the point: the Hotel Waldorf-Astoria has decided that it is time to pay attention to me, and is giving a large tea and dance in my honor on Saturday, Feb. 18th. In addition, my photographs of people in Venice are to be displayed on a terrace of the ballroom on silver screens. The whole thing is to be very elaborate, and is being planned on quite a big scale under the auspices of the Princess Chavchavadze of Russia, Mrs. Morgan, Mrs. Whitney, Mrs. Saportas and Mary Garden as patronesses. (Really one couldn't do better!) Elaborate engraved invitations on gold vellum are being sent out next week, and the Hotel Waldorf-Astoria is bringing to bear all its publicity pressure and social pressure to make it a great event. It is to be a Going Somewhere party, as well as another Carnival of Venice. Harold Stern's orchestra will officiate, and God knows what else.

Now, I want very much to have Mother here for it. She is sure to protest that it is impossible on account of the store, the fires, my grandmother, economy programs, etc. Now, can't you in some way make her see that this is a major event which tops all those others in importance? That it is her duty to be here more than to be on the job at home for a few days? I have worked for the last eight years towards just the sort of success that is attending me now, and I want her here to share it if only for a few days—or even a few hours. It is already too late for Dad to share it. And one never knows when it will be too late for Mother to share it. I know that it is extremely difficult for her to get away. But she ought to make the effort, and I hope you can in some way persuade her of this. AND PLEASE do not let her suspect that I told you to do it. Just say that I wrote you that I hoped she might come for the Waldorf-Astoria event. Then in your own way you can add that in your opinion she ought to do it. She has a great respect for your opinion, and perhaps we can swing it.

And while we are on the topic of coming, I wish you and Aunt Lotta could come too. At any rate you will receive invitations.

        Yours,
        Max

Monday evening [about February 6, 1933]

Dear Mother,

I am so happy. I am on all the crests of all the waves! This is all beyond all my most extravagant hopes for this winter. The Waldorf-Astoria thing is progressing. Mary Garden has consented to be a patroness even though she will not be in N.Y. by the 18th. Anyway she has invited me to have dinner with her and Muriel in her suite at the Ritz Tower this week Wednesday night.

I told the publicity man at Knopfs today about the Waldorf-Astoria tea, and, he was quite staggered. He said he never heard of such a thing, and that it was quite unprecedented. He said no other Knopf author had ever had such a thing given in his honor. At first I don't think he even believed me. Blanche Knopf is in Miami.

Another great new project is this: I am rounding up fifty people to go to a special midnight show of the Hollywood puppets the night of Feb. 16th. All the people are fans of Gary Cooper, and it is a night in his honor. The organization is called the Garyflappers, named after the old Gerryflappers! I have had cards printed and stationery printed. I will probably make a nice profit too, as more than fifty people will want to be there, and I'll get the excess money. I have interested Peggy Fears in it. You have probably read about her all winter. She is the ex-Follies girl who married A.C. Blumenthal and all his millions. Blumenthal is Jimmy Walker's closest friend. He and Peggy live in an entire floor of the Hotel Ambassador on Park Avenue, and she is giving a big dinner party for me the night of the Cooper affair. We dine in state with her at the Ambassador, and then go on to the puppet show. I am also photographing some of the puppets of Greta Garbo, Katharine Cornell, etc. for my show at the Waldorf-Astoria. It is getting to be too amazing. Peggy Fears is a grand girl, and a good person for me to know, for she is producing shows all the time on Blumenthal's money. She is Lenore

Ulric's producer, and Dorothy Hall's producer, and she is the one theatrical producer in town with unlimited funds behind her. I am seeing her again tomorrow night. She said she would like me to be her new Noel Coward and it begins to look as if I might be!

Today I had a charming note from Douglas Fairbanks junior who said he had my book and was looking forward to enjoying it on his trip back to Hollywood next week. He says that when he returns here in May he wants to meet me. This feeling is mutual.

Sorry to write you so often but something tremendous happens almost every hour, and I have to keep you posted. I wrote about the Waldorf thing in my usual extravagant urging way. I have urged you before, but this time I hope it works.

Yours,
Max

Max used his address for the Gary Cooper fan club: "The Gary Flappers

A New Cooper Union
19 West Thirty-First Street
New York City"

Wednesday [about February 8, 1933]

Dear Mother,

Your letter just came, and worries me more than I can tell you. I had a sneaking idea you were not feeling well. I didn't know what was wrong, but I knew your letters weren't right. Do, make every effort now to get well quickly, and obey every single thing the doctor tells you. For you to get well is the only important thing now, and I am sure you will if you do the right things. You have a good constitution and have always enjoyed wonderful health. But you have always overdone on that account. Nothing seemed to wear you down, and you got the idea that you could you do anything and survive without any bad results. But now you can't and you must be careful. You must get some rest, and stop worrying about minor things, and you must eat with more sense. You have always lived on a diet that few people in the world could live on—I mean whatever happened to be at hand, or whatever could be fried quickest. It is impossible to criticize it, because you seemed to flourish on it, but I always knew it wasn't right. And—like Vainglory—you ate too much meat. Have your doctor prescribe a sensible diet, get rest, and take medicine, and I'm sure you'll pull through this attack of nerves. Don't forget that in addition to the nervous strain of your work and of Doddy, etc. your nervous system has had very severe shocks over the past year. You held up wonderfully through the crises themselves, but this is doubtless a natural reaction that comes a little later. All I am trying to say is that your present run-down condition is probably a natural result of understandable causes, and not an independent condition by itself. It will take time and effort to get back in good shape, but you can do it, if you will MAKE the effort and TAKE the time.

    Your coming to the Waldorf-Astoria party must depend entirely on how you feel next week. Take good care of yourself this week, and try to relax about everything, and by the middle of next week you may feel like coming. But if the doctor thinks it would be a risk or too much of a strain, then of course don't do it. I would like you here for this event in my honor, but there will be other events in my honor later, though I don't know what they will be. You know I want you to come, but your coming must depend primarily on whether you would enjoy it. Don't come just because you think I would be hurt if you didn't. Don't decide until next week, and then you can come or not come on short notice as far as everything here is concerned. You never can tell about the weather. Here it is zero one day and balmy the next. Half a day's shopping would buy you the necessary clothes. I would go with you, and I would also go with you to do your buying for the store, as you suggest. We could get you some good looking clothes very easily, and clothes are cheap everywhere. And even if you do not look your best you will look good to me. You needn't feel uneasy about being left with strange people. I could put you at a table with the Frank Bishops or the Paul Osborns or someone like that while I circulated in the crowd, if you do not want to be burdened with making conversation with Romanoff princesses! Of course if you prefer to be next to the princess Chavchavadze I can fix that up for you too . . . Just anything you say. You could come here Thursday instead of Friday if you would like Friday to rest up. Settle it all to suit yourself, and consult the doctor first. I don't want you to take any chances with your health even if Queen Mary had asked us to Buckingham Palace. I will leave the whole thing to your good judgment.

Last evening was another very eventful one with Peggy Fears. I was invited to dinner at seven thirty, but it took Miss Fears so long to get herself decked out in the Blumenthal rubies and diamonds that we did not leave her hotel until after ten o'clock. By that time she decided it was too late to go anywhere except the Casino in Central Park, so she ordered an elaborate midnight supper there, and took her party of six there. A dinner for six at the Central Park Casino would cost enough to bankrupt any little bank, but that is nothing in a Blumenthal's life. It became very dramatic at the Casino because at the next table sat Lupe Velez and Johnny Weismuller. Lupe and Peggy are having a feud, and Lupe would not speak to Peggy. So to annoy her Peggy spoke to Johnny, while Lupe held her head to one side. Everyone expected fireworks for Lupe is famous in Hollywood for her fiery Mexican scenes, and is apt to take off her slippers and throw them at anyone who annoys her. But last night she was very lady-like and didn't throw anything. Anyway, Peggy decided her party should be the last to leave the Casino. Apparently Miss Velez had the same idea. So finally everyone had left the place except our party and Lupe's. The waiters were longing to close up and go home, but Lupe wouldn't budge, and neither would Peggy. This went on for an hour or more, and we finally were worn out and all left together. So you see there is quite an effort involved in being a friend of Peggy Fears! When Mayor Walker retired from office and went to live with the Blumenthal's at their countryhouse last summer Albert Carroll in his impersonation of Walker in a show sang a song which went "You can have your City Hall—I'll take A.C. Blumenthal." That's what Peggy Fears took too, only I think she takes more of his money than she does of him, though he may be at the dinner she is giving for me next Wednesday night at the Ambassador.

The man, Mr. England, came here yesterday to discuss the party at the Waldorf. He said it would gain much more newspaper attention if some particular person could be announced as giving it, rather than just that the hotel were giving it. In that case he said he was afraid society editors might dismiss it lightly as a routine hotel affair. He asked if he might announce that Muriel was giving it. I roared with laughter, and said that would be preposterous because everyone knows she hasn't a spare cent to give a party with, let alone engaging orchestras and all that at the Waldorf-Astoria! So we may pin it to someone else. It is all very extraordinary. He also asked if the press stories would annoy me if they referred to me as the American Noel Coward. I said no, but that they might annoy Noel.

I shall be very uneasy until I hear from you again. Do send me a prompt report of what the doctor thinks. What is his name? I wouldn't rent the house. Even while you are staying at Doddy's you always know in the back of your mind, that you can go home whenever you want to. It would be more disagreeable than it is if you knew you could not go back there. The rent money wouldn't be worth what you lose. Besides, if you ever did have an illness that necessitated your staying in for awhile there are no facilities at Doddy's house. Your staying there this winter was just a temporary makeshift arrangement. Don't think of giving up the house now.

I have been wondering what circumstances Josie is in, and whether you might make her any offer of any kind. If Norman left her in any way stranded or very hard up, why don't you offer her the house, and a job at the store, or a percentage interest in the store or something? She might be glad for a place for herself and congenial girlfriend. She is business-like and conscientious and attractive. She drives a car, and you could sail around the countryside together. She might consider it if you put it to her tactfully, not permanently of course, but as a temporary measure while she is in suspense and you are too. Let me know what you think. I hope to see you next week if you feel up to it. If you don't I will understand perfectly, and will see to it that there is something just as good for you to come to whenever you do feel like coming.

All love,
Max

Thursday [February 9, 1933]

Just a word to tell you about last night with Mary Garden. Muriel and I dined with her, just the three of us, in her suite in the Ritz Tower. She was looking marvelous in silver pajamas, and had ordered a very delicious dinner, consisting of oysters, chicken soup, and a lamb roasted with onions and potatoes. And the point of this story is that she didn't touch the lamb. She has eaten no meat at all for years, and that accounts to some extent for her marvelous looks and health and vitality and figure and youth, or so she claims. Also she touched no coffee—she only takes it in the morning. I tell you this in the hopes that it will make your own diet more acceptable, knowing that Mary is on a rigid one too, and flourishing on it! She and Muriel talked like mad for hours. Mary called Insull "an old stinker" and feels no regrets over his collapse in wealth. She also said that they are erecting a monument to Debussy in Paris, and that every city in America had made a contribution to it except Chicago, and that last summer she wrote to Harold McCormick and asked him for $400 for this purpose, and he wrote back that he just couldn't spare four hundred dollars for any cause, and that as for Edith, she was almost penniless. Mary herself is not suffering any financial embarrassment, as she has signed up to sing in moving picture houses for the next two months at three thousand dollars a week. She leaves tomorrow to sing at the White House in Washington Saturday night. She is bored to death at having to spend an evening with the Hoovers, and she is taking my book to read on the train.

I hope to hear from you right away that you are feeling better. And any plans you make for next week will be ok at this end. Just let me know.

        Love,
        Max

Friday [February 10, 1933]

Dear Mother,

I am wondering how you are faring in the cold wave. It is very cold here too, but not nearly as cold as the Middle West, according to the papers. Wednesday evening when Muriel and I went to Mary's it was like a May night, warm and balmy and we were uncomfortable in our coats. When we left Mary a few hours later it was like the North Pole. Wednesday evening was the warmest February weather on record. Wednesday night was almost the coldest on record for years. It is crazy, all of it.

Plans seem to be all set for the tea dance on the 18th. They are featuring the photograph exhibition aspect of it more than anything else now. They are going to show all the pictures I showed at the Levy Gallery except the Negroes, who do not seem to rank showing at the Waldorf-Astoria! The list of the people I photographed is to be reproduced in the announcement, and so is the blurb about me written by Gilbert Seldes. It is funny how things happen. I study the piano for years very seriously and people do not make any particular effort to want to hear me. Then I start taking pictures of people in Venice as a joke, and people fall all over themselves to see them and show them and so on. It makes everything in life seem so casual and so accidental . . . Two orchestras are to be on hand for dancing, and Kay Francis has been added to the list of patronesses. My personal friends are to be admitted guests. The public at large is to pay $1.50 for the privilege of being there. Thus the Waldorf-Astoria makes back its expenses, which even the Waldorf-Astoria is obliged to do in these times. If you are here it will be grand. If you are not it will be too bad, and you will have to come in the spring, when I will try and have the pictures hung in Madison Square Garden for you!

Love,
Max

Monday [about February 13, 1933]

Dear Mother,

  Just got your Friday letter. I'm relieved you feel less dizzy and a little better. But I think your condition sounds precarious to take a long trip if this weather keeps up. It is still fiendish cold here. Snow is banked up knee deep in the streets for almost the first time since our great visit here in 1920. The sidewalks are icy, and walking is no treat. Of course all this may disappear overnight if it warms up, and by the end of the week it may be fine and dandy. But this is the way it is now, and if anyone has any signs of flu left over, let alone anything else, it is no weather to be travelling around in. I tell you this against my will, because I would rather have you think it was fine and dandy now. But I do not want you to run any risk in your present condition, and frankly, I do think it would be a risk in this weather. However by Thursday it may be different, and if it is you can hop on a train and send me a wire that you are starting. There will always be other teas and things to attend if you would rather wait for spring. This one happens to be something special, that's all, and my first thought, when it was suggested to me, was to send the word to you and have you enjoy it too.

    Don't get excited and don't WORRY about things like the Garyflappers. I never start what I cannot finish. I have more than the necessary fifty subscribers already, and still three days to go. The dollars have been pouring in. Everyone wants to attend. Rita Romilly rang up Muriel yesterday very indignant because she had not been asked to be a Garyflapper. She said everyone in N.Y. whom she knew had become a Garyflapper and she was insulted at being left out. I hadn't meant to leave her out but just hadn't gotten around to her. So I called her right up as if I hadn't heard of all this, and she was all smiles, and said she would send me two dollars right away.

    I enclose a note which just arrived from Natalie Hammond's secretary. Natalie consents to be a Garyflapper but she cannot come to the show as she is going to be away. I went last night to see her Miracle Plays which she put on for two Sunday nights at great expense and effort. John Glen danced as Saint Joseph. He rehearsed for a solid month and only got $35.00.

    I enclose also a notice about Muriel's magazine article called American Deserta. It is the first section of her book, and has just come out in the Hound and Horn for January. Smudge has lost his job at Macy's—just because they are turning off dozens of employees and he has only been there six months. Paul [Draper] is dancing this week at Radio City.

Terrible about the Bailey boy. Was he run over, or in an auto smash? I'm in favor of you trading the car for a smaller one if you want to, but I'm not in favor of your driving until you are absolutely well and in no way nervous. Driving a car is the last thing for a person to do who is apt to lose control for even a second. Get a smaller car and get yourself a chauffeur. Plenty of young fellows would be glad of the chance to Go Somewhere. Don't wait to depend on the Touses, etc

I remember vaguely all that trouble with Joe [Riste] and the money drawer. But that was years ago, and she was a wild girl then. I'm sure that her own children and her feeling for them has put an end to all that sort of thing in her. She has settled down into something quite different—just as Theo has and many other people—and I'm sure that nothing irregular would happen now. Personally, I think that even if she did take things you should have her anyway. It would mean much less stuff to unload in the end, and you'd never know the difference! And she would be such a help and such good company. There is so little good company for you now in Pioneer, I should think you would welcome even Jesse James. I'm sure he was good company, no matter what hold-ups he had staged.

I don't think you would need the shawl if you come here, but you could bring it along just in case . . . George Lynes is having a big opening of his new studio on Friday, so you could go to that perhaps too. Let's leave the whole matter up to weather. If it is impossible now, then <u>without fail</u> you will come in the spring. OR ELSE!

Take every care of yourself. You MUST.

      Max

Thursday, Feb. 16 [1933]

Dear Mother,

 Just got your Monday note. I'm disappointed of course that you don't feel able to come. But I'm not going to shed tears, and you must not either. Put ALL your efforts into getting well and I'm sure you'll do it. I want you to take this experience as a lesson, and never let yourself get run down again, because you never can tell when I am going to send for you on short notice to come and be my right hand woman at some other event. It is true what you say about my Pioneer problems being very serious if anything should "happen" to you. But even though serious they would be solved and settled in some way. They always are. But nothing could be done about you by that time. And what happens to you is the main thing to consider. I couldn't bear to have anything bad happen to you. I feel very close to you, closer now than I think I ever did before. We are not together much in point of time, and yet I never think of us as being separate or apart. I keep in constant communication with you, and have you always in the back of my mind, no matter how much I am seemingly absorbed in something else. You must stay with me to give me incentive to do more things and better ones.

 But enough of this. The other news of the week is very bright, and I hope it will cheer you up. I just received news that my book is being published in England. Copies are just out. The English publisher is Cassell of London, and the actual printing was done in Edinburgh. I'll send you a copy of the English edition very soon. I've had one review from the London Daily Express, and others will probably pour in from all the English and Scotch papers. Isn't it exciting? I enclose a letter I received yesterday from the London Society Press features asking me to pose for photographs at a London address in Burlington Gardens. I'm afraid I cannot keep that appointment with Messrs. Hughes!

The Garyflappers Gala was great fun! First there was dinner at Peggy Fears'. We dined in state in the Blumenthal suite at the Ambassador Hotel—dinner for ten. Then the Puppet Show, which was a success and everybody loved it. Photographers were taking pictures for the papers—pictures of me and Peggy Fears and Dorothy Hall and Tullio Carminati and other celebrated people I had assembled. Then when it was over, Peggy took us all out to the Casino again where we danced for hours. She was looking magnificent in a dress made of white beads, and strung with diamond bracelets, and an ermine wrap. Dorothy Hall was also wrapped in ermine and enormous ruffles of black Moline. So much for that. Now I am concentrating on the tea dance Saturday, and next week I hope to RELAX. I really wouldn't be awfully good company for you, as I really am almost tired out by excitement of so many events. However a night or two of twelve hours sleep will fix me right up.

England now wants me to begin a series of photographs of Russian nobility to show at a Russian ball he is planning for April. He wants me to photograph Prince George of Russia as a starter. Why don't you plan to come to New York for this event? That gives you six or eight weeks to recuperate, and the weather and all other things should be much more favorable then. Try and do it. Try hard. The weather here is still very cold, but not at all the way it was last week. Last week was fierce. I'll look forward to seeing you here in April. Things are going on at that time, and people are still in town. In the summer they all go away and it is too hot to come here anyway. Spring or fall is the time for you to come and I hope you'll make it spring. I'm sending you some extra announcements of the Waldorf thing that you can give away or mail.

All my love,
Max

Friday night [February 17, 1933]

Dear Mother,

    Here's a page from today's Journal that will interest you. Especially the column headed "Points about the Fashionables!"

    The large lady in the picture between Prince Toubetskoy and Princess Obolensky is Mme. Alma Clayburgh who is a patroness of my tea tomorrow. Sorry you will not be there. Better luck next time.

        Max

The tea and dance at the Waldorf-Astoria came off splendidly. About 200 people attended the affair, paying $1.50 for admission. Two bands provided music. Max's photographs from the Carnival of Venice exhibit were on display, too.

Sunday Feb 19 [1933]

Dear Mother,

    Just a note to say it was a grand party yesterday, and that everything went off with no hitches. Mr. England was pleased with the crowd I provided, and I was pleased with the crowd he provided, and everyone is happy. The first of my guests to arrive was Mr. Knopf, and the last was Cobina Wright, and in between came all the people you might expect, and a lot more that you might not expect. Everyone was amused by the photographs which were displayed in a double line for forty feet along one wall. When the party was over I went upstairs to Cecil Beaton's suite in the Waldorf-Astoria Towers for a bit, and then came home and flopped into bed at nine o'clock, where I stayed until this afternoon! I feel better now, but the last day or two, I had been living on nothing but overflow reserve nervous energy. This week I am going to make quiet—if I can. The Garyflapper thing which I started just as a joke for one evening is attaining quite surprising proportions. It is considered NEWS everywhere, and pictures are being circulated to the rotogravure sections. The pictures are very good and I will send you prints of them even if they do not appear in the press. One shows me surrounded by Peggy Fears and Dorothy Hall looking like a million dollars. In another group I am surrounded by Mary Dangerfield, Mary Badger, and Dorothy Sheldon. Tonight I am dining at Mary Badger's. In my next I will, tell you who she is so you can keep up. This is just a brief note AFTER THE BALL IS OVER . . .

    Love,
        Max

Tuesday [February 21, 1933]

Dear Mother,

    Here's an article about Aline [Macmahon] that may interest you.

    In a separate envelope I am sending you a photograph taken the night of the Garyflappers show. I am shown standing with a group of three ladies. Reading from left to right, they are Mary Dangerfield looking very prim and English. Dorothy Sheldon looking not exactly poverty stricken. And Mary Badger who is putting my carnation into the hand of the puppet of Gary Cooper. I am holding the puppet and looking quite the Impresario of the occasion which I was. This picture and others may appear in the press, but I am almost unable by now to keep track of what appears about me in the press. My clipping bureau is quite efficient but even it misses things. Anyway this picture will give you an idea . . .

    Mary Badger works at Elizabeth Hawes' dressmaking establishment, the best of its kind in America. Elizabeth Hawes is in fact the only American designer of clothes who ever took a collection to Paris for an opening there. She did this two years ago, and Paris was aghast at her nerve. The French designers were furious and tried to freeze her out, but her show had a big success because it was unprecedented. She is now well established here, and her clothes are about the most expensive possible to buy. The striped silk affair Mary Badger is wearing in the photograph is a new Hawes creation. The Hawes spring opening is to take place on two nights—Feb. 28 and March 1. The first night is for the very rich clientele, and the second night for the faster and smarter theatrical set. I am ordered to be there both nights and to bring people from both sets, because I know the rich and the smart. I am going to do it, but I think I ought to begin to charge high prices for bringing people together, and do it professionally—like Elsa Maxwell.

Mr. England says that Mr. Lucius Boomer, the manager of the Waldorf-Astoria was very enthusiastic about the affair on Saturday afternoon, and told him I must be a very extraordinary young man to have attracted such a brilliant gathering in the afternoon. So you see . . .

I am also sending you today a copy of the English edition of GOING SOMEWHERE. It seems to be going quite a lot of places itself.

The weather is nice again now, and I hope you are feeling better, DO EVERY SINGLE THING your doctor tells you to, and don't do a thing he says you shouldn't. Put all your efforts to taking care of yourself, and let everything else take care of itself for a while. And please write and let me know more.

    Max

Max's health was precarious most of his life. Before his thirteenth birthday he missed weeks of school because he was "sick with indigestion." A few months later he had an unspecified operation, possibly a tonsillectomy, at a hospital in Toledo. "I took gas," he wrote to Doris, "and didn't feel it at all." As an adult he suffered from painful sinus infections. In a letter dated May 30, 1934, A.E. commented to Max that "the real source of your terror is due to physical ailments," specifically "sinus trouble."

Sunday [February 26, 1933]

Dear Mother—I got both your letters and the check which I banked yesterday. That makes only about $100 dollars you will owe me in April doesn't it? I can imagine how panicky the Michigan situation makes people feel. People here are concerned about it too, and Eddie Wasserman asked me the other night whether your money was in Michigan banks. I said no.

    I wish you would send me the [Toledo] Blade mention of the Garyflappers if you can find it. I hope you got the photograph, and the book. Roy Meyers ordered a book from me and I am sending it tomorrow. In an answer to some of your questions: I didn't write more about the party the first week because I had a hard cold. Not a grippe or flu but just a cold in my head of the kind I hadn't had for ages. I'm all over it now, but my sinuses feel all stuffed up and I think longingly of Florida. I've had quite a quiet week. A great many people paid $1.50 to come to the Waldorf tea. I should say about two hundred, so of course expenses were made. People wore day clothes, no formal evening clothes, I do not mean to try to get into other activities there. Give me time to get my breath again.

    Yes, I too thought of what the fortune teller told me about England. I didn't tell you about possible publication there until I was sure it was coming off. I knew there was negotiation. But negotiations so often have fallen through in my projects, that I'm superstitious now about discussing them. I've seen an excellent write-up from the London Times which calls GOING SOMEWHERE "one of the most entertaining affairs of the kind ever printed." Tell Mr. Hodson's nurse that the twins are fictitious entirely. Eddie Wasserman asked me to dinner and took me to the Metropolitan Opera Thursday night, where we heard Lily Pons. Everyone wonders whether the opera can survive another year. Everything is going to rack and ruin so fast nothing can stop it.

But everyone seems much gayer and more abandoned this year than last. Up to last year people seemed to be still deluded into thinking that prosperity was just around the corner and that if they were cautious and scraped along things would be better. Now nobody thinks they can possibly get better without an upheaval of some sort, and that the whole world is in such a mess it can't get out without drastic scrapings of existing orders, and that if the gold standard is going to crash we'll all crash together, and that if nobody has anything then nobody will be any worse off than anyone else. It's like living in the wild days before the French Revolution. One of two things is certain. Things will have to get better, or else they will swiftly get much worse and there will be open revolt. Millions of men won't starve through another winter. They'll begin to take whatever they can get their hands on, and I don't know who will blame them. At the movies people applaud Zangara. Nobody applauds Roosevelt. The times are very sinister.

You ask about Marion Walton Putnam. I enclosed a card announcing a show of her sculpture. The picture of it in the card looks pretty odd.

I'm glad you feel a little better. Now I want to hear that you feel a lot better.

   Love,
    Max

Adolph Hitler's rise to Chancellor of Germany promoted the causes of the Nazi party and a concomitant increase in anti-Semitism. Max was perceptive in recognizing so early the warning signs of Nazi persecution of the Jews.

Thursday [March 2, 1933]

Dear Mother,

Here's a little note after a big night—last night—which was the opening of Tallulah Bankhead's play. I had to cancel my date to go to the fashion show, for I had had the date for the Bankhead opening for a month with Marion Saportas and Peggy Fears, on whatever night the play opened. It was postponed several times, and finally got here last night. We dined at Marion's, and got into the theater with the assistance of the police. I wrote you about the opening of Tallulah's first film two years ago. I drove to that with Natalie Hammond, and that was bad enough. But last night was much worse, for Peggy Fears is far more famous than Natalie, and her Rolls-Royce is unmistakable. Well, as I said, the police helped us through the mob and got us inside the theater. Between the acts it was awful. Peggy wanted a drink of water, and we tried to find a drug store or soda fountain near the theater, but we had to go half a block to find one. Peggy was in a yellow satin evening dress with fur sleeves, white fur. She had to run to keep warm. And then a whole mob of people ran after us, and when we came out of the soda fountain the whole mob was pressed against the doors and windows and we had to fight our way out. Everyone wanted Peggy to sign autograph books. Marion Saportas was in a new dress for the occasion made of figured lavender organdy with long trains in all directions and a big ruffle of shirred organdy around her shoulders like a cape. She had a very hard time of it on the sidewalk. After the play it was like Bedlam. Hundreds and hundreds of people were lined up in the streets hoping to see Tallulah come out. Police clubbed them into submission, but they were like wild men and women. Tallulah is the only person who affects crowds like this anymore. People howl and trample each other half to death to get near her. It's her first play in New York in about nine years. She is very good in it, and the play itself is not good. After it was over we all went to a big party given for Tallulah by Ilka Chase, the daughter of the editor of Vogue. It was very brilliant. Madame Schiaparelli, the most fashionable of the new fashion designers in Paris was there, and all sorts of extraordinary people. Tallulah told me she thought she was well-received, but that her welcome was nothing like what she was accustomed to in London. I don't see how it could have been much worse—or better. The people in the streets half killed her as it was.

I did go to the fashion show of Elizabeth Hawes the night before. The clothes were very nice not very startling. They showed a movie of Miss Hawes made by Ralph Steiner who was there with his wife. I enclose a letter from Aunt Alice. Probably you got one too.

        Love,
        Max

Max in front of an Art Deco poster, dated March 3, 1933.

Inaugurated on Saturday, March 4, President Franklin Roosevelt declared a nation-wide "bank holiday" from March 6 through March 9.

The holiday was then extended to March 13. Some banks took longer to re-open.

Monday [March 6, 1933]

Dear Mother,

 Your letter enclosing the coupons just arrived. But as we are in the midst of a bank holiday too, there will be no depositing of them right away! They say banks will be open on Friday. And that new accounts will be able to be drawn upon. This is to encourage re-deposits of funds that had been taken out for hoarding purposes. So if I can deposit the coupons and draw on them we will be alright for a while.

 I generally go to the bank on Monday to get my week's expense money. Fortunately, this week I have ten dollars left over from last week, which was not a very expensive week. So ten dollars will keep me in meals (half-rations) for quite awhile. And there are no other immediate expenses to meet. Of course things like rent, etc. will just have to wait everywhere, as no one ever has eighty dollars in his pocket. The landlords will take checks and cash them when they can. Everybody is now in the same boat, and everyone here is taking it very calmly, and with considerable amusement. Everybody knows that a hundred million people are not going to just lie down and die because of a fantastic to-do about little bars of gold in underground vaults. If the present system fails, something else will take its place. And with all the banks closed, the situation is far less serious than when some were closed here and there. At any rate new and drastic legislation will take place now, and with all the banks closed together, they will be able to open together on some sort of new basis. And the Toledo banks which have been in the dumps for years will probably come out with the rest. So there is no need to worry as your letter expresses yet. I only hope you have enough "change" for a week or so. But in a town like Pioneer you can of course get credit for groceries and all the necessary things. You can even here. All the big stores are advertising, urging credit accounts. Theaters take checks. Everyone is living and exchanging on confidence. It seems in fact to be the first manifestation of confidence in quite some time.

Saturday night, after the news broke, I went to what was called a Depression Party at Paul Flato's—the 5th Avenue jeweler's. It was called a Depression Party but there were no signs of Depression. Everyone was blazing with diamonds, and feeling very gay. Most of the people there were new to me. Then last night I went to a supper party for twenty people at Mrs. [Ilka] Chase's, in honor of Tallulah Bankhead. Tallulah got bored at this party, and asked eight or nine of us to go back to her place which we did. We bought the morning papers and sat around reading all the bad news, and Tallulah decided to put her new play on a check accepting basis. Later on she sent for sandwiches and coffee for everyone—charging both! Marion Tiffany Saportas was there, looking very elaborate. She is accustomed to receiving three thousand dollars month alimony from Jack Saportas, but this has all been curtailed recently. And last night she had exactly twenty-five cents for the rest of the week. Tonight John S. Cohen Junior, movie critic of the Sun, and Tallulah's current boy-friend is giving another enormous party for her. The parties go on just the same. People walk to them instead of riding. That is the only difference!

Everyone talks about nothing but the money situation. Saturday afternoon I went to tea at Howard Rothschild's—a scion of the multi-millionaire Rothschild family—and banks were mentioned and nothing else. Everyone agrees that it is very exciting to be living in such times with history being made before our eyes. That is all very well, but I suppose it is less exciting if you are actually hungry. Peggy Fears asked me the other night to motor to California with her and two other friends in June—in Jimmy Walker's former Rolls Royce and with a chauffeur doing the dirty work. I said I certainly would do it. But as she is very flighty, it is not safe to count on that. However, if things do straighten out before summer, I am going to try and get out there some way. I had a long letter from Namara this week begging me to come. She says she and Mindret [Lord] have taken a lovely six room house, furnished, and very well furnished, with a terrace, and a garage, and a flower garden, and a lovely view, FOR $65.00 a month, and that such places are plentiful. And if I do go I will of course stop by to pay a visit to Pioneer and you! There's nothing like making elaborate plans with nothing definitely in sight to do them on. But I have an idea there will be by June.

Anyway, love,
Max

I would like to know whether you ever receive half of the things I send you. Did you get the English edition of the book? Did you get the photograph of the Garyflappers? Did you ever get the column I wrote about Mary Garden? Or the picture of Peggy Fears? Or the photograph of the Tellegens which I took? Or the London Times review? Or the letters from Miss Henry and Louise Hellstrom which I asked you to return to me? Or various other clippings, items, and miscellanea which you never acknowledge? I find so many things to send you that I think will interest you or please you, but as you never refer to any of them I don't ever know whether you get them, and it is very discouraging to mail them out so excitedly only to have them received in complete silence and never heard of again. Gold standard or not, you should be a little more polite!

Tuesday [about March 7, 1933]

Dear Mother,

Here I am on Tuesday with just about as much money as I had on Monday. I dined at Mary Badger's last night, and we had planned last week to go last night to see Mae West at the Paramount, but we decided to resist doing anything giddy under all the circumstances. So we didn't go. Later I went to John Cohen's party for Tallulah. She is elated because she has packed houses every night, and they are going to do three matinees a week. Police reserves have had to be on hand outside the theater at every performance to handle the mob that wants to tear her to pieces with love. Naturally she is quite pleased—especially since she has her own money in the show.

Papers today say scrip will be ready sometime today or tomorrow. I can't send you that as it won't be transferrable from state to state, but you can get plenty in Ohio apparently. I am waiting a day or two before depositing the coupons just to be sure that they can be drawn upon. The papers insist the new deposits can be drawn upon at any time and in any quantity. So everything seems all set. No one seems worried. Everyone seems very much encouraged that the bottom has reached, and that at last something is being done.

I dreamed last night that you and I were on a train on our way to California. I hope it is prophetic. Had a lovely letter from Mary Garden yesterday in praise of my book, and saying that while she was in Chicago she gave away many copies of it to her friends. She is now in Louisville Kentucky, but will be here again March 18th, and says she wants to see me, and Muriel then. I adore her.

If there isn't any business at all, and there probably isn't, why don't you close the store part time? People can get used to a curtailment of business hours just as they have got used to a curtailment of a lot of other things. When they are not only buying a fraction of what they formerly bought there is no reason why you should serve the public a hundred percent in hours. If people know you're only open at certain times they'll make more of an effort to get there. Spare yourself everything you can in this hectic period. It's a year this week since I was so frightfully sick with the flu. I've been writing to Alice all winter that I might come down in March, but of course I'm not thinking of it now, with the money situation the way it is. You can go to Jacksonville and back by boat for fifty dollars—with a thirty day stay permitted, and that is certainly a bargain. I don't suppose the boats are very swell, but still it's a bargain. Dorothy Sheldon went to Florida last Saturday morning to visit some relatives who are there for the winter. I suppose she got on the train just as the bank news broke out, so she may be stranded when she gets there. I'll keep you posted on all developments. Take care of yourself, and please don't get upset.

    Much love,
    Max

Wednesday—Fourth Day of Plague [March 8 1933]

Dear Mother,

  Here is another day, Wednesday, and still no sign of the promised scrip for another day or more. I still have money—only seventy cents less than I had yesterday morning! I got through the day yesterday on 70 cents, and feel quite proud of it. It was a very good day too. The Civic Repertory Theater called me up in the afternoon and offered me two free seats for last night to see Nazimova and Eva Le Gallienne in "The Cherry Orchard." They were giving away all the tickets in order to have an audience at all and not close up. So I took Dick Clemmer to see the play, and it was pouring rain and I couldn't afford a cab, Peggy Fears gave me her Rolls Royce and chauffeur to drive me to the theater, where I had seats in the second row. So I couldn't exactly complain of the bank holiday last night!

The events are fantastic all around. Mary Badger, the Social Register lady, was hunting around yesterday for mushrooms to make sauce for spaghetti to feed all the girls, seamstresses, etc. who work at Hawes dressmaking establishment. They had no money to eat on, and Miss Hawes had no money to pay them, so the establishment was <u>feeding</u> them.

Marion Saportas, who, as I wrote you before, is used to having three thousand dollars a month income, was without a cent before last night. She had to WALK to Eddie Wassermann's apartment for dinner, which was quite a jaunt for her. When she got home that night, she found a telegram from Lilyan Tashman in Hollywood, asking Marion to wire her fifty dollars. Lilyan said no one in California had any money at all. As Marion had none too, she couldn't even answer the telegram!

So it goes. I'm lunching at the Selde's today, and I'm starting early because I mean to walk quite a distance. They live on 86th Street! Fraulein Kopp, the Swiss woman who lives downstairs, says she will advance me five or ten dollars whenever I need it. So I'm not in any straits, and please don't worry about me. I try not to worry about you, but I do just the same.

More soon,
Max

Thursday [about March 9, 1933]

Dear Mother,

This is to tell you that my bank let me in today, and cashed a check for twenty-five dollars without any difficulty. So now I have more than thirty dollars in real money, and I feel very rich. If you want me to send you five or ten dollars in bills, in a registered letter, let me know promptly. The man advised me not to deposit the coupons just yet. They don't want to do any business that is not absolutely essential until things straighten out a little. He said the coupons would be delayed in getting credited anyway, and that it was more sensible to hang on to them until the situation is less topsy-turvy. So I will. Anyway, it is reassuring that my bank is in good condition. If it were not it would not be open today when most of them are not supposed to be open until tomorrow.

There is no other news today. But you should be satisfied with this much!

I had a letter from Doddy, largely concerned with matters of your diet. It may be a comfort to you that all the country is on a diet now with you. Thank Doddy for her letter and say I'll be answering her.

    Love,
    Max

Friday [March 10, 1933]

Dear Mother,

Your letter just came and deserves a prompt reply. I realized perfectly well that the financial situation is very critical. If I sometimes seem casual in referring to it in letters it is only to spare you any added gloom from me, and because I am temperamentally not a type that worries, and I never really expect the worst until it is at hand. I am not unaware that it may eventually be at hand. But honestly, I do not think it will. I think that a crisis like this when EVERYONE is involved is less serious for us than the minor crises of the past few years when some of the people, including ourselves, were involved. In the days of the Toledo bank closings, and the Florida bond defaulting, and all that, it did seem as if we were especially harassed, and were particularly unfortunate. But only a comparatively small number of people were affected and nothing was done about it. Things were just allowed to slide. Now everyone is in the same predicament, and something HAS to be done. Things can't just slide now. There has to be a readjustment everywhere, and while it may be slow, it will have to be sure, and while we may not end up having as much as we thought we would, I'm sure we will come out better with all the nation working towards readjustment, than we would have with scattered straggling committees, etc. the way it was before the general bank crash. I am able to face whatever has to be faced. I'll spend summer at Clear Lake if necessary or in a box car if necessary. I've never been faced with many emergency situations, but I've always survived whatever I have been faced by, and so have you. All you say is true, about how I have always been supplied from what seemed a dependable source. From the time I was conscious at all, and sick half the time, I always had it implanted in me that unlimited protection was behind me, and I was to be spared practical responsibilities in order to indulge my own talents and fantasies. I wish too that I could do something that brought in a reliable income. But with hundreds of thousands out of jobs here, people all trained for jobs, there is no job for untrained workers. I am a highly trained person but not a trained worker at all. I can play the piano very well at a time when pianists are starving, and when musicians as a class are probably in greater distress than any other class. I can write for theater when half the theaters are closed, and the rest closing. I can write at a time when the book business is at the lowest ebb since the invention of the printing press. The fact that my book was published at all in a year like this is a sort of miracle. And though there is nothing of the "financial wizard" in me, I have managed to make a definite place for myself among many very rich people, and have as my friends many of the world's most distinguished people, and coming to New York eight years ago without even an acquaintance here except Andy Haigh, I have built up a circle of literally hundreds of friends, and have organized a life here in a way that is unprecedented by anyone we know from the

Middle West. Naturally I cherish it, and would hate like anything to leave it. To return to Ohio to live would be not like turning my back on just New York. It would be like turning my back to life itself. I mean it would seem too much like accepting defeat, and I don't consider that it is defeat. I mean I think I should stick here if it means taking a two by four room. I have often suggested this before more or less as a joke but this time I would do it. If you find it impossible to come here to see me then I am certainly coming out to see you this spring or this summer. But I am not going to relinquish New York on account of this temporary disorder on the world. Up to last week Hollywood was still the one place where money was to be made. People unable to afford to go to the theater still did go to the movies. This week nobody can even do that, and the studios may have to close, or dismiss a lot of people instead of taking in any new ones. So going to Hollywood doesn't seem very sensible, except from the point of view that living is much cheaper there than here. If I were to motor out with anyone, I would go on ahead to Ohio on the train, visit you, and be picked up on Road 20 later. Anyway, none of this can be counted on. Peggy Fears is very sweet but very vague. She doesn't retain!

    To change the subject to Peggy Fears—she is very young. She came on to New York from Texas to study singing some years ago. While she studied she got a job at Texas Guinan's. Producers saw her and put her in a show. Ziegfield saw her and glorified her in the Follies, and she became so successful in the theater she gave up singing in a concert way. Then A.C. Blumenthal married her, and she had millions. He didn't want her to stay on stage, but he said she could produce shows on his money. So she has done that for two years, and has made herself as well-known as any of her stars. She still wants to go back on the stage and she probably will next year. My association with her is not just a pastime. She likes my songs and wants to use them whenever she does a new musical show. A young man named Clyde Kelly who has a glorious voice has learned several of the songs, and sang them for Peggy last week. He is also going to sing them for radio executives soon.

In spite of bad book business, magazines go on forever. I want to write articles for film fan magazines about film personalities. I was sent to one editor, Miss Waterbury, who edits the magazine called Movie Mirror. She said she couldn't tell how I would write unless I wrote something and let her see it. So two weeks ago I wrote an article about Gary Cooper. She read it and liked it, but said it was over the heads of her public, and she is sending me to meet May Allison who edits the magazine Photoplay. I have something like this on foot all the time. I write to you about parties and people because it makes it more interesting reading. But I have business lines out at all angles all the time, and the minute any business is being done, I am in line to have some done with me. It seems slow, but something always happens in the end. Nothing would ever happen if I gave up and went home.

I do appreciate all you have to go through untangling the maze of taxes, etc. It was miserable about that National Dairy payment. It makes me sick to think of you being so harassed by these difficulties at a time when you ought to be comfortable and secure. I am back of you in all you do. And when you send out the final danger signal I will heed it. In the mean time I don't want you to be panicky. And don't believe a word you read. The news changes every hour. Last night big electric signs in the Times building announced the banks would be closed indefinitely. The next edition of the Times said most banks would be open today in N.Y. It's going to take a few weeks to straighten the banks out, and it was foolish of Roosevelt to announce it would take a few days. It is too jumbled for that. But let's not get worked up until April.

        Max

Monday [about March 13, 1933]

Dear Mother,

    Your letter just arrived with tax list. I realize perfectly well that the tax calendar is just one damn thing after another, and that almost everything else is too in these times, I haven't a word of criticism for anything you do, and I'll make no more suggestions. All I know is that you are the only extremely valuable personal connection in my life, and that you are not well and that you are overworked. So naturally I protest against it. I realize that income is cut down to next to nothing. But I believe that there are some things in what is known as Life that are more valuable than what is known as Capital. And I wish that in a time like this when income is curtailed and your need for cash is increased that you would part with some stock, sacrifice them, as you call it, for half their value or less, and get some ready cash to tide you over the wintry months. Or sell a bond at a sacrifice to a "shark" and get some money. I know one hates to do it. But the sacrifice of a bond ought to come before the sacrifice of one's self. Once you are well and on your feet again, you can pull in your belt and economize again to the limit. But your health should come before any economy program. I just know that if I were sick and a doctor ordered this or that, you would raise heaven and earth, and dispense with anything to see that I got the care demanded. Well, you are as valuable to me as I am to you only I am not in a position to dictate to you. I can only say I wish you would do this or that. All I want you to do is get well, if we have to be church mice together!

    Mr. Weber's letter makes sense. We all know that the bank legislation acted to open the Federal Reserve Banks first. My bank here is a Federal Reserve Bank. The others will follow in due time unless they were unsafe to begin with, and the Spitzer Rorick was sound before the holiday.

It is terrible about Mr. Hodson, Hogue, Solier, and the rest. The world is certainly in the dregs of its existence. The newsreels at the movies show nothing but hair raising scenes all over the earth. Nothing but persecutions, revolutions, floods, havoc of all kinds.

Dorothy Sheldon returned yesterday from Florida. She visited her brother there, and an old lady drove her down and back, with a chauffeur, so it cost her nothing. She gets back to find Roy's salary is cut in half, so they may have to move into smaller quarters again. Anyway she enjoyed the last three weeks . . .

Beatrice Locher leaves tomorrow to get a divorce in Reno. Almost nobody knows it, so don't tell anybody. Bobby is in the West Indies. So there is something very unpleasant gone to smash. A friend is motoring her to Saratoga tomorrow and asked me to go along. But I don't see any pleasure in motoring to Saratoga and back in this weather. And I am not going. The sun is peeping out today however, and spring may show up eventually.

I'm glad Fae [Johnson] was heard from.

Mary Badger went to hear Rachmaninoff in Carnegie Hall last Wed. and said it was two thirds empty. He is one of the five or six most popular pianists, and three years ago you couldn't fight your way into his concerts. If the hall is nearly empty now for him, one can imagine what it is like for the lesser pianists. I write everyday on my play. I think it is good. But of course it may be "unintelligible" to everyone else. I'm no judge I guess! Anyway, I hope we'll be living on royalties a year from now. I'm living cheaply at present.

I hope Doddy is improving. It's too bad she has to be miserable.

More whenever you can take it.

Max

The earthquake Max refers to in the following letter occurred on March 10, 1933. Centered off Long Beach, California, the 6.4 magnitude quake killed 120 people.

Tuesday [about March 14, 1933]

Dear Mother,

    Your letter which came today sounds reassuring, and quite like your old self. I do so hope you continue to get better fast, and I'm sure you will, and still faster when it begins to warm up, and you have fewer fires, and more fresh vegetables, etc. A regulated diet can't fail to improve you, I'm sure, for your diet was most unbalanced for years. And when you get back to the house take lots of warm tub baths which will get the winter poisons out of you.

    I lived for a week on nothing but food bills, and they were slight. This week I am obliged to buy necessary accessories like shaving cream—and even toilet paper! I am going back to my bank today or tomorrow and if it still doesn't want to take the coupons I'll go directly to the Hanover where they are payable and see what they say there. Anyway the strain of suspense is over, it seems, and now it is just a slow process of reconstruction.

    The earthquake capped the climax. No one we know out there seems to have suffered any damage. Marion Saportas rang up Lilyan Tashman right away on Saturday, and Lilyan seemed quite unconcerned about it. She said Beverly Hills had escaped entirely, and that she was just going out to a luncheon party at the Hoffensteins.

    I felt very much suspended all week and unable to concentrate on anything—even though my own life within four walls was not materially changed. I felt "up in the air" all the same. I am making no plans in advance at all. Alice told me to come South whenever I could, and I told her I would let her know, but I don't know what to do even about that.

Last year I went to Palm Beach on March 17th. We were having blizzards of snow here then, and I was sick. This year I'm not sick and there are no blizzards to send me south, though the weather is nasty and damp and raw. March is always the worst month here. I know Florida would do me a lot of good, and it is not nearly the expense it sounds, since I have next to NO expenses once I get there. Also I have everything I need in the way of sport clothes, as I got them last year down there. As for California in the summer I know it is hot and dry, but it is probably no more uncomfortable than New York which is hot and muggy, and more oppressive than the dry heat of the South. And again, I'm not going to plan on that at present. I still think I could go on an Italian liner or even a North German Lloyd liner and do some writing to pay my way. But I would not feel comfortable on a trip like that until you are well—either well enough to go along, or well enough that I wouldn't worry about you getting worse. People tell me I could get a free trip to Bermuda for ten days if I pulled the right strings with Henry Dell who runs the Castle Harbor Hotel there and who is a friend of Mr. England. He sent the Seldeses there for ten days. But I'm not sure I'd enjoy going to that wretched little island alone without anyone I liked going along. What is to be done?

    I'm still in favor of your hooking up with Josie in any feasible way. Of course I don't mean that you should "support the Ristes" as you called it in a recent letter. You would make terms, of course, but you would enjoy Joe's company, and the girls would add a lively touch, and Joe is approachable on the subject, as you can see from her letter between the lines. She certainly doesn't mean that you would take her to New York. But she does suggest that you get together, and I wish you would at least have a talk with her.

    The Florida governor sounds sensible don't you think?

I've not met A.C. Blumenthal, though I've seen quite a lot of Peggy Fears in the last month or two. They live in a whole floor of the Ambassador Hotel, in more rooms than one can count, so they don't see much of each other unless they happen into the same suite of rooms at the same time. I think he is very fond of her. But he is fond of Pola Negri and Constance Bennett and any other lady who is famous enough, and I don't think he is ever exactly lonely. People think he has less money since Jimmy Walker is off the scene. He was always in on Jimmy's "big deals."

Few people have seen Carl Van Vechten all winter, as he takes pictures day and night and sees only the people he is photographing. He does all things by extremes. When he was going out all the time he went to parties and to Harlem every night all night. This winter he refuses to go out at all. He has been a photographer now for a year, and the novelty will be wearing off soon, I should think, and then he will be in circulation again. Fania Marinoff had appendicitis last month and was in the hospital quite a while and then convalescent at home, so she has had a quiet season too.

Yes, I too wish more people would buy books, but I suppose it's too much to expect. I haven't bought a book all winter!

The week-end was moderately quiet. John Cohen, who is in love with Tallulah, gave another party for her Saturday night. Fannie Brice and Beatrice Lillie and Fannie Ward and other famous stars were there. Tallulah now has New York by the ears just as she had in London, and her two years of lack of success in Hollywood are forgotten in the general rejoicing over her success. I saw Ina Claire again at the hotel Algonquin last Thursday night. She was with her prince whom she is in love with now. He is the Prince von Liechtenstein—one of the few remaining reigning princes over a principality in Europe. It would be most amusing if Ina married him and became a reigning Princess. He already has a wife but she is morganatic. Still, it is complicated. Paul Draper danced at the Algonquin affair and had a success but he has no job.

Mary Badger asked me out to lunch on Sunday with Elizabeth Hawes, the designer, and Freddy Paine who runs a book shop. Mary's nurse was away Sunday afternoon so she had her two children on her hands for two hours. We all took them for a walk on the embankment along the East River and through Carl Schurz Park in 86th St. I hadn't been with small children for years and they seemed very odd. On the embankment many people were walking their dogs and their children, and the dogs and the children were all dressed alike, in blue and green zipper suits and red woolen costumes. The dogs looked very smart in the red suits, and so did the children. It was quite cold, so of course the dogs had to be all dressed up.

No more today. Tell Doddy to keep her money or to spend it on herself. I'm all set for the time being . . .

          Max

Thursday [about March 16, 1933]

Dear Mother,

To tell you I have banked the coupons, and that all is well again. If you want any of the money back in any form, let me know. This is an uneventful week—the March lull. It is bloody cold, and seems colder than it did in January, because you expect it to be cold then, but you don't expect it now.

I enclose a note from my London publisher. It says the book is "doing very nicely." England is so used to depression by now, that I suppose the times seem perfectly normal there. Here we can't get used to it yet. Can't think of a thing to tell you today that would interest you. Peggy Fears has closed her show, Music in the Air, on account of a salary cut fight with the stage hands union. I saw Frank Bishop two days ago. He is glad to be out of Detroit which seems to be the world's lowest depths this season. Everyone is surviving nicely.

    Max

Sunday night [March 19, 1933]

Dear Mother,

    Outside the rain is raining, the snow is snowing, and the sleet is sleeting, and I don't know whether I can face it to go around the block for a bite of dinner. I guess I probably can. I wish I could slice a chicken with you in the cupboard. I mean not you in the cupboard, but the chicken.

    You can put down last night, March 18, as the night I met Pola Negri. She was at John Cohen's party for Tallulah—his third in three weeks. I was very glad to see the Negri in the flesh. She looks just as she should. She wears her face chalk white like a mask, and she is dressed in an outfit of white satin with leopard skin around the top and leopard skin around the bottom, and a golden girdle around the middle. She came with Tade Styka, the Hungarian portrait painter, and she was in an amiable mood. She is sailing on Tuesday. She has been trying to sail for weeks, but the government wouldn't let her because she wouldn't pay her back income tax. So at last she paid it, and now she is off, and she seemed quite relieved. I'm anxious to hear what the Toledo and Pioneer bank developments are. Here everything is open save the Harriman bank—where Carl has his money. My bank is said to be one of the soundest in the city, but they are practically all sound now, and everyone has forgotten all about bank closings, earthquakes, and all. Thursday night Marion Saportas took me to dinner at the Seton Porters' whom I had never met before. They must be inconceivably rich, as they live in THREE FLOORS of an enormous apartment house in Park Avenue, with a private entrance on the street up a black marble staircase to their apartment. It was like a movie setting, all rooms ten times their normal size. Early English rooms, and Japanese rooms, and any kind of rooms you preferred. Then they took us to the opening of the Club Garron which was packed to the ceiling and to the floors with people like Marilyn Miller and Walter Chrysler junior and George Raft and Madame Schiaparelli, etc. The bill there was eighteen dollars for four bottles of ginger ale, and fortunately I was not paying for it! However people seem to be beginning to spend the way they did four years ago. And everything is looking up.

    More tomorrow or next day.
Max

March 21—Tuesday [1933]

Dear Clara Olive:

    Here is a page of considerable interest from the Los Angeles Times. Aline MacMahon sent it to me, with a message at the top of the page. It is very flattering to see myself teamed up with George Bernard Shaw—even if Miss Delicia Allen is between us! The review of the book is good—but probably nobody read it, as March 12 was the Sunday after the California earthquake on Saturday, and I imagine no one had his mind on books that day. Still it may do some good. But the book business is pretty well shot this spring. They say even best sellers aren't selling—whatever that may mean.

    The weather keeps up being ghastly. It hasn't stopped pouring for more than an hour since I wrote you on Sunday. The sleet has stopped. That is all. Such weather makes my sinuses feel like mountains in my head, and even my finger throbs and aches like a volcano. I'd like to omit drizzly March from the calendar every year, or else be able to sleep it off. That is what I've been doing mostly these past two days. It is about time I should hear from you now.
Max

Sunday [about March 26, 1933]

Dear Mother,

    Just in case you might think there is any change in things here, let me reassure you that the rain is still falling, that it is still dark as dusk all day, that all the lights are on, and that the air is heavy with mist. I continue to sniff it and wheeze. It was like this yesterday. And tomorrow will be tomorrow, and doubtless the same. We are resigned.

    I am at work on my play again. It is supposed to be a light comedy, though it may turn out as gloomy as Macbeth under these atmospheric conditions.

    This afternoon I'm going up to Osborns to see their four new kittens. They now have seven cats in their small apartment and they fear they will have to move into a larger place because they cannot bear to part with any of the offspring. If they would I'd be tempted to take one.

    I saw Pola Negri again Thursday afternoon at Marion's. She was in black fur and black veil and black Russian leather boots which reached to her knees, all very odd. She said as soon as she returned from Europe she wanted to be photographed by me in Venice because she liked Marion's picture so much. I told her I did the snapping in my bedroom and that I'd be delighted to have her come. She wants to spend April in Paris and then come back. I haven't taken any pictures of anyone since the Waldorf show.

    I'm glad you and Mrs. Beard are friendly again, and that you have a "gang." Let me know when you are moving home. And let me know about your last blood pressure test. What will Joe and Besse DO if their little income is lost?

I bought myself a lovely white turtle neck sweater yesterday for 45 cents and am trying to look like Clark Gable. I guess it will constitute all my new spring wardrobe.

More soon.

Max

>
> Aren't
>
> you
>
> glad
>
> you
>
> are
>
> not
>
> a
>
> Jew
>
> in
>
> Germany?

Monday [about March 27, 1933]

Dear Mother,

Here starts a new week, just like all the past weeks—sun under a cloud, and dampness in the air. The sun looked out for a minute one day last week, but then went right back under again, and it has been rainy ever since.

The Seldeses invited Muriel and me to go out dancing, of all things, on Friday night, which we did at the opening of the Carlton Club, through a splashing rain both going and coming. However it was dry and quite agreeable inside. On Saturday I took Dorothy Sheldon to tea at the Waldorf-Astoria—on the invitation of Mr. England, of course—I never pay for anything anywhere. She was under the impression that she was quite dark from the Florida sun, but she looked snow-white to me. She had gone over to Palm Beach from Lake Worth several times, but had not seen Alice, as Alice does not like her. We got to the Waldorf in a dry condition, but by the time we left it was falling cats and dogs, the rain, I mean, so we were soon wet. It rained all last night again, and my bronchial regions feel like soaked prunes.

    The French boy whom Ettie Stettheimer brought here took me up to Harlem the other night to the house of a singing teacher named Bonds. When we got there I found he was occupying the same flat Alelia Walker lived in before she died. Various people came and went throughout the evening, some of them coal black people I had never heard of. But they had read my books. One colored boy knew it practically by heart and mentioned almost everything in it. I was quite amused, and asked him how he ever happened to read it in the first place. And he said he got it on the advice of Gifford Cochran, of all people. Gifford Cochran is a Cochran who married Ganna Walska. So, you see, Harlem makes for strange and surprising link-ups. I enclose a letter from the editor of Photoplay, which makes it increasingly clear that the movie magazines seem able to get along without any of assistance from me.

    I wrote to Fae [Johnson] and asked her for the Los Angeles page.

    I hope things are brighter north of Road #20.

    More as soon as there is more.

                Max

Wednesday [April 5, 1933]

Dear Mother:

    Daylight again at last!

    I got your letter this morning, and have signed the card promptly, and returned it to the People's Savings Association. It is probably a sensible move. Your letter sounds as if the "slough of despond" is easing up a little. I do hope the Pioneer Bank plan goes through and that you can do free checking again. I can't imagine what you would do without a bank there over a long period, or what any of the business people would do. As soon as there is any free money I wish we could get a monument for Dad. It seems as if a year is long enough to wait. I don't believe in extremely expensive monuments in country cemeteries, but I do think there should be one before too much time goes by. You know best about the funds. Can't a payment be made, and other payments to follow?

 Doddy does sound like a miracle of resilience. That is what you both are. It is a pity that you are not more chemically attuned to each other to appreciate each other's presence and performance! I hate to hear of the deaths of Pioneer people—even those I hardly know like Charlie Cogswell. It seems there are always deaths and departures from small towns, and never new arrivals. Of course I suppose new babies keep being born, but there isn't much companionship in a new baby—except for its family!

 Gas on the stomach ought to be easy enough to get rid of, I should think. What is the new report on your blood pressure? Jimmy Walker has it too, but he is getting married next week.

 Of course, whether I go to California or not, I will see you this summer one place or another. If I go west I'll stop on Ohio on my way, and if I don't go west, I'll stop there anyway that is, unless you cannot come here. I still want you to do that, and the trip would do you good, in good weather. It is not unpleasant here until July. We will make plans soon.

 This letter ought to reach you on my birthday, and it gives me great pleasure to send you the enclosed notice by Ernest Newman as a symbol of recognition on that day. As I wrote you yesterday, he is the most looked up to, and most widely recognized of all modern music critics, and a great writer about music on his own account. So, such attention makes me feel that my first thirty years have been pretty well spent, and I hope you will think that the money spent on me has been well spent too. Please keep this clipping on tap because I may want it back if I cannot get hold of another for my own scrap book. And do not say that you cannot find a big enough envelope for it if I decide I want it back on short notice!

Did you arrange for me to be born on April 7th, in order that my birthday should coincide with the rebirth of beer in 1933? They say Friday night will be like New Year's Eve. Are you going to sell beer at the store? The banks seem to be about the only places in New York that are not going to sell it. But nobody seems to care, as there has always been plenty of it in every block in town anyway.

Was very much pleased this morning to have a letter from Romaine Brooks, saying she had enjoyed my book very much, and had laughed aloud. She has been in Italy, is in Paris now, and is coming here next fall to become an American citizen again.

All love.

Max

Thursday [April 7, 1933]

THE WEATHER

**Today: Cloudy followed by rain;
Little change in temperature
Tomorrow: Probably rain**

Dear Mother,

Daily weather report.

I was at John Becker's gallery this afternoon, and on leaving there to get a bus home I had to walk three blocks in the rain. I am now drenched and soaked to the skin, and am preparing to take a bath and stay in the tub the rest of the season. What sense is there in getting out of the tub? The whole outdoors is nothing but a tub, only the water outdoors is cold, and in the tub it at least is warm.

I hope you went to Toledo with Clara Sweet and that you escaped any cloudburst. Thank you for the birthday note. I wouldn't mind being thirty if the weather would change. I'm sorry about Nellie Gilpin's bankruptcy. If it will comfort her any, tell her that Brentanos went bankrupt this week—the world's largest bookshops.

Peggy Fears and I are not on the "outs," but she is absorbed in personal problems and I have not seen her lately. A Blumenthal divorce is in the offing, and she is having trouble with her plays and her players and stage hand unions, and is planning to leave for London.

Excuse me now while I wring out my trouser legs.
     Max

19 W. 31—New York—April 11 [1933]

Dear Uncle,

Once before I was writing my novel I consulted you as my literary-legal advisor in regard to the status of twins. Now I am writing a play and I need to consult you again. About wills and on what grounds they can be broken, and where I can read up on some legal terminology relating to them. The situation in the play (do not tell a soul!) involves a family of four daughters, middle-aged daughters, whose mother has died and left all the family property to a second husband, whom the daughters detest. They want to contest the will, but they do not want it to appear that their mother was irrational or in any way "crazy." They summon a young lawyer and he must tell them something or other. And what would he tell them? Are there any other grounds on which wills can be broken except the incapacity o the person making the will? What would you say to four rather odd sisters who found themselves in this predicament? Please tell me what you would tell them. At your leisure . . .

New York is rainy and moderately uneventful. George Bernard Shaw is in the harbor today but disdains to come on shore until evening.

I wrote to Doris yesterday, calling her all kinds of a toad.

Hoping to hear from you—
                Max

Wednesday [April 13, 1933]

Dear Mother,

Twenty-four more hours of driving rain have turned now to sleet and snow, and even that is quite a welcome relief from just plain water. You probably think that I am very exaggerated about the weather, but as a matter of fact I do not exaggerate. I went with Jimmy Amster and his mother to dine at Mary Badger's last night. We intended to go out somewhere after dinner, but there was a downpour, so we stayed in and listened to Bernard Shaw on the radio, which was worth listening to, and I hope you heard him. Then today when I woke up it was pouring down so hard that I thought it must break the skylight. I stayed in bed until noon, hoping it would let up enough so that I could get across the street for some coffee without getting drenched. But there was not a chance. I finally got into my oldest coat and an old felt hat and slunk out to breakfast like a drowning rat. The major problem of everyday is how to get in and out without getting soaked. The weather in itself is a matter of no importance, but in my case it does affect me physically and psychologically, and six weeks of rain with practically no let up leaves me feeling just like Jeanne Eagles or Joan Crawford in RAIN. We ought to be above being affected by such things, but I guess I'm not. I'm not much of a nature fan, but the one thing in "nature" that I do love is sun—as you know from my sitting on a potato box in the backyard in

Pioneer for hours!—and we haven't seen the sun for more than an hour at a time all spring here.

There seems to be no news at all this week on any front. Everybody is just existing and swimming around. I saw the movie of Noel Coward's "Cavalcade," which is marvelous and breaks your heart. Besse [Durbin] would go mad over it.

Love, and more soon.
    Max

Thursday morning [April 14, 1933]

The enclosed just came from Fae [Johnson]. Also your letter. I'm sorry Fae didn't send the whole newspaper page, but anyway, here is the main event. Frank B [Bishop] got off to Tennessee without me. He is a good driver as far as that goes, but his car is too little for such a trip. And he is so unpredictable, he might stay away two weeks instead of one, so I gave it all up.

I wish I knew how to inject some variety into Pioneer life but I don't know how it is to be done. I'll be out there in June to sit on the potato box again, if that will help any!

I don't think the new beer is enough of a "stimulant" to do you much harm—anyway not an occasional glass of it. But do as your doctor says, anyway.

If I go to California I'll of course be economical. I know some people out there like Tashman who live extravagantly. But I know many more here who live extravagantly. It is the same everywhere. People who can live extravagantly do. If they can't they don't. And I know plenty of people out there who don't—like [Marguerite] Namara and Mindret [Lord] and Jack Becket [Becker] and Mercedes de Acosta. Even Aline Mac Mahon and Kay Francis save their money. Especially Kay, because she knows she is a star by accident, and won't be one forever. I'm sure I'd not spend as much as I do here. The only real expense would be the transportation.

The sun is out! That is news like man biting dog!

Monday [April 17, 1933]

Dear Mother,

Here's a cold and drizzly Monday following a cold and drizzly Easter Sunday. Lots of people seem to have paraded thru the mists of Easter, but having no new wardrobe to sport, I went only to Muriel's to Easter breakfast which we ate with Paul and Smudge and the cat. A man named Samuel Putnam arrived in the middle of breakfast, from France so to speak. He is an editor and translator of French books and magazines. So he had lots of news of Europe. He says everyone expects war within six or eight months, and that he is installing his wife and children in a small village in the Alps which he thinks is less apt to be bombed than a city. He says the outlook is absolutely gruesome everywhere, which was none too pleasant an Easter thought.

Mary Badger had a large party Saturday, and at it was Leonie Sterner, just back from her year out west. John Becket [Becker] and Douglas Parmentier were on their way out to visit her when they passed thru Pioneer last spring. She lived in Santa Fe for a while and in Arizona for a while, and most of the time in Hollywood. She enjoyed it all very much, and said one could live on one fourth what it cost here. We said that sounded too impossible so she thought for a minute, and said, well anyway, one third. She said she had a whole lovely house in Hollywood, next to Elissa Landi's house, for what she would have paid for a small flat in New York. All these stories sound improbable, but I am more and more anxious to give it a trial and find out. I think by the end of June I could afford to go by train. I have stayed away from Florida, and economized in many ways, with a Western trip in view.

And it looks more desirable every day, as every day we wake up here to the same black weather, thick with mist and fog.

In addition to the rigors of the weather, the problem of eating is becoming a serious one in this part of town. All the restaurants have radically reduced their prices, but they have simultaneously reduced the quality of the food until it is now practically un-eatable. Meal after meal I leave untouched, and generally end up having a sandwich in a stool at a drug store. There isn't a decent restaurant for blocks and blocks. You probably think that I am full of complaints. I don't mean to be. I know I have less reason for complaining than most people. Only, with all signs of quality disappearing from the world so fast, it does seem unnecessary that cooking should disappear too. And yet it is fast becoming a lost art in New York, except in speakeasies, where all the real cooks in captivity are engaged.

I had a card from Frank [Bishop] in Tennessee, saying his car rode like a Rolls-Royce. I doubt that! I'll be glad to hear that you have moved home and given up the hill-climbing.

      More soon,
         Max

Tuesday [April 18, 1933]

Dear Mother—Got your letter, and suppose you are in Toledo today. I hope you are having a good day, as we are. We had a gloomy Easter weekend, but today the skies are clear, and look as if perhaps it might be permanent this time.

I'm sorry to hear about Mr. Hodson's death, but of course it is better than lingering half-life. Also I'm sorry about Doddy. You do not mention your own health, and I assume it is better, or at least no worse. I went to dinner at Marion Saportas' last night, and later other people came in and we all went upstairs to Tallulah's where we played games—

of all things—and finally scrambled eggs and ate some crab meat. Tallulah's father, Senator Bankhead, had a bad heart attack this week in Washington, and she is worried. She adores her father. Her mother has been dead since Tallulah was a small child. Marion Saportas expects to go to California this spring with Mrs. Lionel Barrymore. She will probably stay with Tashman when she gets there. I hope she does, so that I can hook up with her there.

I'm sorry my letters about bad weather have given you the impression that I am "miserable." I most certainly am not. It is depressing, of course, to have so much rain, and it does make my nose and throat troubles seem worse. But there is always something going on here to take one's mind off bad weather, and it is only because the weather has been so exceptionally bad that I have written about it so often. After such a bad early spring, the late spring is bound to be more sunny. The first sunny days which are really warm, I am going to the beach to my favorite sun-parlor, and let the sun beat on all of us, breathe the salt air, and get rid of the soaked-prune feeling. That wouldn't be possible in Pioneer. Besides, I don't want to come out there at just this time of year. It would seem too much like a repetition of last year, and it would be depressing for all of us. I'm coming later, but not yet.

Alice De La Mar returns from Florida this week, and that is a good sign of spring. Muriel may really go to the country next month. Everyone has been under the impression that she has been in the country all along. Blanche Knopf has recently given Muriel a good share of her winter wardrobe, which happens to fit, and with a few added accessories make her look very elegant again! I'm glad Libby Owens [Glass Company] are prosperous. Chicago, Milwaukee, and St. Paul are not!

Who is the new girl you have? You haven't mentioned her before. I'm delighted you have her, and it is a comfort that she is a GOOD COOK!

The restaurant problem seems critical around here only on those days when it is raining so hard that I don't want to go far away. And the only places near at hand are Armenian places, Jewish restaurants, drug stores, and Childs. And Childs has become terrible. I still go there from force of habit, and because it is convenient, but there are no other adequate reasons for going there. And when they serve hot things cold and cold things warm, I get furious! These are infrequent occasions, however, I am invited out a good deal, and pleasant days I walk a few blocks where I find good meals. So don't let my outburst of yesterday disturb you too much!

I received a fan letter today from an unknown admirer named Marco Carson who wants me to sign his book if I will let him stop by for that purpose. I suppose I will. I always wonder what these unknown quantities will be like.

Peggy Fears goes out only with her mother these days!
      Max

Thursday [April 20, 1933]

Good morning—

How do you feel being off the gold standard? Shall we buy a lot of everything before prices go up? I enclose two letters for your pleasure—one from Doris, and one from a man, Mr. Rainey at the National Broadcasting Co. It took me two weeks to get an appointment with Rainey, and then took two weeks more to get the audition itself, and then it took two more to get this note from him today. And I doubt that anything will happen about it even now, because the radio "clients" have diminished rapidly over the past few months. There are fewer and fewer advertising programs, and the others don't pay anything.

Anyway—

Doris' letter is full of praise for you, which is of course justified. You, as well as Dad, have been more than kind to the Grand Rapids clan. Though your present life may seem full of outside irritations, there must be considerable inside satisfaction in knowing that you are so SQUARE and so very GOOD! In spite of present-day mishaps, your life has been in many, many ways an enviable one. I especially envy you the world you grew up into. I don't mean the personal day-to-day, Pioneer world, but I mean the atmosphere of the world, in general. In those days though it was a world of struggle for advancement, still everyone did believe that they were advancing, and that there was something to advance toward. People believed that they were getting more and more civilized and enlightened all the time. Then came the War and everyone was shocked to learn that the world was still savage and beastly, and that nothing had improved since the dark ages but lights and locomotion and such things. The after-the-war conditions are now worse for more people than the days of the war itself, and no one foresees any solution now except more war as a solution of the chaotic peace. Every country is overflowing with unemployed men, and a war would provide something to do with them. They can go to various fronts and shoot each other. Prices would go up and there would be another semblance of "prosperity." In the meantime there is nothing but absolute chaos everywhere, and all young people necessarily have what Noel Coward calls "the Twentieth Century Blues, with nothing to win or lose." I am very glad I grew up when I did. For people growing up now the whole world must look like a cesspool. I at least had twenty-five years or so of agreeable illusion.

After months of appealing to the public for funds, the Metropolitan Opera now is assured of a short season next year, opening after Christmas. And today's papers say that unless Carnegie Hall makes more money next season, it will have to become a movie theater. If that happens, then there will not be a large concert hall left in the city of New York. In the meantime it is going to run a beer garden and see if that makes things break even.

Marion Morehouse just rang up to say Goodbye. She leaves Saturday on her first trip to Paris. Paris is going to be very expensive this year for Americans because of the exchange rates. But probably Marion will make some money over there as a fashion model. She is one of the best, and she will be new to Paris. Still, it is the last place I would want to go this particular year. Enough now.

      Max

Wednesday [April 26, 1933]

Dear Mother,

  Here's a note on a sunny day that might be any bright Wednesday in January. I enclose also a note from Fanny Butcher, the literary editor of the Chicago Tribune, who wants to see the Venetian pictures when she comes to New York next week. I have written her that they are no longer on public display, but she can come in and see them here. I hope she does. And if she does, then we will see her in Chicago—so it all ties up . . .

  Last night was Cobina Wright's big circus party at the Waldorf, which I did not attend—the tickets being ten dollars. I had a quiet evening instead, with Cary Ross and Walker Evans.

  Monday, taking advantage of a sunny day, I went to my sun parlor at the beach, and lay in the sun for three hours. Many people I know were there. I swear it was like lying on the golden streets inside the pearly gates, the feel of the sun is so wonderful. I could feel the whole soggy spring being baked out of me, and I am longing to go back, but today is it is cold.

I saw Florence Osborn at John Becket's [Becker] yesterday. She is negotiating to get a Vermont farm for this summer, with cows and chickens and a farmer and his wife to work for her. She says Paul hates the country and won't go there, so she intends to go alone to the farm and leave him to his own devices. As I left there I ran into Marguerite d'Alvarez in the street. She has been in Europe for two years and I was surprised to see her. I asked her how it seemed to be in New York in these times, and she said she found it thrilling—the careless way New York progressed to its destruction. I asked her if she was convinced that it was on its way to destruction. And she said, "Of course, the whole world is." And on this cheerful note we went our ways.

Sunday I was in the neighborhood of Gramercy Park and took a look at my old neighborhood in general. It is a rather ghostly feeling. I went past the Hearthstone where I often used to lunch with Helen Lynch. It is now boarded up and deserted, and the houses around it on the park have been torn down to make way for big brick apartment buildings. Helen Lynch is out of the world, as far as anyone knows. Bob Chanler's house stands gray and gloomy in 19th St. All the curtains and furnishings are out of it and you can look in the front windows and out the back ones. FOR SALE signs are all over it, but there are no buyers. Then in 18th St. I passed the buildings in which Elinor Wylie lived, and which Rita Wellman lived with Edgar Leo. Elinor is dead, and Edgar too is dead, shot by his own hand. The whole neighborhood throws out an air of violence and disintegration.

I am planning to come out to you early in June, and spend the rest of that month with you, and maybe longer. Anyway, I'll wait around until after the July coupon harvest, and see if we have enough dividends to afford a trip. If we do you can go as far as Chicago with me. If we don't we can both go to Chicago anyway. Even though summer trains are hot, it would not be a bad trip west from Chicago. I could go to San

Francisco and visit Noel Sullivan there before starting south. The length of time spent in Hollywood would depend on expenses, the possibility of getting something to do, and the general hospitality of the people. But whenever I came back, I would come the southern route and stop off in New Mexico or Arizona. I am determined to have a month or so in mountains and desert air to see what effect it has on my health.

I am not in poor health, but I am never over-supplied with energy. I always have just enough to get through ordinary routine, and none in reserve for DRIVING POWER. This year I am going to try to get it. When everything else in the world is at such low ebb, there are still plenty of bracing physical stimulate and I can at least stock up on those. I won't mind being away from New York for five or six months, if I can make some satisfactory arrangement about the apartment. Will let you know soon about that.
     Max

Later Wednesday [April 26, 1933]

Dear Mother,

Your letter came today just after I mailed mine to you. So this is just to follow it up, and tell you that the coupons are here safely, and I'll bank them promptly, and hope for the best. I did not expect any money at this time, and do not need it, but it will be safe here, and will be on tap if you ever want it for any purpose. It sounds good to hear you "say" that you feel moderately prosperous again. So do I with such a reassuring surplus in the bank. In spite of our "losses" or curtailments, we have come out better than most people, I still maintain. It is now 1933, and we have not been forced to change our 1928 mode of living very drastically. Of course we economize more, and think twice before taking a taxi, or buying a theater ticket, and all that. But we are still living in the same places, with only incidental differences in our modes of living. So many people have been absolutely uprooted, and forced to do everything on a different scale, and we should be very grateful. The Toledo bank situation will clear up, I feel sure. I don't know about the Pioneer bank, because I don't know its condition or resources, without Mr. Hodson as a bulwark. But our investments continue to pay pretty well, sometimes on time, and sometimes late.

    I am very glad that you have gone ahead and bought the monument for Dad's grave. I think a year is long enough to wait, if we have the money to pay for it. And I can trust your selection in matters like this. I am glad you approve of my enlarging my wardrobe. I have tried to be so extremely economical all this year because I felt I shouldn't let an unnecessary cent go out as long as I was not bringing any in. But clothes are a good investment for anyone in my position. The trouble is I am not quite sure what to buy if I am going out west, because I am not entirely sure what sort of things I will need, and I don't want to carry around any things I won't need. Summer days in California are hot, but the evenings are cool the year around. I would wait until I got out there, but they say it is hard to get clothes out there and they are expensive. Everything else—food, rents, are said to be cheap. New York is undoubtedly the best clothes market. Today I am wearing my blue suit I got in London in 1927, and it still looks pretty well when it is pressed! Some days I even wear my Paris 1926 suit, but not when I expect to be seen by anyone.

    Sorry about the friction between Doddy and the maid but it has a familiar ring!

    Alice De La Mar is back, and is coming down to see me next Monday. Muriel has gone to the country, really the country this time, to a little house in Connecticut near the Whitall's house. It belongs to Hob Erwin who has gone to Hollywood. I am curious to meet Fanny Butcher. I have read her reviews ever since Ann Arbor days, when I read her columns about Carl's [Van Vechten] early books. I'm sure she would introduce me to amusing people in Chicago if I looked her up out there. Albert Carroll is in Chicago, doing something or other about amateur dramatics at Hull House, of all places. Several N.Y. shows intend to play in Chicago this summer, so we can connect with a lot of people if we go there. I think of Mrs. Lundberg in connection with the Chicago school teachers, and I wonder if she has come to blows with Charles D. Dawes! I did not hear from any of the "Chicago girls" about the book. But for that matter, I didn't hear from any Pioneer people either, except H. Meyers, who ordered one, and Nellie Gilpin, who didn't! However, there are no hard feelings!

      Max again.

Monday, May 1 [1933]

Dear Mother,

  Just when you are beginning to feel sort of prosperous I am sorry to have to return to you the enclosed coupons and slip. When I banked these April Pasco County coupons they were returned to me. I said nothing about it and put them away, meaning to send them through again the first of May, hoping there would be funds at that time. Today when I got them out to bank them again, I found the enclosed slip which I had not seen in the envelope when the coupons were returned to me. It advises holders of the bonds to send information to the Chicago bank, as you can see. I suppose you had better do this instead of me. And you can put the coupons in the safe for safe keeping. So there it is—another nuisance. I banked the Snow Hill coupons and hope they can be redeemed. I guess I'd better buy no clothes after all until I see how things turn out. I have no URGENT need for clothes. It is just that when spring comes you feel like having something new to wear. I can easily do without in the meantime.

George Lynes gives himself a farewell party tonight. He leaves for Paris Friday. Last night Dorothy and Roy Sheldon came here and brought an Argentine moving picture editor from a Buenos Aires magazine. He leaves for Hollywood today and says he hopes to see me out there.

Saturday night I went up to Harlem with Marion Saportas and Tallulah Bankhead and Mrs. Lionel Barrymore and Mrs. Paul Whiteman, and various other cronies from Tallulah's play. Peggy Fears organized the expedition, but she did not appear when the time came. She went to the Mayfair dance instead and hooked up with Lupe Velez.

The Bishops came here on Friday. Frank made very good time in his trip to Tennessee. He enjoyed it and said the weather and the country were beautiful, but that the people were unbelievably backward and uncivilized. He said he stopped in one house where they had no stove and had never seen such a thing. They had only an open fireplace. I don't know why he happened to be in such a house however. His rich lady backer, Lucy Cotton Thomas Ament Hahn Magraw married her newest husband, Mr. Macgraw, only a month ago, but she has already discarded him and thrown him out of her house.

I had a letter from Frances Ewing today—something quite rare and the first in two or three years. Her chief reason for writing seems to be to express her "pride" in me, and to ask for a photograph of myself. She says I inspire her to do things she never does.

Will write again soon, now that the weather is agreeable it seems there is less to write about!
        Max

Thursday [about May 4, 1933]

Dear Mother,

Your letter arrived today, and being rare they're always welcome! Too bad about Doddy and her behavior, but the only thing to do is just let her go her own way as far as it is possible for her to do so. She can't stand being directed, and I guess she never will. The only thing one has to realize about her is that she really enjoys commotion more than she does calm. So that the things that would really distress most people excite her and please her in some way. So you shouldn't feel bad when she seems to be having a bad time. For that is really her kind of a good time. I should think it might be a relief to you to be alone this month. I still plan to arrive there early in June. My rent here is payable up to the 8th or maybe a few days sooner.

    I am making negotiations with two agencies to handle me in Hollywood, and see if anything can be done about me out there. Last Saturday night with Mrs. Barrymore and Mrs. Whiteman, I met an agent named Minna Wallis, who is part of the firm of Curtiss and Wallis. She lives in Hollywood but is here for a week or so, and she is said to be the best agent out there. I am seeing her today at 6:30 at the Biltmore, to talk business. Then too, I have been negotiating with the William Morris agency, which is the biggest international agency of its sort, with branches in Hollywood, Paris and London. It generally handles "big names." I have the papers signed by this agency to handle me for three months, but I haven't signed yet. I don't know which to sign with. People say you get more personal attention if you sign with an agent on a smaller scale like Wallis, because such a big agency as Morris has less time for people who are less well known. Still Wallis, handles quite important people too, such as Clark Gable, etc. Morris got Sam Hoffenstein his job, and Mae West, etc. Anyway, by the first of the week I will have signed with one or the other. It doesn't mean an awful lot to have signed, since they do not guarantee to get you anything to do, and you do not pay them anything unless they do, and in that case you pay ten percent of what you make. It just means that nobody else can represent you for a period of ninety days. And I won't be out there before sixty days anyway, at the least. But I want some sort of negotiations to precede my going, and it is well to start them from this end.

Alice de la Mar came in yesterday, and so did Muriel, who is in town for a few days. And also I asked two boys who are movie actors— David Rollins, and Tom Douglas. Tom Douglas is practically a star. They live together in Hollywood, and it developed yesterday that Hob Erwin is living in their house in Hollywood at present, while Muriel is living in Hob Erwin's house in Connecticut. So it was accidentally quite a ring around the rosie. Alice said she might go west this summer instead of to Europe where she has gone every year most of her life. She wants to go to Russia with Muriel if Muriel ever gets ready to go. Anyway—everyone is getting ready to GO SOMEWHERE. George Lynes had an enormous party Monday night, paid for by two English boys who have been around the world and just arrived here from the South Seas. Everyone was talking of departure in the next month. George sails tomorrow. The Julien Levys are giving a big party tomorrow night and then they leave for France. The Askews leave for England. Dorothy Crawford is going to the Dalmation Coast. I have told everyone that I am going to California so I hope I won't have to disappoint my public!

Too bad about the fire. It must look awful around the "Bridge" now. Maybe we can spend some time around Clear Lake in June. I might ask Dick Clemmer to visit us there for a few days. He has gone back to Ohio after two years of being unable to get anything to do here. His family which was extremely rich, has lost everything, and they are still living with relatives in a town outside of Cleveland, on Lake Erie.

Of course he is so miserable he can hardly bear it. Some of his friends here think he might kill himself if something doesn't happen.

Anyway, we will try and liven things up for you in June, and see if that makes you better.

Paul Draper danced at Radio City this week and had a success. But all his write-ups in the papers said he danced, and was the son of Muriel Draper, and then went into long accounts about her and her past life and her conversation and her personality and her parties and her writing and her clothes and everything else about her, and Paul was quite forgotten. This annoyed both him and her. But that is the penalty of being the son of a celebrated woman. Ruth Draper was dragged in too.

I am dining at Mary Badger's tomorrow night before going to the Levys. She plans to go west this summer too, and wants me to go with her, and she says she would come to Pioneer and pick me up there. But I am going to discourage this. I want to enter Hollywood alone, and on my own. I'm like Doddy, and I'm like you. I want to go it alone, in most cases at least.

Esther is divorced, and staying in Paris. She writes that she thinks the new financial theme song in this country should be "Silver Threads among the Gold."

Mrs. Lucy Cotton Thomas Ament Hahn Magraw has announced she wants to marry Frank Bishop, and that she is going to ask Claire to divorce him "for his own good."

There is a get-together in Grand Street tonight of all the Neighborhood Playhouse people. Most of them who were particular friends of mine, like [Albert] Carroll, and Aline [MacMahon] etc. are scattered, so I doubt if I'll attend,—though I may decide to when the time comes.

I am drying out these days, and coming out of the fog I got into for awhile.

                Max

Monday [May 8, 1933]

Dear Mother,

    In reply to yours on Thursday:

    I don't understand entirely what is meant by "refunding" the Florida bonds. But I honestly think it might be sensible to sell a few of those defaulted bonds at a sacrifice, and re-invest the money in government bonds. There would be less money, to be sure, and smaller interest rate, but anyway what there was would be sure. The interest on those Florida bonds is very high. But 4 percent goes almost as far in 1933 as 6 percent went in the nineteen twenties. One can adjust one's self to a smaller budget when one has to, but it is very hard to adjust one's self to a budget that is never settled from one month to the next, and which may be available at a given time or may not until six months later, it becomes impossible to PLAN anything, and live in a continual state of suspense. I'm no authority in these matters, God knows, but that is just my idea. Just for a few of the bonds, of course—not all of them by any means.

    I'll go ahead and get some clothes, and if Snow Hill comes back, well it will just be too bad.

    We have a dry warm day every now and then to cheer us up and give us hope, and then comes a succession of cold ones. Today is a cold wet one. Yesterday was a warm dry one, and I went to the Winslows at Fieldston.

    It worries me very much about your falling downstairs like that. Stop using the back stairs. Only go down where there is a railing. It is probably just dizziness, but you might have a serious fall, just the same. How often does Clara Sweet go back and forth to Pioneer? It might be an idea for me to hook up with her in Toledo. Then I could hop on a fast train to Toledo and ride out to Pioneer with her, instead of taking a slow milk train to Bryan, and having someone make the trip to meet me there. What would you think? I don't know how big a car Clara has. I mean to bring a lot of baggage, enough to last me several months. I saw Eddie Wassermann Thursday night at Kay Mills' supper dance at the Algonquin. Eddie said he thought I was terrible to go to California instead of Europe with him. He said California was like Woolworths while Europe is like Tiffany's. I said I thought everyone ought to see Woolworth's once, and that I didn't think Europe was going to be much like Tiffany's this season anyway. Lewis Galantiere is just back from there, and says London is moderately gay, but that Paris is so depressed and deserted it is pathetic. He didn't even look up any of our friends there. He just did his business and came away again. Kay Mills is going to be in Chicago all summer doing publicity for the Fair [Century of Progress], and tells me I can stay with him at his place whenever I come there—just to let him know when I'm coming.

  The Levy ball on Friday night was quite festive. All the ladies looked very elaborate in their spring outfits—lots of white ruffles and long trains of white organdy and lace ruffles—all very much like 1870, and very difficult to dance in. Muriel made a sensation in a black gown Blanche Knopf gave her, and to go with it Muriel had bought a huge Moline neck ruching which stands out from her shoulders a foot in all directions and makes it look as if her head and arms were coming out of God knows what.

  Yes, I'm afraid that Doris is "gone for good." I understand so well how she feels, I mean about the impossibility of permanent return, after making such a departure as she has made, or as I have made. Istanbul is a lot farther away from Michigan than New York is, as far as distance goes. But New York is just as remote from Michigan as Istanbul in its mode of life, I mean the section of new York that I know.

The agent, Minna Wallis, has gone back to Hollywood, taking a copy of my book with her and some of my old Grand Street songs. She says she will not handle me for less than a year. I hate to sign up for a year with someone I know so little about. But people who know say she is a very efficient agent, and has all the necessary contacts. She is Norma Shearer's closest friend, for instance, and Norma Shearer is Mrs. Thalberg, and Irving Thalberg is head of Metro-Goldwyn-Mayer and there you are. I have written to Sam Hoffenstein to ask his advice, and I hope he answers, but he is so vague you never can tell what he will do.

At Muriel's on Thursday I met a Miss De Witt who is here from Hollywood on a visit. While she is here Adrian is living in her Hollywood house. Adrian is Metro's [MGM] first costume designer, a young man who does all the costumes for Joan Crawford, Garbo, Shearer, and Marion Davies. Miss DeWitt told me I must come to see her because she will be there by the time I am, and that she will introduce me to Adrian at once, who will introduce me right and left. I have just as many contacts with important people in Hollywood now as I have here, and I feel sure this is the year for me to go, if we can scrape up the cash to get me there.

More soon,
Max

Tuesday [May 9, 1933]

Dear Mother,

Correspondence thick and fast! Just got your Sunday letter, and hope you didn't eat too much! You are right, that I am emphatic about going West. I will know definitely about the apartment this week. I have not been able to pin the landlord down to an actual sum per month while I am away. But tomorrow I am having a man from the Manhattan Storage Company (where I stored my things safely both times I went abroad) come in here and see what I have and make an estimate on what it would cost per month to store my things. Then I will know exactly where I stand when the landlord makes me a price. If the storage price is cheaper then I'll go into storage. The storage men do all the packing work for me, and it means only two days or so of being torn up. In some ways I would rather be in storage. I would feel a little more comfortable if I kept this apartment when I was away I would feel obliged to return to it when I came back, and I'm not sure I want to. It is a nice roomy apartment with lots of advantage which are hard to duplicate. But it has just as many disadvantages. The building is not run as well as it was formerly. That is because it is only half full, and the landlord can't afford to run it as well. He means well, and in time it will be in ship-shape again, but in the meantime it is not. This neighborhood deteriorates all the time, and the restaurants are fierce, and I have to go out for every bite, since there is no food served here.

Also, I feel a need for a clean sweep of some sort this year. I don't want to feel that I have to come back here at a specified time if I don't want to. And of course I can't expect the landlord to keep me going in this apartment at a cheap rate indefinitely. So don't be surprised later this week if I tell you I'm going into storage. At present it's an even chance either way.

I expect to be very much refreshed and brightened up by the West, and when I return to N.Y. I would like to make a whole fresh start of some sort, and not just fall back into my old routine. I feel that this year is a turning point of some sort. Dad's death definitely terminated something. And the appearance of my book in some way terminated something else, or rather started something else. I feel as if I were bringing the nineteen-twenties, as well as my own twenties, to a close, and that a new period is beginning. I have lived nearly ten years in New York, and I have loved every year. I haven't done exactly what I planned to do when I came here, but that is the result of many new circumstances, and I am just as pleased over what I have done as over what I might have done. New York is a different city entirely from what it was ten years ago, and the whole world is a different place. Everything is caught up in a whirlwind of change these days, and we have to change too, or be left behind in the rush.

Ten years ago I was very snobbish about movies and would not have thought of doing anything about them. But I have become much more tolerant, and the movies have become much better. I am anxious to make a stab at them. I realize perfectly well that they are at low ebb this year, just as everything else is, and I will not be surprised or particularly disappointed if I don't get something to do. But I want to try it anyway. Even if I do not get anything to do, it will be a stimulating and interesting sojourn for me out there. And certainly what few opportunities there are in my line are more out there just now than here.

Then too, apart from professional interests, and apart from just having an enjoyable trip, one of my main objects in going out there is for purposes of health. I'm not sick, but the fact remains that I've had a catarrhal and bronchial discharge for the last twenty years, and while it doesn't seem to get any worse, it's plain that it isn't going to just cure itself at this late date. And, a long damp rainy spring like this one leaves me feeling a definite need for physical bracing up. I want to know what Colorado feels like, as well as California, and Arizona. If there is hay fever on the Pacific Coast, the mountains and desert are near by. I know dozens of people who spend summers out there. They say it is very hot around noon, but never any more unpleasant than New York midsummer heat, and that every night is cool the year round. And everyone agrees that living costs are cheaper. So I'm determined to try it.

Of course I will have my things insured, if I do keep them in this apartment. My piano is insured up until October 1933 now.

I think it is worth the $25 license for us to have the car while I am home. But I don't think it is worth $40 insurance. We don't take long trips either on dangerous roads or in heavy traffic. The chances of accident are so slight in our small trips that I think such insurance is exorbitant.

Libby-Owens advance was front page news in N.Y. papers yesterday. It is sure to advance, still further. My railroad and utility stocks are pretty well shot, but I'll bring out my certificates and put them away in a Toledo box when I come, and we'll forget about them, and maybe some day we can buy a hat or something with them.

I can't give advice about the Fellsmere district coupons. You should better consult your Toledo broker, and act on his advice.

I went to see my tailor yesterday and looked at samples. Suits are $10 cheaper than they were last fall, but are apt to go up in the fall, he said. I didn't select any stuff yesterday, but I will soon. People tell me that ANYTHING goes in the way of clothes in Hollywood—sport clothes, sweaters, even bathing suits on the street. However, I do not look my best in a bathing suit, and I could scarcely wear one to Tashman's. So I think it's a good idea to have one very smart and brand new suit to wear to the BEST PLACES. I'm sorry Dietrich is leaving there this summer. But anyway, Garbo is there, and that probably adds something to the atmosphere, even though no one ever sees here.

More in a day or two.

Max

Max's Bela Lugosi look.

The disturbance Max refers to in his next letter may have ensued from Diego Rivera's speech the previous night, claiming that he came to the United States not only to paint murals, but to advance the cause of the proletariat. The Rockefeller family had dismissed the muralist because the work he had been commissioned to paint at Rockefeller Center contained a portrait of Lenin.

[about Sunday, May 14. 1933]

Hotel Warrington
Madison Ave. at 32nd Street
New York City

Hello,

    Here are some morning-after reflections, from the press, that spare me going into detail further. It was like that. Everyone was there. The walls were bursting. People screamed and clapped and hissed and threw paper and booed and waved odd objects and generally Bedlam was raised. Whatever the evening was worth musically, it was certainly the most extraordinary social and artistic gathering in New York in years. The best of the audience and all the performers went on to Club Deauville where there was dancing and supper all night, and then several dozens went on to T.R. Smith's party in 47th Street, and when that was over great groups swarmed over to Childs Fifth Avenue for coffee and eggs at daybreak. I have slept very late and am up just in time to go to Alice de la Mar's tea. We did such a good Black Bottom together last night we made a tea date for this afternoon in her roof house on top of a Park Avenue skyscraper, and the most delightful house in town. Life in this city becomes more and more fantastic and dizzy from day to day. I enclose all those things. Digest them. You may be glad you didn't hear it. Anyway, be glad I was in it.

    About the coupons, they were the $120.00 of the Town of Broken Bow. They were sent long ago to Broken Bow, and no funds were forthcoming. The bank says there is nothing to do but wait till the taxes come in.

    Save all these clippings.

        Max

Friday night [May 19, 1933]

Dear Mother,

Have been out to dinner with our usual little group—Marion Saportas, Peggy Fears, Mrs. Lionel Barrymore, Tom Douglas, and Dave Rollins. They all seem to be headed toward California eventually, but no one knows just when. Marion is going with Mrs. Barrymore, but Mrs. B is vague about the dates. Peggy Fears is vague about all things. She was supposed to go to the country—Larchmont—today, but instead, she went to Jimmy Walker's tailor and ordered some new suits. She still wears skirts, but she goes to a men's tailor, and has men's coats. She went to the theaters with Marlene Dietrich last Saturday. She took Marlene to the Casino to lunch, and Marlene checked her wraps in the men's room. When Marlene goes out with a man she appears as a woman, and when she goes out with a woman she changes her sex and appears as a man, which is quite obliging of her. I'm sorry I missed seeing her, but she was only here overnight. I hope to see her on the Coast when she returns in the fall. She did not have a single woman's garment on as she went through the streets here and she was a 5th avenue sensation. Mrs. Barrymore is excited over Harriman's disappearance tonight. She has known him and been a friend of his since childhood, but just two years ago he got her to invest a lot of money in his bank. So she doesn't care now if he lives or dies.

The weather is warm and the sun is out and has been for three days, thank heaven. I am going to Muriel's place in the country tomorrow and will be back on Monday. Alice Robinson is going out on the train with me.

When I suggested riding out with Clara Sweet I supposed she was in Toledo and making frequent trips to Pioneer. I didn't know she was staying in Pioneer, so I think it would simpler for me to arrive at Bryan as usual.

I had a prompt letter from Marion Morehouse in Paris. She is established there in a lovely flat with a terrace and a garden, and she loves it.

Dined at Alice's with Hans von Herwarth Wednesday night, and she took us to the Film Society showing of a French film of Cocteau's. Saw Carl and Fania there, and practically everyone else I know.

There was great commotion at Joe Brewer's the other day. He has been on a motor trip down south with Douglas Parmentier, and sent word to Ella, his colored cook, to prepare dinner for him and Douglas that night of his return here. When he got here he found Ella dead on the kitchen floor, shot to death by her boyfriend who was jealous of her. It was quite a disturbing homecoming for Joe. He has had Ella for years, and we all knew her, as she always officiated his parties. She was always very nice and amiable, and an excellent cook. Many things have happened to my acquaintances in New York, but this, I believe, is the first one to have been murdered . . . Joe has no job, and his father has next to no money apparently. He owns all sorts of hotels and property in G.R. but hotels are worth nothing with nobody in them. Joe is still trying to sublet his apartment here, as he has a long lease on it and doesn't want to keep it. In fact the real estate agent was showing the place to a prospective tenant the other day and that was how Ella was discovered. It must have given the prospect quite a shock—and needless to say the apartment did not rent! More the first of the week.

      Max

Wednesday [May 24, 1933]

Dear Mother,

Nothing but blue skies these days. What a relief. I spent a delightful weekend in the country at Muriel's. Alice Robinson went along and came back Sunday night. I stayed over and came back

Monday night. Alice is going to take my statues of Muriel while I am away. I am glad, for they are so hard to pack. Jim Whitall came to Muriel's house to see us Sunday. He and Mildred are renting their Connecticut country house for the summer and are taking a Rhode Island country house for the summer. Nobody is going to be in the same place this summer, apparently.

Went last night to a large party at the Stettheimer's a party for Baroness Hatvany, the German woman who wrote Maedchen in Uniform, on which the famous German film was based.

I do a little packing each day, clearing away odds and ends, throwing out junk, so it will be less of a job when the time comes. Will write again as soon as there is news.

   Max

Saturday [May 27, 1933]

Dear Mother,

  You are very bad not to have written me for two weeks, but I had a note from Lettie Belle [Finkel] saying she had heard from you, so I guess you can be heard from. I left word at her hotel, which is practically next door to me, for her to call me or to come in and see me the first of the week. My apartment is not looking its best by any means, for I have been slowly packing away ornaments and non-essentials for some time now, so that it won't be such bedlam at the end. But I won't mind Lettie!

  Here are some clippings—one about the popular song situation, just in case you may think my own ideas about it are exaggerated, or in case you might think my case was an isolated one. There is just no such thing as money in popular music or in serious music either. There isn't any money in anything as far as I can see, except Libby Owens stock! I hope its rapid rise from day to day cheers you up. Its profit will soon make up the losses in some other stock, and then we will feel we have quite a lot of money back that we had practically lost hope over. The other clippings concern my friend Dorothy Hall, and my friend Mrs. Blumenthal . . . but not each other's friends, over this weekend, at least.

I read all the Morgan testimony and feel quite a financial authority . . .

I'm not quite sure in what form to remove my surplus money from my bank here when I leave. There is no sense in keeping a small account here while I am away. There is no sense in making a deposit in Pioneer or anywhere else. And there is no sense in carrying cash. I think I will buy travelers checks. I carried them all over Europe with me. They are safe and convenient, and readily redeemed anywhere on the globe. And I don't mean to go off the globe.

I went to see Betsy Hildreth two days ago. She is the friend of Alice de la mar who went to the Bahamas with us on our "flying trip." She has been out west all this winter for her asthma, and loved it, and means to go back next winter. She was in California and Arizona. She motored everywhere. She said it was all delightful and cheap.

My physical trainer of last fall, Jack Pollock, has been fighting in Texas. Now he has landed in Chicago for the summer, and says I must come to see him there. You can see for yourself that we will have an awful lot of social obligations in Chicago! I am very anxious to see you. I plan to leave here June 8th, and arrive in Bryan on the 9th, which is a Friday. I will be thinking of you on Decoration Day, and hope you will not find it too difficult a day. I hope too that the monument will be up in time, and that you are pleased with it. I have no plans so far for the Decoration Day holiday, but will undoubtedly Go Somewhere.

It's very hot and I love it. Am wearing my new suit for the first time tonight, to dinner at the Dangerfields.
Love,

Max

Tuesday [May 30, 1933]

Dear Mother,

   Glad to hear from you at last. You did not mention receiving the second set of no-funds coupons which I mailed you, but probably it just slipped your mind, it being such a common occurrence . . . I saw Lettie Belle [Finkel] and her husband at their hotel yesterday. She seems just the same as ever, and her husband was agreeable enough. He spoke to me in the lobby of the hotel when I came in, because he recognized me from the photograph in the Los Angeles paper! They may come in here one day to hear me play for a minute. I told them I was torn up, but they said they would sit on the trunks and like it. She says I will need both summer clothes and winter clothes even in the summer in California. I am getting ready a box to mail to you—full of things that I may not need in California, but that you can forward to me in case I do—things that would be inaccessible if they were in storage.

   I dined with Eddie and Carl last night. Eddie is very much excited over his trip to Greece and Turkey. Too bad he will miss Doris and the Dardanelles!

   Natalie Hammond and her rich girl have gone to Spain to live in the mountains with the Gypsies. You can see it is quite a season for getting into remote spots.

   This is Decoration Day, and rainy and nasty. I thought of going with Carey Ross to the races at Belmont Park, but gave it up because of the weather. I didn't care enough about the horses, and I'm afraid the Belmonts wouldn't be on display in the rain. So I am staying in and taking down the photographs in my Gallery, and filing them away in order. It is a little bit upsetting to end an era like this, and I hate taking down each separate picture, because it is like taking part of myself down. But in another way I am quite pleased with the prospect of a new place when I return here. When I return to N.Y. I want to take a place, unfurnished, that I can make more or less permanently my own. It will mean having a certain lump sum to spend on furnishings, but I guess we can afford it be that time. And I think that by the time a person is thirty years old, it is about time to own a bed of one's own, and a chair or two. I want a place with an extra room where I can put you up on something more than a sofa. And I want a place where I can have breakfast and lunch prepared without preparing it in the bathtub. I want a bedroom with an outside window. I have reached the conclusion that the disadvantages of this place outweigh the advantages, so I'm not exactly shedding tears at leaving.

Eddie Wasserman and I are going up to Muriel's in the country this coming Saturday, returning to N.Y. Sunday night. So this week I am getting all the little odd jobs done. Monday I will be ready for packers. Will be moved out by Wednesday, and will leave N.Y. on Thursday. Will let you know definitely on what train a little later.

Love to Doddy and you.

Max

[about June 2, 1933]

Dear Mother,

It is Friday night, so now I can say I will see you a week from "tonight." Just a year since my motor trip with Franz Solier now.

This afternoon I went out to the old Paramount studio on Long Island to watch Dudley Murphy direct Paul Robeson in scenes from the movie of The Emperor Jones. It was the first time I had ever seen an important film actually being shot. This is a special film feature being made in the East, of Gifford Cochran's money. It was very interesting. I stayed there for four hours, but only one short scene was shot. They rehearse it over and over, and then they shoot it over and over and over. No easy job under blinding hot lights. The scene in the film will last less than two minutes, but a hundred people worked more than four hours over it. Of course Dudley is the vaguest man alive, and how he ever gets a film together at all is a miracle. I don't see how he remembers from day to day that he is at work on a film even. He said he would be glad to give me letters to people in Hollywood, but that there would be no use in his doing that, because I knew so many more people out there than he did. I protested that this might be wrong, since I had never been there and he had lived there for years. But he insists I know more people out there than he does. Blanche Knopf told me yesterday to look up Mrs. Sam Goldwyn and give her her love. Phyllis Walsh is sending me a note to Elsie Janis. Marion Saportas leaves for the Coast on June 14th, with Mrs. Lionel Barrymore. She is going to stay at the Barrymores', and Mrs. B told me to look her up at once, and Marion says they will be at the train to meet me when I arrive. So I guess I will arrive with plenty of "good connections." I am not signing with any agent until I get there. I may not even need one.

    I sent you a package of clothes today. You needn't unpack it until I get there if you don't feel like it. There's nothing in it that needs attention.

    Now I have torn up this place, I am eager to get under way towards something new, and I feel all livened up for the first time in quite a while.

    Glad you sold the motor boat, as I would never use it. I want to do a lot of boat-rowing instead. I wouldn't sell the cottage though, as long as you must be in Pioneer. Even if you are not there much, it is a diversion occasionally, and diversions are few enough. Also it is a delightful escape if only for short periods. And, when you do get ready to pull out, the cottage will always be the most readily saleable of the real estate properties. Also this particular year you probably wouldn't get as much as it is worth.

The Seldeses had a party yesterday for various departing friends—chiefly Dotty Crawford, who is off to the Dalamatian Coast. Joe Brewer said he had sub-let his apartment and had stored all his furniture in the Whitalls' barn in Connecticut, because he couldn't afford storage in N.Y. warehouse—which sounds pretty odd from Brewer! He leaves today for Grand Rapids, and wants me to drive up and see him there. Shall we do it? I want very much to see Doris if she comes, and I don't suppose Aunt Lotta would want to spare her for a minute out of Michigan. Anyway—all this we will discuss next week.

    Much love,
    Max

How did you like the midget on Morgan's knee?

On June 8 Max boarded the train to visit his parents. Rev. Bready meet him at the depot in nearby Bryan and drove him to the family home in Pioneer. Three days later he and his mother motored to Clear Lake, Indiana, where the Ewings had a cottage. Max returned to New York near the end of June.

Friday [about June 23, 1933]

New York

Dear Mother,

Here I am, more or less settled again. The trip east was very pleasant, and nothing to worry about. Franz [Solier] is a very careful and very skillful driver. He drives fast when he is on a long stretch of good road with nothing on it, but he takes no chances of any kind, and is a model of cautiousness in every way. We picked up the other men at Holgate and Napoleon, and they too were nothing to be alarmed over. They are schoolboys. We got to Wooster about eleven o'clock and I thought of Doddy. We lunched in an Ohio town called Minerva, and then hurtled on to Pittsburgh. Pittsburgh is just another word for the inferno if you ask me. It has a magnificent location on hills and on three rivers, but it is hideous and stricken looking and it took us nearly two hours to plow through it. Then we got into the mountains and it was beautiful driving. The roads are perfect and entirely safe—no steep ups and downs—all graded on the Lincoln Highway. We kept right on going and got to Hagerstown Maryland for the night. It does make the country seem pretty small, when you can leave Pioneer in the morning and drive into Maryland for dinner. Then we went straight to bed for Franz was tired. We got up and went on to Annapolis for lunch Wednesday. Bob [Solier] showed us all over the place and was very sweet. In the afternoon there was a dress parade of all the midshipmen, and a presentation of trophies of various kinds by the Secretary of the Navy. During all these ceremonies the boys had to stand rigidly at attention in the boiling sun without moving a muscle, and after about half an hour they began to faint away. One after another toppled over and had to be carried away. I don't see why they didn't break their noses and put their eyes out, falling over face forward on the ground. I suppose no more than a dozen collapsed, and they say this always happens because their uniforms and their collars are so tight. But it did seem pretty savage, especially when you saw two toppling over at the same moment. This was over about six in the afternoon, and then I left for N.Y. that night. The town of Annapolis was crowded and jammed with relatives and visitors for the Commencement week, and rooms were expensive and hard to find at all. Franz and his two friends had to rent a library in a private house and sleep on emergency cots. This didn't look very enticing to me, and there was nothing for me to stay all night for anyway, since I would just get up and leave again next day. So I took a tram car to Baltimore, had dinner in the station there, and took a train to

N.Y. which got me home an hour or so after midnight. I was tired by that time, and my own apartment looked good to me. Yesterday I got unpacked. The two boxes I sent ahead were here O.K. Annadella Winslow rang up and asked me to come out there to dinner last night, but I wanted to stay in town and dine with Muriel last night, which I did. Before dinner we went to the Seldes to a cocktail party, their farewell before they sail tomorrow. Gilbert was pleased with my letter about the road signs and is using it for a column. Almost all of my crowd of friends was at the party so I saw them all at once. Then at night after dinner we looked in at a party at the Duke d'Arcas. Esther was there and Sam and Edith Hoffenstein. We did not stay late. We left together with Leonard Amster and went to Childs for coffee. I had a long talk about Hollywood with Sam and Edith. And I am going to see them at their suite at the Elysee today.

Everything here falls into place so normally, and is so much the same as ever, it is hard to realize how things are changed at Pioneer and for you. There is no denying that they are changed for you. But I want you to try to accept it as a change not for the worse and not for the better, but just as a CHANGE. Everything changes. And we must try to think of this, not as the end of a period in our lives, but as the beginning of a new period, which will be different, of course, but which we must try to make as pleasant as possible.

I will write again soon.

Much love,

Max

P.S. The suitcase was just delivered. It is in good shape, and also the mail you sent with it.

[No date, but apparently written in June, 1933]

Dear Mother,

Yesterday the sun came out for the first time in two weeks, so I went to my beach sun parlor and came home in the evening several shades darker. I feel better now!

Today is Eddie Wassermann's party for Kay Francis. I was asked to come out to the [Lawrence and Roberta] Conrads today to attend their Commencement rites, with John Erskine as speechmaker, but passed it up in favor of meeting Kay Francis. Will write you about that later.

I enclose a letter from Dr. Cameron. I wrote to him some time ago, asking for any details he might care to send me about Dad's passing. I hardly thought he would answer very much for hospitals never do, but I did want to know a little more than I did. His letter adds but little to our knowledge, but as it does add a little I am sending it on to you.

I enclose also a picture I took of Taylor Gordon last Sunday, one of the best of the lot so far. Eddie took me to dinner and the movies Tuesday night. He stopped here for me, and brought Bonnie Goossens in with him. She was in town only for two days, and sailed to France yesterday. She looking very handsome and I was glad to see her for a minute. She said Zena was learning to croon. Things get stranger all the time.

I am lunching with Leonard Amster today.

Any news there is will follow.

        Max

[Apparently written on a Monday in June, 1933]

Dear Mother,

Here is Mary Garden's interview on arriving in town a few days ago. She must not have been following American events very carefully, when she says that you don't see Otto Kahn and Samuel Insull taking any income cuts!

Last night, Sunday night I dined at the Amsters Fifth Avenue with Jimmy Amster and Muriel and Esther. Papa and Mama Amster had gone to the country so Jimmy entertained. After dinner we sat on their roof and it was beautiful overlooking Central Park.

Wednesday night I am dining at Alice de Lamar's.

Today it is very hot. I spoke too soon.

No more news this morning.

            Max

[about June 30, 1933]

Dear Mother,

I don't expect you to answer all of my letters one by one. I write often because I have more events than you have to write about, and I am under the impression—though it may be an illusion—that a letter provides a welcome diversion in your day. Anyway that was the case with me. I do like to hear from you though as often as you feel like writing.

The Uncle A.E. case is certainly deplorable. It does seem as if the trouble worked on him surprisingly fast. I don't know what we ought to try to do about it. I would hate to think that he went without adequate care. But hospital and doctor care does not require immediate payment, and I suppose Walkley could pay it slowly over a period of time. Anyway I suppose we should certainly pay the taxes in such an emergency. I got $1.50 interest from J.P. Morgan today—I mean dividends—so J.P. is still solvent, I guess! Am glad to hear that things are moving well in the store, and I guess you are a miracle to unload anything. Shop after shop after shop along Broadway and Fifth Avenue are closed or just empty. Had a strenuous night last night at Eddie's.

Muriel and Esther and Kay Francis and Kenneth McKenna and Spivvy Devoe [Spivy Le Voe] and Bernie Bandler and I were there, supposedly to listen to the convention over the radio. But it went on and on and on forever. Kenneth McKenna finally went home to bed, leaving Kay Francis on my hands. I finally took her to her hotel at three o'clock. Eddie called up today and said he went to bed after that and left the rest of the people listening. Muriel and Esther stayed and listened all night, but still no one was nominated! Esther is a great political enthusiast, and a mine of information. The night before that Esther and the Crawfords and I dined pleasantly on Alice De Lamar's terrace overlooking the city.

Rita Romilly came in yesterday to be photographed in Venice. She was supposed to bring Paul Robeson, but at the last minute he couldn't get away, so I was disappointed.

Had a note from the Seldeses from Stockholm today.

Today Betsy Hildreth, Alice's friend, is giving a party, rounding up all the winter visitors at Alice's at Palm Beach. She has taken a penthouse upstairs in the same building where she lives downstairs with her mother who is very old. Every day to be free of her mother for awhile, she gets dressed and goes ostensibly to luncheon or the theater etc. But in the elevator she does not go down, she just goes upstairs to her penthouse and entertains or relaxes there. Her mother thinks she does a lot of gadding about, but she is just upstairs all the time. An excellent plan don't you think, in such a situation? I am going there today for the first time.

Beatrice Locher showed up for lunch yesterday. She is back and forth between their Staten Island house, and her family's house in Boston, and her family's country estate in Vermont. She and her sister are taking a house on the Cape somewhere for the summer. She said I could come and stay there for $12.00 a week! She said she would have to charge something because they are all so broke. Bobby can't even sign a check, because he is being sued for breaking the lease on their business place which they had to give up. So it goes. I might go there for a week or so but I doubt it. I wish I could buy Muriel one or two of your dresses. She used to have such magnificent clothes but she doesn't buy any new ones now. As soon as she gets the telephone bill paid the gas is turned off, and after that the lights are apt to be turned off. And I should think she would go mad, with the annoyance of little bills like that.

    I have no plans yet for over the 4th. I hope you can get a rest and some fun at the lake. I approve of your going to Grand Rapids if you can see your way clear. Let me know any plans.

                       Max

4. Hollywood

On July 24 Max was on the train again, this time headed for Chicago and a tour of the Century of Progress. The next night at 9:35 at night he re-boarded the train and set off for San Francisco.

Wednesday P.M. [July 26, 1933]

Chicago & Northwestern Ry.
Union Pacific System
Southern Pacific Lines
The Overland Route

Dear Mother, This message comes from Nebraska. It has been a day of uneventful passage past miles & hundreds of miles past corn and cows and nothing that might be passed between Montpelier and Bryan. A few low sand hills are beginning to appear in the west, and by tonight we will be quite high up by the time we reach Cheyenne.

Weather is splendid. There was a big breeze off the Lake all the time I was in Chicago, and last night on the train it was so cool I needed all the blankets. Today is warm but not uncomfortable.

I had tea with Betty at the Palmer House. She looks as young as she did ten years ago but more attractive—you will be distressed to hear! Certainly she looks smarter than anyone else I saw in Chicago—either on the streets or at the Fair. Most people look like the kind who attend country fairs rather than world's fairs. You will find it easy to go to the fairgrounds. Busses go there from the Morrison Hotel corner & when you get there you can ride around in more busses or be wheeled in chairs or in a jinricksha! The grounds are far more attractive at night when lighted up—so don't go until toward evening.

Taylor Gordon said he was at Noel Sullivan's house when he gave a concert in San Francisco several years ago, and he says it is a magnificent estate overlooking the bay, with beautiful grounds & sunken gardens and a real show-place.

Some features of this train are rather odd—for instance at lunch time a Japanese boy goes through the coaches playing on a set of chimes. If you are bright you get the idea that the dining car is open. If you are not I suppose you'd be quite mystified!

I bought a San Francisco paper & find that the weather is around 60 degrees.

When we take our motor trip west we will have to be very patient getting across Nebraska! It's just a big desert of corn and cattle & creeks with towns few & far between & very scrawny looking.

This writing is pretty rocky looking in spite of the flat country—so it will probably be still worse tomorrow when the land is rocky too. But I'll try to write again then too.

Good bye—

And Get a Woman!

Max

Thursday [July 28, 1933]

Chicago & Northwestern Ry.
Union Pacific System
Southern Pacific Lines
The Overland Route

Crossing Nevada

Dear Mother,

No use saying it isn't hot today—because it is! The temperature is well above 100 degrees, but there is no humidity and we are up so high and the air is so dry that it doesn't feel nearly as hot as it is. Last night going across Wyoming it was quite cool & I wore all the blankets. It didn't get hot until around noon today. The train stopped for half an hour at Cheyenne last night around nine o'clock. Everyone got off &

listened to a noisy band of hill-billys playing at the station. A rodeo was in progress & the town was festive.

Crossing the Great Salt Lake this forenoon was fantastic. To save time, the train does not go around it, but goes across it for miles & miles on a trestle. We were practically out of sight of land & the lake was covered with billows of salt that resembled white caps.

Nevada seems to be completely uninhabited. We go for hours & miles & miles and never see as much as a house for what seems like a hundred miles at a time. Wherever the population is, it isn't near the railroad! At Ogden Utah I received a wire from Noel Sullivan just to say he was expecting me, & to welcome me. There is no one of any interest on the train though it is quite full. The food on the train is excellent—far better than on the N.Y. Central out of N.Y. And it improves the farther west we go. We have a new dining car in this state which is very fancy, with gay flowered China & gay colored table cloths & napkins. Negroes and Japs both are in service.

We get into the state of California tonight around midnight. Then it will be cool again. We reach Oakland around 8:30 in the morning & then take a ferry across to San Francisco. The trains don't go into San Francisco from this direction.

More will follow.
           Max

On August 4 he left San Francisco for the short ride to Hollywood. Five days after his arrival there, Max wrote to Muriel, "I met Gary Cooper on Monday at lunch and on Tuesday I <u>shared a napkin</u> with him at tea. He is at once amiable and anti-social, poised and restless, and more <u>detached</u> than anyone alive. In the middle of tea (in Lilyans dressing room which adjoins his) he got up and went out and rode a bicycle—just rode around, going nowhere, and saying nothing. He is taller and thinner than anyone we know and he has a secretary who is *shorter & fatter than anyone we know—a sort of exaggerated Joseph Stella! The secretary says that what Gary likes most is to roam around his ranch playing a mouth-organ."* Jack Moss was Gary's secretary. On September 2 Max was an invited guest at Kay Francis's Barn Dance, held at 6666 Sunset Boulevard.

[September 9, 1933]

Hollywood Roosevelt Hotel
Hollywood, California

Dear Uncle,

I'm very much upset and worried about Mother again. She seems to be getting worse, and losing weight rapidly, and seems to be very frightened and worried about herself. I really don't know what to do about it—whether to stay here and try to get established or whether I ought to go back to Ohio and see it through. The thing is that there is nothing that I could do personally for her that medical care and complete rest couldn't do. If only she would go somewhere and get that attention and above all take the rest. We have all begged and implored her for so long to slow up and take things easier, but she would never listen. Now she has to apparently, but she seems panicky about what to do. I'm sorry you did not get down to see her at the time of Henry's funeral. But I know how busy you are too and what a commotion Doris' imminent departure must provoke! At any rate I wish you would use all your persuasive powers to make Mother go away to a sanitarium or some such place for a while where she can have rest and care and proper food and above all A CHANGE. I have written and urged her to do this. I don't know what else to urge. Doddy is a terrible problem of course. But if the worst should come to Mother and Doddy would be left, then the problem would be well nigh insurmountable and I just don't know what I would do.

I have had a marvelous time out here—have met everyone I wanted to meet—and I think I am off to a good start professionally. Nothing is signed up yet but my agent is confident that I can be placed here and make big money. I am crazy to do it, but I feel my hands are tied until something begins to improve in Pioneer. I don't know why I worry you with it, for there is nothing you can do, I know. But I do feel so far away from the scene now, so much farther than when I was in N.Y. I do wish you could go down and see her again, or persuade or coerce or kidnap her into going to Battle Creek, some place where she could pull herself together. If she could build herself up enough to stand the trip I would insist on her coming out here for the winter, leaving Doddy as a "paying guest" somewhere. Doddy is far more able to stand the rigors of another Pioneer winter than Mother is. I'm honestly afraid she won't pull through another winter there if something drastic isn't done this fall. I feel that a whole new pot of gold is waiting for me out here and I do hate to pull out and leave it unless it is utterly necessary. On the other hand I feel like a pig to stay on out here if I really am needed at home. If you can send me any inside news of the situation, I would appreciate it.

Doris is probably leaving any day now. Give her my love if she is still there. And to all the others.

    Max

Saturday [September 9, 1933]

Dear Mother,

Your letter written Monday, Labor Day, just arrived today. I have had a bad four days wondering about you, but have assumed that no news is good news.

I am very much worried about you, but I do not feel hopeless. I think you have every chance to get better if you will devote all your efforts to it. Your efforts are great if you turn them into one channel. You have a good constitution, but you have abused it and overtaxed it. I think what you absolutely have to have is a period of absolute rest. I think the Wilderness would be quiet and refreshing. But like Clear Lake, it is too far away and inaccessible. You must be where there is immediate medical attention if you need it. If you go away anywhere I should think a sanitarium would be the place. There you would have rest and care in any emergency, proper meals, etc. Why don't you try Battle Creek? You could have Ruth R. stay with Doddy. I do so wish you would do this. Go away somewhere and take a real rest in a place where you have proper care. Build yourself up in a new surrounding. I'm sure you would improve faster anywhere else than you would in Pioneer. Don't be discouraged by Franz' [Solier] scares. He may be just scaring you into doing something drastic because he knows you won't do anything unless you think it is serious.

  I feel too upset to enjoy myself much here. But apart from worry about you things here look very promising. I still have not signed that five year contract with Mrs. Schulberg, but she is going ahead anyway to make some appointments for me, and she is absolutely confident that she can place me. If she does we will have a lot of money coming in. But all I want of the money is to please you. If you are not able to enjoy it I won't give a whoop about it, and I don't know what I will do or where I will go. If I get to making steady money out here and you get yourself into better condition I will insist on your coming out here this winter, and leaving Doddy as a "paying guest" at someone's house. She will just have to face it whether she likes it or not. For she can get along there better than you can. And if she realizes how sick you are and that you HAVE to get away, I'm sure she will be reasonable. The store is the last of the worries. The stock can be closed out or the whole place can be closed. These are emergency times. And we must make plans for a N.R.A. [National Recovery Administration] all our own!

Thank you for the two checks. The hotel here will cash them. I still have $150.00 of my original funds, which will carry me up to October if nothing unforeseen intervenes. Before this money is gone I hope to be able to send you some!

Last night I dined at William Hurlbut's. He is a playwright from N.Y. whom I used to see at Muriel's and Mary Lawton's. He has just built himself a house out here, Early New England in style, and it looks very odd out here among the Spanish palaces! He has five immense and beautiful cats, and delicious food and it was a very pleasant evening. Billy Justema was there too.

Muriel is at last in New Mexico. I heard from her yesterday. I had not heard from her for nearly three weeks and I didn't know what had happened to her. She and you are my two most valuable connections, and I want to keep you both in order, and to know all about you all the time!

Keep me informed. I'll come home any time you say so. But I hope it can be reversed—and that you will get better and come out here to a warm winter of rest, no fires, no worries, and no duties. And I'm sure that will turn the trick, and you'll start all over again.

Max

[about September 11, 1933]

Hollywood Roosevelt Hotel
Hollywood, California

Dear Muriel, Gertrude Stein and Alice B. Toklas are the only topics of conversation everywhere. I hope you know that Gertrude is on the COVER of 'Time' last week, and that her book is even reviewed in VARIETY! Her publishers now hope to make even 'Tender Buttons' a best seller. She preoccupies people here more that Greta Garbo. Variety agrees with her own opinion that 'in her time she is really the Only One.' I feel sure that before the winter is out she will be on the cover of The Saturday Evening Post, and that she will take the place of the Japanese Girls in the newsreels. She and Mae West vie now for press attention . . . Jack Pollock showed up suddenly and unannounced from Reno. He stayed three days and then went off to some indefinite destination in Idaho. It was all what you are no judge of."

September 21, 1933

Hollywood Roosevelt Hotel
Hollywood, California

Dear Uncle,

    I sent you a card yesterday acknowledging your first letter. Then today your 2nd letter came. It worries me, as it contains new material for worry. Mother had given me to understand that she was getting along pretty well since the tooth extraction—and this business about going to Ann Arbor is all news to me. However I am glad you told me—and I will not tell her that you told me. It begins to sound involved doesn't it?

    I do hope she will go to Ann Arbor or somewhere and get a first class diagnosis from someone better than the village doctors she has gone to so far. For years she was in despair over Dad because he would not go to a good doctor. But he just would not, and nothing could make him do it. If this recent scare of hers is sufficient to jolt her into some drastic change, it will have served its purpose.

    I think the Wilderness would do her a lot of good, if you do not think the remoteness from doctors is a disadvantage. Anywhere but Pioneer would be a help, I'm sure, so please help me to pry her away a little. I'll pin a blue eagle on you for this service sometime!

Almost all my friends here are down with grippe, flu, pneumonia, due to the eccentricities of this famous climate. I have a cold too but I'm keeping it a secret from Ohio!

More later. I hope Mrs. Worth is improving. Give her my love.
Max

Thursday [September 21, 1933]

Hollywood Roosevelt Hotel
Hollywood, California

Dear Mother,

I know you too have a birthday coming soon but I am not going to pay any attention to it this year. Forget birthdays for awhile. But I will send you a present with the first money I make. There's no way of knowing just when that will be. Mrs. Schulberg says all the executives are out at the Tennis tournament this week and can't be bothered with business!

Things have been fairly inactive these last few days because I have been "laying low," nursing a cold. Not the flu, grippe, and pneumonia that most people out here have. Just an old fashioned cold in the head. But I've been "greasing" and "dosing" and it is about over now. It's impossible not to catch a cold in this climate. One day is like Florida and the next is like Canada. And very often it is both ways in the same day. If you go out for a few hours in the afternoon there is sure to be at least 30 degrees difference in temperature before you come in. So no matter HOW you dress you are sure to be uncomfortably warm when you start or uncomfortably cold when you return. No two rooms you go into are ever anything like the same temperatures, and no room you stay in stays at the same temperature for long. So your system has to learn to get adjusted to the most violent changes every few hours. And some systems don't ever seem to learn. Sam Hoffenstein says most of his income goes into paying for flowers sent to friends in hospitals! The hotel chambermaid assures me that the recent weather has been the "most unusual." Other people tell me that it is ALWAYS "unusual." So I'll just have to wait and find out for myself what is usual.

If you are not getting better, then do go somewhere and consult a GOOD doctor. For years you begged Dad to do that, but he just would not. Please do not go on in the same way that you begged him not to. Get yourself some real medical attention, the best there is. The best is not good enough for you. But you will have to make the effort of going to the big doctors. They won't just show up in Pioneer. Please do it for me.

Love and more soon.
Max

Saturday [September 23, 1933]

Hollywood Roosevelt Hotel
Hollywood, California

Dear Uncle,

I commence to feel very Masonic, don't you? Such a secret society we are working up, and such a big one too . . . So far I have not betrayed any of the confidences, but yesterday I was tempted to, when I received letters from both you and Mother which seemed to bear directly contradictory messages. I was in the verge of writing to her, and "telling all," and claiming that I was being treated unfairly, by being kept misinformed, etc. Then someone telephoned me and asked me out to the Tennis Tournament which is taking all of everybody's time out here this week. So I went out before I got the letter started. The tennis matches were very exciting, as Lilyan Tashman was there in a box making it very plain that she was the world's best dressed woman, with a tiny toque perched on top of her stiff cream-colored curls, and black gloves reaching her shoulders. Then, in the box next to us, sat Charlie Chaplin, alone, and bundled up for dear life in sweaters and coats, for the California climate is that of the North Pole. Also there was tennis being played and that was exciting too . . . after all this I was taken to dinner and stayed out all evening, crawling home at midnight thru the heavy California fog which puts London fog right off the map. Don't believe any fairy tales about southern California climate. They are all as false as Amy McPherson, its major product. Well, anyway, this is all by way of saying that when I got home it was too late to write a letter. Then this morning yours arrives, showing that Mother wrote you more or less what she wrote me. So I won't complain to her just YET. Probably she DOES need rest, and I'm glad she is resting, but I wish she would get some GOOD medical attention too. But I'm sure she won't unless she gets scared to death or unless someone forces her too. It is such a mix-up and all so unreasonable, I don't know what to do about it, or what to ask anyone to do. Anyway please keep me informed of whatever you or Mrs. T [Touse] or any other confederates find out.

    Love,
        Max

Sunday [September 24, 1933]

Hollywood

Dear Mother,

    Got your Wednesday note today. We get mail on Sundays for some reason around here. So glad you have had three good days in a row and hope they keep up. Take a lot of treatments from Dr. Jones. I can worry about you, but you mustn't worry about me. My accounts of the weather here are probably exaggerated simply because it is so different from what one expects. It really isn't bad in itself. I will probably want my overcoat eventually but there is no hurry. My trench coat serves perfectly well as a wrap. It is not so much big outside wraps that one needs as it is a lot of little sweaters and things like that to put under things, and I have plenty of them. My cold is gone now. I am lucky that it was so brief. Peggy Fears is still sick and going to doctors every day. Irene Barrymore is still in the hospital, but I guess she doesn't mind it. So many of her friends are there it is sort of like being at a party.

I went to Los Angeles again yesterday and posed again for Billy Justema's picture of me. It is really beautiful, and I think it is one of the few portraits done of me that even YOU will like. I will send you a reproduction of it eventually. Billy hopes to do portraits of movie stars this winter as covers for the movie magazines. I hope he gets a chance, but he is really too good for that sort of thing. Carl Van Vechten was very enthusiastic about his painting when he was in San Francisco last month, and thought that Billy ought to go to New York and have an exhibition. But Carl has since written to Noel Sullivan advising him not to let Billy go to N.Y. this year. Carl says it is not a year for ANYONE to come to N.Y. And Carl is New York's greatest enthusiast, as you know. All the news from there sounds pretty bleak. Dorothy Sheldon writes that she and Roy are moving into a still smaller flat in the building on First Avenue in which Elsie Arden lives. She says Aimee McPherson is "preaching" at the Capitol, and Dave Hutton is singing at the Palace. He is singing "I Wonder Who is Kissing Her Now."

It seems Muriel is a sensation in New Mexico. Mabel Dodge has been giving colossal parties for her and all the countryside, white people and Red Indians are flocking to see her.

Hope the agents get going on me next week, but you never can tell. Time means nothing to movie executives. They are like Dan Cox and they go by their time. The fact that you may be in a hurry to get a job does not make them in a hurry to give you one. In fact it works the other way. If you act eager it makes them think you can't be very good! You've got to seem indifferent to make them interested. They like to coax you. The ideal way is for them to coax you away from New York. I still think this is the only place where there is even a CHANCE for me to make any money this year, and I will stick it out for months if necessary, waiting for a break. That is, if you get better, and I feel justified sticking. It all depends on you . . .

I have a plan for a new novel, and I will get to work on that shortly, if nothing else turns up in the meantime.

Adrian is buying a new Mason and Hamilton grand piano this week, and wants me to come often and use it, as he does not play himself.

I enclose clippings about Hollywood parties, which does not seem to indicate Depression at all! Also picture of the Foujitas, who along with myself were the guests of honor at the Hoffenstein party when I first arrived here.

Too bad about Mary Garden having to sell that house. She really loved it. I went there to see her once but she was not at home. I see Studebaker is flat broke. Betty Compson is flat broke. Gloria Swanson is practically broke. She had to take off her bracelets in the courtroom here and hand them over to pay debts. I hope you feel comfort in the facts that you are healthier than Tallulah Bankhead and richer than Gloria Swanson!

    Max

Hollywood, Tuesday [September 26, 1933]

Dear Mother,

Had a comforting card from Mrs. Touse yesterday, and feel quite proud of your improvement. Keep it up and then keep on keeping it up. And keep on keeping me posted. This begins to sound like Gertrude

Stein. I have just read her autobiography. After nearly twenty years of being laughed at, she is at last a Best Seller! Her picture is on the cover of "Time." It is strange to think of Gertrude Stein and Mae West being the most discussed women of the moment!

    I spent last evening at the house of the boy friends of Jack Becket [Becker]—Tony Purdy and Richard Ames. Jack Becket is now at Taos where Muriel is. I had a long letter from her yesterday which is quite fantastic. She says the Indians come to the house where she is visiting and dance like mad and beat on drums for hours without stopping in the dining room! I mean all this in the dining room without stopping. I should think it might interfere with her writing, but she says she is writing well. She said Mabel Dodge who is well past 50 years old met her dressed in a child's embroidered white dress and a pink shawl. And that Tony, her Indian husband, wore pink braids in his hair and a blue shirt and turquoise and silver jewels and a purple tie and English boots and breeches. And as if this were not enough, the servants wear boots, made of white deerskin and dresses of violent and scarlet cotton! It must be like living in a rainbow. She also says that Beatrice Locher is married again already to a Southerner named Farrar.

    The weather is better. It is agreeably cool and not too foggy. Just about right at the present. I may be going to Los Angeles again today for another portrait sitting. The contrast between Hollywood and Los Angeles is fantastic. It reverses the usual formula. In most cities the core of the city is fashionable and the outskirts are not. Here the outskirts like Hollywood, Beverly Hills, Brentwood Heights, etc. are fashionable while Los Angeles itself is a hick town. The people in Hollywood look smartly dressed and cosmopolitan. In Los Angeles they look like nothing you can imagine. The other night after I left Billy Justema's I stopped in at a downtown Los Angeles movie theater to see Marlene Dietrich in "The Song of Songs." This is the play Irene

Barrymore (then Irene Fenwick) made her big N.Y. success in a long time ago. It is a beautiful film. But what an audience. Oh dear what an audience. It was my first experience with the typical corn-fed Los Angeles crowd. The theater was full. And there they sat, row after row of farmers and farmer's wives, all looking as if they were in their way to Kay Francis Barn Dance in their horses and buggies. Los Angeles probably has more farmers in it than any spot on earth. All the retired farmers from Iowa, Kansas, Nebraska, and all that region, come here as fast as they can. They come by the thousands, they come by the hundreds of thousands, and once in Los Angeles, they remain just the farmers they were. Other cities too have big populations recruited from the farms, but other cities seem to assimilate them, and eventually the population becomes more citified. But not so in Los Angeles. There were only farmers there from the start, and only more and more farmers have been added. So that it is primarily a gigantic community of farmhands, and in spite of it being a city of around a million people it is quite a lot like Primrose multiplied thousands of times. For a city of its size it is probably the most illiterate in earth. Only a supremely illiterate city could take Aimee McPherson seriously as a spiritual leader, and build her up into the powerful legend she now is. Of course New York is flocking to see her too, but with a different point of view. Broadway goes to see her because she gives a good performance. Los Angeles considers her a messiah. And there is quite a difference. As soon as the movie was over I fled on a streetcar back to Hollywood and felt as if I were back in the domain of civilization again! Another night Billy took me to an authentic Chinese restaurant in Chinatown, and even there one found farmerss in overalls at dinner! I guess they bring their overalls right along from Iowa and that's what they wear even on a night out in Chinatown! What a country we do live in! And I guess the strangest products of the whole country make their way to Los Angeles county!

I spoke with Lilyan on the telephone yesterday. She hopes to be able to work within two weeks. Do you? Don't let me catch you at it. Too bad about Fae [Johnson]. What operation does she need?

More to follow.

Max

[September 29, 1933]

Hollywood Friday

Dear Mother,

Your card came today. Also a little note from Mrs. Touse. It begins to look like progress, even if slow progress. I did not get any letter from Nellie [Gilpin]. You wrote that she sent one this week. From time to time I do get messages from various friends, all of which seem to contradict each other. I get stray messages about a second tooth being pulled, about chiropractors at work, and Franz writes that he is in control of the case, and that you are now on a regime of COMPLETE rest. It all leaves me in a haze of confusion, but I have stopped worrying and am just hoping. You know that I am with you and behind you in every way, and that I would come to you if my presence would add anything helpful, but I can't see how would under present conditions. I realize what an effort it must be for you to be quiet! But there is one consolation about being quiet in Pioneer. It is not much more boring to stay in that it is to go out! Just try to relax completely and give your body which has been on the go so long a vacation. I have all faith in your pulling through. I can understand how an illness seems much more of a burden to you because you have always had such perfect health. Muriel too has had perfect health for years and great vitality, so that whenever she does have an illness and has to slow down, people give her little sympathy, and say to her, "Now you know how most of us feel most of the time!" I'm glad you've got a good girl, and I'm sure Mrs. Touse is efficient at the store. So now you concentrate on yourself.

You write that you are trying hard to get ahead but that it is a slow process. It is just the same for me in a professional way. I have not seen Mrs. Schulberg for two weeks, but I keep in touch by telephone. I feel she is doing all she can, but agents can't perform miracles. Enclosed page from Variety is illuminating. Read it. Studios won't give opportunities to newcomers unless hounded into it. They know that with their filthy lucre they can get anyone they want. Agents are in the business for the one and only reason anyone is in the movie business— the money. No one in the whole industry is in it apparently because they like it, except perhaps Mary Pickford. Everyone agrees that it is too awful but that there is money in it. Agents get ten percent on the salaries of all the people they place, so of course they work harder over the people who can command the biggest salaries. I don't suppose I could command more than $200.00 a week at best, and that means only $20.00 for the agent which is more chicken feed. Obviously they will push harder for someone who can make $1000 a week or more. This is the reason why the agents want you to sign for several years, because after a few years you will undoubtedly be worth more money and thus they will make more out of you. I have agreed to sign for three years any minute there is a big "bite" for me. But I won't sign just blindly before there is even anything in sight. So it just means waiting. Meanwhile I enjoy myself quite a lot, play tennis everyday, see delightful people. And spend less than I did in N.Y. so there is no ground for complaint so far. Also I am accumulating stray data for a novel which is going to begin in Hollywood.

Last night I had a new experience—my first attendance to a spiritual séance. It was at William Hurlbut's new house, the early American house I wrote you about. He is an ardent spiritualist and as I had never had any experience at all, I was anxious to attend. About ten people were there, including Mercedes de Acosta. We sat in the dark around the dining table. The medium was a plump old lady named Mrs. Gaynor. She sighed and went into a trance. Then odd white lights appeared around the room, trumpets bounced here and there, water dripped into our faces, breezes blew, and then a spirit arrived and said he was an Indian Chief named Seneca. He whooped and did a war dance. Then other big chiefs arrived and talked about Arizona. Various dead relatives came and said they were glad to be there. Then the spirit Doctor Bounds, whoever that is, came and gave me a message. He said I was trying to accomplish something that would take me three years to accomplish, but that I would accomplish it with glory and with the help of a dead Indian and an uncle and old writer! Dr. Bounds then told Mercedes that her past two years had been most peculiar, and she agreed heartily. Spirit hands touched several people, one woman was pushed all around the floor on her chair, the table gave a lurch at Mercedes and me. We asked for hands to touch us, but instead a trumpet came out of the air and hit us very hard on our heads! A woman named Mrs. Patton was worried about her health, and asked for some reassurance. The spirit said that she was not wanted among the spirits and that she would enjoy health on earth for a long time. Then the spirits said that because the house was so new it was hard for them to do any more and that this was enough for one night in a new house. So they slapped the medium in the face and she came to, and the lights were turned on, and we were served coffee as if nothing happened. What had happened I'm sure I don't know. It is by no means convincing, but it is at least disturbing. Mrs. Patton said she thought it had been a very good séance, but that she was disappointed that President Wilson had not been heard from! Mercedes de Acosta drove me home, and said that she had had dinner last night with Greta Garbo, and that when she told Greta where she was going Greta wanted to come along. But Mercedes would not let her. She thought that Greta's appearance would disrupt the session and I guess it would have! Mercedes too has been sick and this week she is being sued for $50,000.00 because she drove her car into someone else's, so her life is quite troubled.

Am going to Pasadena tonight with [Marguerite] Namara. She is appearing there in the play, "Enter Madame." She has waited more than a year for this chance, and she gets no salary at all.

Where have Lettie and her husband gone?

The other day by chance I ran into Vadim Uraneff, the Russian boy I knew long ago in New York, to whom I am eternally indebted because it was he who first introduced me to Muriel. Many people have claimed to have brought us together, from Bob Chanler to Robbie Nederhoed. But it was Vadim who really arranged it. He has been out here for seven years and looked very broke and ghostly.

No more today, my lady.

Max

Eventually Ad [Adeline] Schulberg, owner of the Schulberg Agency in Hollywood, eventually did take Max on, but terminated the agreement on November 5, 1933.

Sunday [October 1, 1933]

Hollywood

Dear Mother,

Got your letter just today, and it sounds as if you had been pretty much unnerved when you wrote it. I mean all this worry about me. You must NOT worry about me. I am sorry I even mentioned that I caught a cold. It was just an ordinary three day cold in the head such as I have had hundreds of and I got completely over it in the three days. I think it was because I was wakeful and worried about you that made me catch it, as much as the weather. The immediate cause of it was probably getting over heated playing tennis on a windy day. At any rate it is all over, so forget it. I have been here only a short time and I have to get "acclimated." The climate is so different from that of the East Coast where I have lived so long. I naturally find it colder than the natives who are used to it. It takes a little time to get adjusted, and I can do it. The same holds true of getting work. I have been in Hollywood less than two months, and the first two weeks or so I did not even approach an agent because I needed to look around and get my bearings and find out about agents. The Schulberg agency only heard of me about five weeks ago and no one could expect any results that soon. So it is surprising to have you urging me to pull out and leave just because the nights are cold and haven't been handed a job immediately.

Before I leave this part of the world for good I will of course go to some other part of the Southwest. I want to see what New Mexico and Arizona are like. But I am not going now. I won't go until I have exhausted all possibilities of work here, or until I feel bad results of the climate. Anyway not before the "rainy season." I don't know when that is and I cannot find out. What people tell you depends on whether they own property or not. Property owners say there is no rainy season, that the weather is always ideal. Others tell you there is a rainy season, but no two people agree on when it is. When it comes I will probably know it. It hasn't rained a drop yet.

And about an overcoat, I will buy one just the minute I feel I need one. I didn't buy it when you sent that money because it was August and I didn't need it. And as far as warmth goes I don't need it now. But I will get [one] for the sake of looks before long. When I wear a sweater under my suit coat and then wear this trench coat and scarf I am warm enough on any occasion, because the air, while it is cold, does not penetrate. You know me well enough to know that I like my comfort, and that if I were uncomfortably cold I would get something to make me warm. I am trying not to spend money unnecessarily and I am trying not to accumulate clothes and things that will be hard to carry around. But the minute I really need a coat you may be sure I'll get one.

All the people who were sick two and three weeks ago are now well except Irene Barrymore who is still sick. And Mrs. Talmadge who died. She had pneumonia at the end, but she has had cancer for years and that is why she succumbed. She has been a great character out here for years and the whole colony is worked up over her death.

It is also surprising to have you write that you are not interested in movie stars or anything they do. You always seemed to me to be distinctly interested. But if you are not then I won't need to write you about that. I have put considerable effort into writing you about them, but if it does not interest you then it has been time wasted.

I am eager to please you insofar as I am constitutionally, or chemically able to. But I CANNOT go out in the country and just sit on a cactus by myself whether in this state or any other. I'm just not made that way, and as Maud would say, it is just too bad! I am sorry too that you feel that nothing I do ever "gets me anywhere." I do not know of anyone who shares this opinion with you. I admit I am lacking in high-pressure money making talents. Perhaps I will fare better when the Communist state comes, in which everyone will work for a few hours at some little thing or other and everyone will share equally in the results. Until that happy state comes, people like me will have to get along the way they always have. Don't take this letter too seriously. It is just a hurried reply to your letter which I realize was written under agitated conditions.

[Marguerite] Namara was very good in the play at Pasadena. But the supporting company and direction was not so good and it is not a very big success. Be good now, and give the rest cure a real chance. Just eat and rest, and rest and eat, and I am sure your nerves will calm down and your body will build up.

I own just one big rug, and a number of little ones. There must be five or six little ones, but they are really little and shouldn't be much "footage." Maybe they won't send the bill for six months. Sometimes they do not.

Had a letter from Marion Saportas. She says N.Y. is livening up a little—

No more today. Probably more tomorrow.

Love,

Max

Monday [October 2, 1933]

Hollywood Roosevelt Hotel
Hollywood, California

You may or may not read in the papers that we had an earthquake last night. It may have been too unimportant to make a news story in the East. But on the other hand they sometimes exaggerate these things in Eastern papers. So this is to reassure you and tell you the truth. We did have one. But it was very slight lasted only a few seconds, and no damage done anywhere. I was asleep. I had been at the Hoffensteins at supper and Edith [Hoffenstein] drove me home to my hotel. I went to bed and went to sleep. I was wakened by the bed rocking like a cradle. The chandelier was swinging in the ceiling. And everything was rattling and groaning. For a second I couldn't tell what was going on. Then I woke up completely and knew it could be only one thing. I decided to just stay still until it was over. Which I did.

Then I got up and nothing in the room was disturbed. Everything had heaved back into shape. A few people were in the hallways, and one woman had been made sick to her stomach. Everyone reassured each other, and said the only thing to do was go back to bed and go to sleep. Which I did also. Though I was a couple hours in getting to sleep! It was just one of those little disturbances which people out here are used to. Today nobody gives it a thought and you shouldn't either. I am glad to have experienced it. Now I know what THAT is like. It is really very odd, Coney Island roller coaster feeling. You do not feel fear. You just feel terrific concern over how long it is going to last, and what things are going to be like when it is over. I guess probably it took place just to welcome Lettie Finkel back and make her feel at home. As if in recompense for the disturbance of the quake the weather today is perfect. It is hot and clear the way it was the first week I arrived, and the way one expects California to be. Maybe the quake was just what we needed to clear the air and get rid of the damp and the fog. Anyway today it is ideal. So calm your nerves and drink your orange juice and get well soon. All love,

    Max

Friday [October 6, 1933]

    Just got your note of Monday. Your line reading "hope to hear you are moving to a warmer place soon" falls on deaf ears. I don't know quite where I could go to accommodate you unless you want me to go immediately to the other world. Enclosed clipping explains.

    I went to the beach two days this week and loved it. And two nights this week I dined at the house of Pancho Muratori, a new Argentine friend. He is a boy who is here for a three month visit. He is extremely rich, one of those fabulous Argentines whose family owns thousands of acres of cattle country in South America, and live in a huge house in Buenos Aires, with scores of servants. Poncho himself owns ten thousand cows. But he says it is awful to own that many thousands of cows, because there is so no market for them, and they have to eat, and they are always having little cows. However he does not seem to be feeling the strain of supporting the cow, as he has taken a lovely place here and bought a big car, etc. Six hours after the earthquake he had a telegram from Argentina from his family asking how he was, so the news must have traveled fast. Scientists at Pasadena say that this little quake was what is known as a "settler" after the major quake last spring. That is, some little earth fold had to settle and now it has settled, and all is over permanently, or at least permanently for a few years.

Last night I dined with Vadim Uraneff. On our way out from the restaurant on Hollywood Boulevard I saw a woman in white sailor pants and blue stripes down the sides, a short blue jacket, and white wooly tamoshanter over wild red hair. This turned out to be Lettie Belle Finkel out for a stroll with her husband. They are living in Hollywoodland, a suburb on a hilltop. They said New York had been terrible and that the storms on the East Coast were so awful, they were delighted to be back here. Lettie said she didn't even mind the little earthquake, it was so much more acceptable than the Eastern storms. They said they would call me.

I'm so glad your pressure is going down. Franz wrote me that he saw an improvement in you, and that he felt sure you would continue to improve if you would submit to his regime, but that it was absolutely necessary that you should submit to it rigorously. So I hope you will. I think the neighbors are pigs who do not go to see you.

I am getting very impatient with Mrs. Schulberg. I have given her a month in which to deliver something, if only an ultimatum, but beginning next week I am going to be active myself, and see if I can be any more active than she has been. Vadim Uraneff is going to send me to meet Kenneth McGowan who is head of a story department at R.K.O.

studios. I may get into trouble with Schulberg by acting independently of her, but I can't help it if I do.

I AM NOT BUYING MY PORTRAIT AND IT IS NOT COSTING ME A CENT. There is no question of buying or selling it. A portrait is being painted. To anyone with any appreciation of creation that is enough. I am simply posing for the portrait. Justema wanted to paint me because he considers me an important celebrity and that it would be to his advantage to paint me and exhibit me. Now he has finished it and it is a fine piece of work. Probably he will never sell it and nobody cares. Some things have value without being bought and sold. I appreciate this fact. You say it sure worries you that I am having a portrait painted. Well, you sure worry me in the way you worry before there is reason to worry. Think Geraldine F. [Farrar] looks frowsy, don't you?

Max

Saturday [October 7, 1933]

Just got your letter about the deed, and about your having your hair done, etc. I think the latter is good idea. You always feel better if you look better. About the deed, of course I will sign off and return same registered mail any time you send it. Will probably receive advice from Uncle A. E. as I hear from him off and on briefly.

I feel more and more convinced that your illness is primarily one of nerves, the more or less natural aftermath of the great strain on you occasioned by Dad's illness, his death, and all the responsibilities of administration and of the store and of the investment and of Doddy and all the others. It is no wonder that you went downhill after going through such a long and severe siege. I feel sure that the rest cure is the thing you need. I feel sure too that the cure would be a lot faster if you could take it in different surroundings from those in which you underwent the strain. But I know how difficult and almost impracticable that is for you at present. I suppose you will have to stick it out in Pioneer even if it does take longer. But it sounds as if you have got good results in these last few weeks. And you shouldn't worry about feeling weak. Anyone would feel weak staying quiet that long. But your strength will return fast once you are up and around, if pressure and heart strain has gone down. Franz says he will write me if he notices any change for the worse, but he seems confident that you are definitely on the mend. So I feel easier. I am very glad that you are getting better, but I am sorry that you are getting "crosser and crosser." I don't understand it. But if what you want is for me to move into an apartment I will do so next week. I am paid up here until Thursday. I have stayed in the hotel longer than I planned to for several reasons, and all of them good. In the first place they made me the very low rate which is but little more than any apartment, and not even as much as the really desirable apartments. During my first weeks here I wanted also to be easily accessible and easily reached. This hotel is a central rendezvous. Apartments are off the beaten track and people never know the telephone numbers without bothering to get them from Information. Then, this hotel is on Hollywood Boulevard, and what street cars and buses there are go past the door. So without a car that is a considerable convenience. These were the reasons why I stayed here the first weeks. But I did look at apartments and would have taken one some time ago if you hadn't gone so sick and I hadn't been so uneasy, wondering what the next message from you was going to be. You were very much frightened yourself, and naturally, I was too. At one time I felt I ought to go back, and I never knew but what you might get worse and I would be called back, and in that case I did not want an apartment on my hands. One does not need to sign yearly leases for an apartment here as you do in New York, but of course you have to pay a month in advance, and in most cases in order to get an attractive rate you have to agree to at least stay at least three months. The place I was on the verge of taking at $50 per month rented at that price only if I would stay until Christmas or longer. I didn't want to get tied up in an arrangement like that as long as you were in a half critical condition, when it was very agreeable staying here, and the saving would not be more than $10 a month or thereabouts. So I have stayed on from week to week awaiting the turn of events. Now that you seem to be definitely on the mend I will take another place IF THAT WILL PLEASE YOU. Your letters are so full of implied criticism, I don't know what to make of them. I came out here with the main idea being that I would try to make some movie money. This implies working with movies and there are no people in movies except movie people. I met quite a lot of movie people and tried to "contact" as many as possible, and to write you about it. But in your letter last week you made it most emphatic that you were not interested in anything to do with movie people and didn't want to hear any more about them. So that leaves me at quite a disadvantage for purposes of correspondence, since movie people are about the only people I know here, and about the only people here that anyone would want to know. The rest are farmers, Christian Scientists, and followers of Aimee [McPherson].

    I wrote a lot about the damp weather in September because it was surprising. But God knows it was not half as bad as all last spring in New York when it rained day and night for ten weeks and there was not even any heat in the buildings. And you did not urge me to leave for Palm Beach during that period! After looking the ground over I put myself into the hands of Mrs. Schulberg who everyone like Sam Hoffenstein, etc. advised me would be the best agent for me. She has not accomplished anything yet, and I am going to do all I can independently of her. But it is a devil of a year for anyone to break into anything. Movies are being made all the time, to be sure, but producers

are feeling their way slowly, the way you would buy goods for the store this year, just sort of week to week and hand to mouth. They want just the old faces and the old names who are tried and true at the box office. They don't know what things will be like six months from now any more than we do and they are not out to gamble with people and take chances either. It is perfectly understandable. All that I am trying to say is that I am doing all that can humanly be done in the midst of the worst economic situation in the history of the world. I have written three stories since I have been here, and will write more. There is not much difference between writing in a hotel room and writing in a one room apartment the same size except the apartment has a kitchen which is not particularly stimulating to literature . . . I am fairly well known in New York. But I am not well known to these movie executives and it is not surprising that they are not jumping to grab me. How do they know I can write movies? They have to be cajoled into believing it. Everything takes time. And I am going to stay here in Hollywood at least until the Knopf money arrives and as long as it lasts me. Then I may have to take to the road, if by that time you are still crosser and crosser. But I hope that by that time you will be imbued with Christmas spirit!
    Max

Monday [October 9, 1933]

Hollywood Roosevelt Hotel
Hollywood, California

Dear Mother,

    Letter came from Uncle A. E. today, enclosing papers for me to sign, which I have signed in presence of a notary public and have returned to Grand Rapids. It sounds like an awfully involved and complicated way out of a mortgage which is so simple to go into. But such are the laws of the lunatic land in which we live, or try to.

Today brought a dose of the old familiar agony. Through Vadim Uraneff I got an appointment with Mr. MacGowan at RKO studio. I was to be there at four o'clock. The studio is of course miles away but I got there. And after waiting half an hour I was told that Mr MacGowen was too busy to see anyone and that I should come another day. So what can you do? You can't smash bolted doors and knock people down to make people see you. If they won't they just WON'T. In New York it is much simpler. There you only have to go for a few blocks to have people not see you. Here you have to go miles and miles. And to do these things without a car is just like is just like living the life of a louse. New York is surely a more comfortable spot for the poverty stricken than this spot is. I am not complaining and I am not discouraged. BUT I AM GETTING CROSSER AND CROSSER!

Tell Doddy I was glad to get her letter and her report on world conditions. Tell her I agree that they are BAD.

I also looked for apartments again today. Could find none for less than $50.00 where there is a telephone, so I guess I'll take one at that price for a month anyway.

      Max

Wednesday [about October 11, 1933]

Dear Mother,

Yesterday morning I received another early morning telegram which alarmed me very much until I opened it. But it was a pleasant message from Muriel saying that she and Mabel Dodge were leaving New Mexico for Carmel, California, and that they would be in Los Angeles four hours between trains last evening. They told me to meet their train with Everett Marcy, an old friend of Mabel's, but not to tell anyone else about their presence here, because they were travelling INCOGNITO. I met the train at the Santa Fe Station at five o'clock, and there they were. Muriel was looking very well, and Mabel Dodge was looking very odd in a printed dress and a black straw hat with a big red ribbon on it and horn rimmed spectacles. She certainly does not resemble a great siren who has worn down four husbands, the last one an Indian, and who has been the storm center of all New Mexico these last ten years, a storm center in Italy before that, and a storm center in New York before THAT. She has also been writing the story of her life and it is now fifteen volumes long. It promises to be one of the important documents of this era [and] in eras to come. Back to their getting off the train. The question was how to spend the four hours. Mabel Dodge was determined to go to the movies. Her one idea seemed to be to discourage any conversation between Muriel and myself. We did not want to sit silently in a movie when we had so much to talk about after so many weeks. But there was no resisting Mabel Dodge. This was her affair and she was managing it and no doubt about it. She was just like Natalie Barney in being a commander in chief. She said we were going to the movies and to the movies we went. Muriel did not want to annoy Mabel since Mabel is paying all her expenses, beginning in New York and continuing all over the continent. So Muriel Draper and Max Ewing met in Los Angeles bursting with things to say, but instead sat in silence looking at a movie that they did not want to see, all because Mabel Dodge is a powerful woman! After the movie (which with the stage show lasted three hours) there was no time for dinner, so they just ate a sandwich in the other station and went off to Carmel. They will be there a week Muriel hopes to have a little longer time here on her way back—if Mabel will let her. Anyway I am glad I saw her, Mercedes and the Hoffensteins and Namara etc. will be furious because I did.

 Yesterday I was invited to lunch by Emily Hahn, the African explorer whom Joe Brewer wanted to marry, and Diana Jenkins the English girl whom Miss Carstairs shipped out West when she went to the West Indies with Natalie Hammond's friend last year. Miss Jenkins seems quite bitter about it, but I must say she is living here in grand style, alone in a 16 room house with maids and cars and chauffeur and everything. Emily ordered a fifteen dollar lunch at the Vendome, and when it was over Miss Jenkins loaned me her car and chauffeur to drive me to Santa Fe station, which was a godsend , as it is many miles away. Then Everett Marcy in his car drove me back to Hollywood after the ladies had been met, so all my problems of transportation were solved for me yesterday without much effort on my part.

 Tonight Everett and I are invited to dine at the house of the Argentine, Muratauri. He has a Filipino cook who speaks almost no English, and Muratauri speaks no Filipino, so it is always a question what will be served for dinner. The Filipino never prepares what they tell him and they never get what they expect. However he is a good cook though he always cooks the wrong things. I am waiting for news of your improvement.
Max

Muriel, Mabel, and Max viewed the movie Night Flight, *starring Lionel Barrymore, John Barrymore, Clark Gable, Helen Hayes, Robert Montgomery, and Myrna Loy.*

Friday, Oct. 13 [1933]

Dear Mother,

 Your card came today, your first message in about a week. I was getting uneasy to hear something from you. Tell Franz that you WILL be well by December 1st. And then try and keep your word. This is probably my last message from the Roosevelt Hotel. I am taking an apartment at

  1825 North Whitely Ave.
  Hollywood

Telephone: Hillside 3121

I looked and looked and this seems the best place. It is $50.00 and that includes everything from maid service to light and heat and so forth. They are getting fresh curtains up for me and getting the place into good shape. I would have moved in today except that it is Friday the 13th. And I need good luck to much to take a risk with bad luck, whether the superstition is silly or not. So I expect to move in tomorrow. And you can address your next letter to me there. I shall stay there a month and probably longer if I like it. Anyway it will mean a saving of twelve or fifteen dollars for the month.

Yesterday I saw Mr. MacGowan whom I was unable to see on Monday. He sent me to see a Mr. Swanson who is a supervisor at RKO and who was very agreeable. He asked at once who my agent would be, and I said Mrs. Schulberg. He said she was about the best I could have, and that he would keep in touch with her office, and let me know if anything came along for me. He said he felt sure something would turn up for me somewhere eventually.

Last night was the second great opening of the year at the Chinese Theater—Mae West in "I'm No Angel." Nothing can give you any idea of the pandemonium it is. People line the street from three o'clock in the afternoon to be sure they have a good spot. Then they stand there until nine o'clock to see Mae West arrive, and then a lot of them stand there until midnight to see her go home. I went to this opening last night, as I was not able to get in at the Dinner at Eight opening. The Chinese Theater holds more than three thousand people and it is an amazing sight on an opening night. All of the fifteen hundred women present are like reproductions of each other. Every single one is laden down with ermine, spangles, jewels, heavy make up, and cream colored hair. It is really fantastic. Outside the theater orchestras played in the street dressed in white satin suits. All the movie press correspondents like Eileen Percy were in the street in a specially constructed platform with their typewriters and telegraphic equipment. Bright lights of all colors light up the distant mountain ranges. Stars arrive and talk into the microphones. Marlene Dietrich looked too marvelous in red and black. Lupe [Velez] was wrapped in mink and pulling Johnny vigorously in a determined Mexican way. Finally came Mae West just smothered in white fur and spangles and orchids. She talked to the world over the radio. The mobs in the street roared. The band played Frankie and Johnnie. And the whole landscape went wild. Then her colored maid climbed onto a platform of red velvet and gold and she too made a radio speech, and she too was laden down with ermine and jewels and orchids. She said she was the happiest black girl alive, and she looked it. At last these people all got inside the theater and the show began. All this other business, you understand, was outside the theater for the benefit of "man in the street." What a place. In Spanish Los Angeles means City of the Angels. What angels!

   Max

By the middle of October, Max had made the move to the Fleur de Lys Apartments in Hollywood.

Sunday[October 15, 1933]
1825 North Whitley Ave
Hollywood

Dear Mother,

  You would be very much surprised today to see me in my new role of householder. I moved into the apartment yesterday and here I am. I feel rather odd, but I think I will like it. I have more room than in the hotel and it costs less money. There is a fair sized living room with a bed that disappears by day into an alcove. A bath and combined kitchenette and dinette. All Hollywood apartments are built on exactly the same plan. They are all exactly alike except that some are more conveniently located, some are bigger, some are smaller, some are shabbier, and some are smarter, but they are all exactly the same plan, and you could wake up in the dark in any one of the dozens I have looked at and feel more or less at home if you had ever been in one of them before.

For the first time in my thirty years I have a sort of kitchen and a Frigidaire. All apartments have these things just as they have floors and ceilings. I'm not much at cooking, but I am going to prepare my own breakfasts and sometimes lunch. Today I went shopping in the market also for the first time in life, came back with a bag full of coffee, sugar, butter, corn flakes, milk, and so forth. So here I am with quarters for a month, and breakfasts at hand for a week. I wish you were here to help me wash the dishes!

I have three windows on southern exposure, so I will have plenty of sun—when there is sun. The weather lately has been alternating three days of sun and then three days of clouds in cycles. It is still considerably warmer than it was in September.

Smart and expensive Hollywood all went to Palm Springs last night for the opening of the season there. Palm Springs is a fashionable resort in the desert a hundred miles south from here. People drive down there to dinner as if it were no trip at all. I hope to see it eventually but not now. Tomorrow night I expect to dine at Adrian's.

Two nights ago Everett Marcy drove me to a deserted castle in the hills near Pasadena. It used to belong to George Gould, and it is an exact copy of an English castle. It is in quite a run down condition now, so it more than resembles an English ruin. There are ramparts and turrets, and a swimming pool, and the whole place is occupied now by two young men who act as caretakers of the estate and who are friends of Everett. So I may go up there quite often.

I shall remain at this address until November 14th, and then we will see what will happen. Write. I hope you are getting up and down stairs now. Why don't you drink Ovaltine for your nerves? It is so simple to fix—just a spoonful in warm milk. I always take it when my nerves are on edge, and a glass of it at night works wonders with me.

    Max

About October 16, 1933, Max wrote to Muriel,
"I have just read Brett's book.
"Write me a bedtime story.
"And give my best to Mabel.
"The last three sentences are not meant to be verse. They are just three Hemingway sentences, but they look odd together.
    Max"

Wednesday [October 18, 1933]

1825 N. Whitley

Hollywood

Dear Mother,

    Your letter came last night after the long silence. It is very good news that you are improving in several ways and in several spots. The financial news is disquieting, but let's not believe the worst until the worst comes, and if it does then we will just take it. I am doing everything to peel down expenses. Now that my quarters cost only $12 a week, I am down practically to my Ann Arbor scale. I used to pay $9 a week when I was a schoolboy there, and just for a room alone, and here I have a bath and a kitchen. I expect to get my own breakfast and lunches. The markets here are wonderful, full of such beautiful vegetables and fruits, and all quite cheap, and the market is only a block away. I stocked up the ice box and the cupboard with the necessities of householding, and of course that took several dollars at the start, but now that I am stocked up I can eat for a long while on very little.

I am going to write to Knopfs to send me some money direct here to this address which will save you worry and bother. I'll tell them to send a certified check or money order of some sort so that I can easily cash it here. As I wrote you before, there will probably be SOME bond money then. If not I will sell some stocks. You have to count on some sacrifice in every investment these days. I have had those stocks so long and been without the money so long that to get any money at all from them would be like finding it. And at even their present values I could live a good many months on those stocks. So there is no need to worry about ME for nearly a year anyway. After that we will see. The world seems to be determined to go to the dogs this century as it has in other centuries before this one, and probably no Roosevelt or no Hitler can stop it. If we go to the bottom with the rest of the world it will be too bad. But at least I was on top of the world for years during the boom. I regret more than anything that you and Dad did not take advantage of those years as I did, and enjoy your money more when it was plentiful. That was your big mistake, but of course there was no way of knowing at the time that it was a mistake. One thing is sure. The next five years will see some sort of world rocking change. Either things are going to get better, or else all will be wiped away and there will be a new start. Because the world will not go through very many years like the last three without revolution. So you must get well soon in case you'll need your strength for the revolution!

We are having boiling hot weather now—95 degrees and I love it. Last night was the only warm night since I have been here. I slept under just a sheet. Every other night I have had blankets and everything. The population is jubilant, as this is the weather California boasts about. It seems there was not even ONE sunny day in June and July and the beaches and all the resorts suffered terribly. August was nice but September was miserable. October is perfect. I am wearing my linen suit to play tennis today at the Gouldings in Beverly Hills.

The Hoffensteins had a little party yesterday from five to eight. Only ten people were there including Adrian and me, and Gloria Swanson and Michael Farmer. Gloria is supposed to be stone broke, but she looked marvelous and much younger and more beautiful than she does on screen. She had with her pictures of her baby Michel Bridget who is three years old and in school in Switzerland! Farmer looked pale and wan after a long session of influenza.

Monday I had an appointment with George Oppenheimer at the Sam Goldwyn United Artists Studio. Oppenheimer used to be in the publishing business in N.Y. and he is one of the publishers who turned down my book when it was going the rounds the way I am now. He is the one who thought it resembled Parties too much. Anyway he is now with Sam Goldwyn and I looked him up. He said he would keep me in mind if he ever heard of anything for me, but he said to get a job was like getting the camel through the needle's eye unless you were an old timer and experienced movie writer. And he said that musicals were the hardest of all to get into, because the number of musical films is small compared to the number of straight speaking films, and there are more old time established composers than there are musical films to go around them, let alone newcomers. He said it is not a question of talent or capacity or ability but just of name prestige. Not what you can do, but what you have done, and how many Ziegfield shows have you done and how many Earl Carroll shows have you done? In short, if you are Irving Berlin or George Gershwin you can always get work because you are Irving Berlin, but if you are not Irving Berlin, who are you? You have to be established to get a start. So I asked the eternal question, how does ANYBODY EVER get a start if you have to be an old warhorse before you are given a chance to start? And he said it was only by accident that anyone ever got a start. Just pure luck, chance, a miracle of God. And that even was a miracle of God couldn't help you without a good agent. So that is the opinion of George Oppenheimer. It would be a novelty to talk with someone in the industry whose name did not end in heimer, -stein, or –vitch. But it is a big Yiddish closed circle. No wonder Hitler wants to get rid of the Jews. It is because they get all the jobs and control them wherever they are! Not that I object to that. Only if I were a Izzy Iskovitch from the East Side I would have more of a chance. There are some disadvantages to being a gentleman!

Night before last I dined at Adrian's. Of all the people I have met here whom I never knew at all before I came here Adrian has been the most hospitable. I enclose a picture of him sitting behind Joan Crawford. And I enclose a note for Doddy. She told me to send her no more post cards because they cost so much! As they cost less than a penny apiece, I hardly knew what to send that might be cheaper.

Write more soon.

   Max

Will wait for further instructions about that mortgage money, if any!

Thursday [about October 19, 1933]

Dear Mother,

Just had a note from Mrs. Touse, saying you seemed a little better and were beginning to see a little sunshine. Good for you. So am I, and in fact a lot of sunshine is pouring in the windows this morning. Our weather is very nice now and it cheers me up a good deal. Pay no attention to my letter of yesterday. I get in the dumps sometimes but I snap out of them again surprisingly soon. I am down to a rock bottom expenditure basis but I really do not mind it, and I am hard at work on my play again. For a long while I just couldn't focus on it, but now I can again. I don't know what determines these lapses. It is mood magic of some kind. But no matter what you say, you cannot sit down at a desk on a schedule and be witty and clever to order just as you would sit down and add up a column of figures. It will be a very good thing for me out here to have a complete play to show, whether it is immediately produced or not. At least it will show that I can handle plot and dialogue more than the book did.

 The Argentines drove in from the Villa Madrid for me last night and took me to a late supper at a place called the Clover Club, which was not very eventful except for the fact that Jean Harlow and her new husband were there. She was just in her pajamas and a white motor coat. And her husband is a horrid insignificant looking middle aged man. People say she married him because she needed an administrator! You need an administrator too but I don't see why it is necessary to marry them.

 A man named Merle Armitage who wrote me the first fan letter I received about Going Somewhere is the manager of the local concerts in Los Angeles. There is a concert about once every three weeks in a big hall called Shriners Auditorium. Mischa Elman plays there tomorrow night, and Merle Armitage has sent me free tickets. Lily Pons was to have sung here this week but her concert had to be postponed. Because of what? You should guess. A severe cold. I have not met Armitage yet in person, but am supposed to meet him Saturday night at dinner at the Arensbergs. He is the man who managed that tour of [Geraldine] Farrar in Carmen, which Dad and I heard in Toledo—my first opera, and the thing that started me off on the thing that I am still off on, if you follow me.

 If you think of any good lines suitable for an Ina Claire comedy while you are there in your bed let me know. I need them!

My cooking is all right except my coffee. I have experimented in every way and done everything people tell me, but still the taste of what I achieve never bears any relation to the taste of coffee as I have known it before. It tastes all right. But it surely does not taste like coffee. I took your advice to buy a big onion. But I got SIX big ones for FIVE cents.

Terrible about Mrs Kesler. Don't think about it. Don't think about ANYTHING for the next six weeks, and you will find you are better.

Max

Saturday [October 21, 1933]

Dear Mother,

Glad to get your note this morning, and very glad you took an auto ride. Get out all you can. You can be judge if it tires you too much or affects you in a way it shouldn't. I think it is a good thing unless you feel bad results afterward.

I am still waiting for cheering word that you are throwing off some of these worries. It is very hard for me to give you advice in money matters because our two points of view about money are so completely different. My conception of money it that it is a means to end. And the only end it can possibly serve, is to bring a feeling of freedom.

The possession of a certain amount of money means a certain amount of freedom for its possessor. But it is not freedom to possess some money and then become a complete slave to trying to maintain the possession. That is just submission to a slave driver which is worse than having no money at all. I could never subject myself to elaborate schemes and machinations to save money at the expense of my peace of mind, because that is going against the very purpose of money—which is to insure peace of mind. And whenever I inherit any property and I hope it will not be for a long time, I shall certainly be completely above board about everything. I shall conceal nothing, evade nothing, take the consequences, and go on from there to something more worthwhile. So as long as I feel this way, why can't you too? I'd rather have a thousand dollars, and have everyone know it, and skimp along on it, than to have thirty thousand, concealed, buried, worrying me and harassing me, and giving me no pleasure and doing no good to anyone. Life is too short and too wonderful a thing to pass in preoccupation with dollars or francs or pounds or marks or any of the rest of them. Of course for feeling this way about it I am called "impractical" and "without money sense," while you are called "practical, with a "good head for business." I can't help help thinking that of the two attitudes mine is the more practical and be far the more sensible. And I wish I could win you over.

Have finished my play and agent is reading it over this weekend. I am very anxious to know her reaction.

More soon.

Max

Sunday [October 22, 1933]

Hollywood Roosevelt Hotel
Hollywood, California

Dear Mother,

A Sabbath note. I have just been across the street at the Chinese Theater where I saw "Dinner at Eight," the film with all the MGM stars in it. It is excellent and quite exhausting. I have written a note of congratulations to George Cukor who directed the film. I know him from New York but have not tried to look him up until I had seen the film. The Chinese Theater is an extravagant nightmare. It is much more elaborate and insane than the Roxy or any other theater I have ever been in on this earth. It is too much for even me to attempt to describe! I just hope you get into it sometime!

Yesterday was warm as I wrote you. But today we have returned to our usual Novemberish temperatures. One wonders how the oranges manage to grow. In fact one begins to wonder if they DO grow out here. I haven't seen an orange since I arrived here. Of course I often have orange juice for breakfast just as I do in N.Y. or anywhere else. But oranges as such are never seen anywhere. One day at a restaurant I asked for a mixed fruit salad for dessert. The waiter asked me to repeat what kind of salad. And I said, "fruit." He looked at me as if were crazy, and said they never had any such thing. Since then I have been afraid to mention fruit anywhere, and I haven't seen any anywhere. I guess they raise a lot of it but they ship it all east as fast it ripens. Nobody out here wants it. Orange juice is about twice as expensive here as it is in the cheapest places in New York. They seem to think you are very eccentric if you order it, and act as if you really wanted it.

I dined at the Hoffensteins last night as per schedule. Richard Bennett and his new wife were there. Edith H. [Hoffenstein] came to [the] table for dinner for the first time since her tonsil operation last Monday. Constance Bennett and Marion Davies are both laid up with flu and bronchitis now. O California climate where is thy Victory? After dinner Edith went to bed, and the Bennetts went to San Francisco. And Sam and I went to a party at the house of Austin Parker, who was formerly the husband of Miriam Hopkins. Of course Miriam Hopkins was there. All the divorced couples in Hollywood are far more congenial after their divorces than they were during the days of the marriage. When they are married they can't stand to be together. But as soon as they get divorced they are together every minute. Ernest Lubitsch was there and the Gouldings and a lot of other people I met before here and there. Emily Hahn was there, a writer who used to be published by Joe Brewer. She says it is all set that Joe is going to be president of the college in Michigan. It is really a scream. Probably not for Joe though.

    I hope for a good report from you soon. Don't be impatient. If you are very weak and run down of course it will take time for you to build up and get accustomed to new blood pressure.

    I'll get my Knopf money the first of November and I have enough now to last until then. So I shouldn't need any more from you until after the first of the year. And by that time all things may be going well in all directions. I hope so. My big storage bill will be coming in soon. I hope you have funds for it. After the first one it will much smaller.

    More soon.

Thursday [October 26, 1933]

1825 N. Whitley
Hollywood

Dear Mother,

    Received your letter today, the double header enclosing the other written days before. It upsets me so to have you worry so much and so constantly and so exclusively. But I know it is no use to tell you not to worry, because you are the kind of person who just does worry, and it is probably easier to worry when you are not well. So all I will ask is for you to try to worry a little less. I think that everything Franz [Solier] says sounds sensible. Undoubtedly your heart HAS been overworked and it will take a protracted rest to cure it. As you say, your illness could have been avoided, and it undoubtedly can be cured. For years you have needed rest but you just would not rest. So now you must take an enforced rest. You must not think of this illness as a phenomenon or a strange affliction. It is probably just nature taking its course. It is the natural result of trying to do too much for too long, and especially of your absolutely insane activity last winter—trying to build furnace fires and run everything in sight. I am not trying to scold you at this late date.

I tried hard enough at the time. But I am just trying to point out that this illness if a perfectly understandable one with perfectly understandable causes, and that you should realize this, and do everything possible to counteract it by trying your very best to relax. Of course it is something that only rest and relaxation would help. That is why I wish more than anything that you could get away for a while. For it must be so different to get your mind off your situation as long as you are right there in it. Apart from the fact that you are not well. We are no worse off than everybody else, and other people seem to sleep. You must too.

    Muriel [Draper] had a hectic three days here, shuttled from house to house as fast as possible, to see all her friends for a little while. Sunday night we were invited to Hurlbut's. Monday p.m. we went to the Arensberges to see the paintings. Then Mr. Arensberg drove us to the Roosevelt [Hotel] where Muriel dressed for dinner. Then Hobe Irwin sent his car for us and we went to his house in Brentwood Heights for dinner. Then he drove us back to Hollywood—miles and miles through the damnable fog. Tuesday we found time to see Mercedes de Acosta, and Vadim Uraneff, and Everett Marcy. And went to the Hoffensteins in the late afternoon. That night Muriel went to dine with John Balderston, and I went to Diana Jenkin's dinner party at the Beverly-Wilshire Hotel. The party included Emily Hahn and Edwin Meyer and Max Baer! The Countess di Frasse was dancing around with Tullio Carminati and Ricardo Cortez, Gary Cooper being still in Montana. Muriel got off to Mabel Dodge's again yesterday, after two weeks in California which she loathes and considers the most dreary hole in the world. Everyone begged her to stay an extra day or an extra week, and Jon Balderston offered her his house in Beverly Hills for the next two months, but nothing could make her stay even another 24 hours. My agents showed a few signs of activity recently and made an appointment for me with a Jew named Zion Meyers at the Columbia Studios. He is going to make some "shorts" and said he might find some use for me. Something else is vaguely pending at Universal. It goes to show that the agents are doing all they can. You tell me to get a "little job" of some kind. But in my line in the movies there is no such chance, because there is no little job. In the first place, I would be glad for a job at $100.00 a week. But no studio would give me such a job. They would think I was not worth anything if I would work for that. Then too, an agency would never let me work for that. Ten percent of a hundred dollars would be only ten dollars a week for them, and they would just laugh. So they insist on holding up the price of anyone they manage and the studio insists on paying a high price to anyone it engages, so it is never possible to get a job at a moderate salary even if you would be glad to. Money means nothing to the studios. They will pay you anything if they want you. The whole battle is in convincing them that they want you. And that is what the agents have to do. It is all an insane circle, but there it is. I will give it a little longer chance. If I got work connections with pictures I could concentrate on it and probably be contented here for quite a while. But it is very difficult and practically impossible for me to concentrate on anything else here at the moment. I mean another book, for instance. A book of my kind of writing has to be light and amusing, and I am just not feeling that way. I am worried and uneasy about you and I feel uprooted and transient. I am so accustomed to the clear-cut rhythm of New York. I find it very hard to get adjusted to this great sprawling stupid misty region. I could never call this place "home" as I can call New York home. If I ever got to making money here I would stay here and make it, but go away to spend it. Nothing could make me ever want to "live" here permanently. It may be God's country, but it is not Man's. Do not think that I am not enjoying it. I am. But I am referring to a long scale of living. That would be impossible in a place like this. For a person like me.

I read that Roosevelt is going to release a lot of money from all banks closed after Jan. 1, 1933, so maybe that will help you little.

I read too that you had a cold spell. Here there has not been a drop of rain since last March. I would rather it would rain once in a while and get it over with. As it is the moisture just stays in the air in the form of fogs and mist.

My housekeeping is working out all right. I don't cook anything much more elaborate than bacon and eggs. But once I cooked a steak.

This is a deadly secret, but Mercedes and Greta [Garbo] may go to New Mexico for a short visit. If they do Mabel Dodge will go mad with delight. I am going to investigate and see what it costs to go to Santa Fe by bus. By train it is a much longer trip than from New York to Pioneer, so it is not a trip one can take too casually.

Cheer up.

Brace up.

But don't get up this week!

    Max

[About October 29, 1933]

Dear Mother,

As you have observed so often, it is SUNDAY AGAIN.

I have just sent you yesterday's Los Angeles paper—not that there is much in it, but it may help you while away an hour. I worry over what you find to do to occupy your time. It must be very tedious. Anyway in this paper you can read about the Los Angeles Navy Day and air meet. The big dirigible, the Macon, and all sorts of planes from all over the country came here and did maneuvers in the sky, but all Los Angeles was covered with a blanket of fog so thick that no one could see a thing. Furthermore, the fliers in the air could not see each other. And finally the Macon broadcasted to the city the fact that it was above the city and then flew away. So the population has to just take it on faith that all this was going on above the city. There was no seeing through the fog to prove it! Of such is the kingdom of the California climate.

Everett Marcy drove me out to San Pedro yesterday. It is the harbor town and Navy base. Los Angeles had no harbor and so they spent millions of dollars and dug one thirty miles away at San Pedro. That is where the fleet stays on this coast. It is a pleasant little town but the trip out there is along thirty miles of godforsaken land like Purgatory. That is where Bob Solier stays, but it was too late in the afternoon to visit the battleships. I want to go out some other day, when perhaps the sun will be out. But that is perhaps too much to ask.

Anyway, that is the Los Angeles harbor. The drinking water supply comes from 250 miles in the opposite direction, as there is no water of any kind here. I suppose there was never a city with such a disadvantageous natural location of its own. Los Angeles is undoubtedly the greatest monstrosity on the face of the globe. I wish you could just see it!

  Max

On November 1 the Knopf publishing company sent Max his first— and evidently sole—royalty check, in the amount of $333.89. Enclosed in the same envelope was another check, this one for $96.47, representing his royalties from the British firm that published his book in England.

Friday [about November 3, 1933]

Dearest Mother,

  What a comfort to get your letter today, a letter that sounds a little bit like your old self, which is your real self. Do try to keep the attitude you had when you wrote this letter. It probably did you good to wash those windows. I'm sure little jobs like that are all right, as long as you do nothing strenuous, and it is good for you to get a little fresh air, even if it is cold air, and I guess from the papers you are having a cold spell. But whenever it gets cold in the Middle West or the East, the Los Angeles papers put it in front page headlines so big you would think it was the Armistice and the Lindbergh baby combined!

  I have surely been in a hellish quandary lately over what to do. Some of our friends have written me that they thought I should come home. Others have written that they did not think it was necessary for me to come home. Still others have said they did not know what to advise me and that I should use my own judgment. Well, it has been very hard to decide what my own judgment was, or is, being so far from the actual scene, and with so many elements entering in. But my judgment so far has been that I had better stay here, so here I stayed. To outsiders it might seem callous of me to stay away when you apparently need someone there so much. But after all you and I know our relationship to each other better than any outsiders can. We are very close to each other, and very necessary to each other, but our relation does not depend on physical presence. We are just as close, just as telepathic, as you say, even if we are not in the same house at the same time. I have tried so very hard to analyze your state of mind and to imagine what I could do to change it. And I have felt sure that the best thing was for me to stay here where all the opportunities are. To go to Pioneer would just simply to turn my back on all opportunity. The main thing now is for us to make some more money to take the place of the past money. Well, I can't make any money in Pioneer. And here I can when I get my break. It is going to take a lot of patience and of wire pulling, but I am not discouraged. I have enough money to last me for months, and I do not mind living cheaply, as long as I am living in my own way. I do not say things like this just to cheer you up. I really mean it. I have never been as enthusiastic about making money as you have, and naturally I cannot be as grief-stricken over (apparently) losing money as you are. I am not "money-minded." I realize perfectly well that a certain amount of money is essential just for physical comfort. I have lived my life on quite a wide field, and I have known all sorts of people in these last ten years. I have known fairly intimately some of the world's richest people, who cannot or could not even count their millions, and they have not been particularly contented or fully rounded people. And on the other hand I have known people like Muriel who have very little money, and sometimes do not know where the next month's rent is coming from, but who are such complete people, and who live lives so rich and full and gracious and inspiring, that naturally I cannot take money as the criterion of satisfaction. Satisfaction comes to the type of person I am from quite other sources. I have been very much excited over this play I writing. And when I come to the end of a scene which I think is particularly good, it gives me far greater pleasure than it would to go out and buy a fur coat, for example. I am not saying that I do not appreciate money. I say the more the better. But I would never feel miserable over the lack of money. It is merely something that limited people use to try to buy the kind of satisfaction that I have inside myself to begin with.

    I have been worried that you might think my letters were not sufficiently sympathetic. But I have realized that we couldn't just sit down and wail. All my sympathy is for you. And you say all your sympathy is for me. So let's exchange the sympathy, and go on from there, to something else. There's not a thing out of your life that was in it a year ago except income from those bonds. And most of that interest you sent to me. If I am contented to go on without it you should be too. I have been "sheltered," yes. But I have not been "spoiled." If I were the kind of person who gets spoiled by self-indulgence I would have gone to hell long ago. But I'm not. I can face this situation and come out all right, if you will try too, and brace up, so that I am not so tormented about you all the time. I can get somewhere in this movie world if I can put myself determinedly and whole heartedly into it. But I can't do that as long as I have doubts all the time that I ought to go home and I am torn in all directions at once.

I am practically finished with the play. It needs a lot of polishing and cutting down but the essentials are all on paper. I am not sure yet whether I will send it to a N.Y. play agent, or directly to N.Y. producers. I have written to both Paul Osborn and Kenyon Nicholson for advice.

My Argentine friends have arrived in New York. They telephoned yesterday and said it is cold in N.Y. They motored there.

Had a long and very sweet letter from Carl V.V. [Van Vechten] yesterday. Lili Tashman is in N.Y. making personal appearances. So now Marion Saportas is giving parties for her there instead of here. Why don't you have an administrator appointed if you want to sell some of those old stocks and get things squared away? The money you would save by not having one isn't worth the constant worry and inconvenience you go through trying to evade the issues. Why not come up to the surface, make everything above board, do what should be done in a legal way, and find a little peace of mind?

      Max

November 10, 1933

Dear Mother,

Here is the end of another day spent at my typewriter. I am absorbed in the play and it is going well, in spite of everything.

It is bad of you to write me so many terrific letters all in a row, and then let a whole week go by without writing at all.

I have had no news of you this week, but I tell myself it is good news that way.

The weather is the hottest it has been since I came out here. Hotter than in August. Hot day and night. I sit around in my underwear when writing. Wear only a sheet and a light blanket at night. September was cold. November is hot. That's the way it is this year. It seems to be different every year. I like it hot. This week Leonie Sterner is here from New York and lately from New Mexico. She is at the Roosevelt. All New York comes sooner or later.

   I feel badly that Texas [Guinan] died.

   I am sending you a movie magazine called "Modern Screen," on page 33 of which you will find my picture with Gloria Swanson, Michael Farmer and several others around a hay wagon. It is the third picture down from the top on the right hand side of the page, in case you have any difficulty identifying us. We all look a little cold. Gloria is in the center in the straw hat. Farmer is bending over Irene Fenwick who has her back turned.

   Everything splendid here.

   I wish you were the same.   Max

Nov. 13 [1933]

1825 N. Whitley
Hollywood

Dear Uncle,

   I heard from Mother today for the first time since she wrote when you were in Pioneer. I did so hope that her attitude would be different or improved by now. But it is not. It is just the same. Her letter is practically word for word what it was two weeks ago just the same things about coupons and taxes and taxes and coupons. And it seems to show that she is right back in the same rut which you tried to get her out of, and apparently did get her out of for the length of time you were there. I was so hopeful over the last ten days, but now it all looks just as awful as before. I still think that to get away briefly would do her more good than anything in the world, but it is useless to suggest it, as she has the idea she cannot buy a box of salt. What am I to do? It is largely hysteria on her part. But one can't cure hysteria with hysteria, and that is what I'll be having out here, if this keeps up much longer.

The weather is perfect here now. Blazing hot day and night. I am doing some writing all the time, but under considerable strain.

Let me know if you get any reports from Mme. Touse.

Max

Monday, Nov. 13[1933]

Dear Mother,

I did not hear from you for more than a week, and I did so hope that when I did get a letter it would show that you had improved, or had altered your attitude a little. But your letter came today, and it is just the same, and now I am sunk again, and I don't know what to do. My play has been going so well, and my living expenses have been practically nothing. I am eager to stay here but I can't stand it much longer if your condition and attitude remain the way they are.

The weather is boiling hot now day and night. Yesterday Dudley Murphy came for me in his Packard and drove me out to his beach house in Malibu where we went swimming and lay in the sand. It was the most perfect day since I have been out here, and so clear that we could see to Catalina Island. He also took me to see his big house up in the hills above Santa Monica. He has just arrived out here after nearly a year in New York, and he says that as soon as he gets squared away he will introduce me to people I should know and who may be helpful to me, in the way of getting work. He himself has no job in sight at present, but he hopes to get something on the strength of the success of

The Emperor Jones, the film he made in New York. I am very glad he is back here.

He is going, he thinks, to Vincent and Edington as agents. And I am thinking of changing to them too if they will take me. Schulberg has been at me for three months, and that is the time an agent gives himself to get something for you. At the end of that time you may leave them if nothing is signed up. I am dissatisfied with what they have done and I am going to change. The Schulberg office is in considerable upheaval now anyway because several of their expensive stars have left them recently. And when two or three $2000.00 a week people leave an agent it means a loss of $600.00 a week to the agent. And the agent has to concentrate on other big salaried people, and hasn't time to devote to "smaller fry" on his list. So I am going to change, and hope for more luck.

I am by no means discouraged. Three months is a very short time compared to the time lots of people, in fact most people, have to wait for their first big break.

If you could only pull yourself together a little, and I could feel I had some "moral support" if not financial. But your letters seem so without hope or faith or charity in or toward anything. Whenever I get one from you I feel I should do nothing but go home. But your letters always tell me not to. It makes me feel up against a blank wall whichever way I turn.

There is no more use in urging you to try to get your mind off these reverses. The business and the investments have been your major preoccupation for so many years, you cannot lessen your interest or take them lightly now. But when you tell people like Clara Sweet that you cannot afford an eggnog! There is just nothing to say. That Spitzer Rorick money will pay an awful lot of your current expenses, even if it is released slowly. You didn't want to spend it all at once, did you?

Spend it slowly. If you can possibly hold on to Libby Owens a little longer I would, for it is sure to advance farther now that prohibition is over with, and bottles will increase. But if you need the cash, sell Libby Owens.

A lot of bonds have defaulted in the past, and then come back again a year or two later. They are in a tight pinch right now like everything else. Don't just lie there and give up, and assume that they will never come back at all.

No, I don't need my overcoat. I don't need anything except I need desperately to have you get better, physically and mentally, and every way. Won't you try harder and harder?

Max

Monday—later

Dear Mother,

Your letter came this morning and I answered it immediately by air mail, while still more or less out of my head. I always go nearly out of my head when I receive a letter from you in the morning, for it always worries me half to death. A letter also came from Clara Sweet, enclosing cards for me to sign and return to the Toledo Trust Co. I have done this and written to her too. So that business is attended to. And now to get back to the more important business of YOU.

I said in my letter this morning that I would come home. That is always my first impulse when I get a letter from you like the one that came today. And I will, if we decide all around that it is the wise thing to do. But we must be sure first that it is. I think it is more and more plain that what you are suffering from is a form of nervous breakdown. As you say your tests show that you have no organic disease. What you apparently have is a case of nerves strained to the limit, and an overworked heart, and last but not least a good case of "scare." I think it was wise of Franz [Solier] to scare you into this complete rest, etc. But you know he has always been a scare doctor, and there is a possibility that he may have scared you too much. You must try and get over your fright. This being your first long and serious illness, it is of course frightening. But you know that people do not die of nervous breakdowns, though they may be very sick with them over quite a period of time. There is no actual danger unless some specific disease sets in. You have been through an awful strain these last few years, enough to make anyone break down temporarily. I think that with rest your body ailments will take care of themselves. But the main thing you need seems to be a bucking up of your MORALE. Your situation is so dreary, you can't help brooding over it, and that necessarily holds back your physical recovery. And that is where I would come in. If my mere presence at home would buck you up then I would come like a shot. There is nothing I could actually do that anyone else could not do. But it might help you just for me to BE there. And on the other hand it might not. As I say, my first impulse is always to go straight to you. But we must stop and remember what it would be like at the end of the third week and the fourth week and so on through the weeks. Shut up in that house with Doddy through the winter, I would soon be at my wit's end too, and we all know it. As I just said, the main thing to buck people up, whether one person or a whole army, is MORALE. And here I can maintain my morale even when things seem very discouraging. Even though nothing seems to be happening, still there is always the chance that something may. Any day something may turn up the next day. And even if professional opportunities do not come, there are always diverting and distinguished people to see, interesting contacts to make, etc. There is in short always something to look forward to whether it materializes or not. But for me—in Pioneer—there is not. Apart from the service that I might be to you, to go there is just to ring down the curtains for me temporarily. There is just the difference, that here something stimulating and exciting and worth while may happen the next day, while in Pioneer there is just the dead certainty that it won't and that it can't. And it is that difference that makes morale or destroys it. My whole aim at present is to be of the greatest service to you. And it is just a question of whether I can be of greater service by returning to Pioneer and adding my jitters to yours or by sticking to my own guns and hoping that you will pull through this crisis. I would not shirk a winter in Pioneer if I thought it would buck you up. But it would just make you more nervous to have me puttering about the winter would be a total loss for both of us. I am very seriously trying to know what is the best thing to do, and I am not being guided by ideas of self-indulgence. Periods of bad luck come to everyone and I hope I can take it if necessary. But I know that my own margin of nervous energy is very slight, and my whole system goes haywire under strain of any kind. And I am not sure that my return to Pioneer would be of any benefit to anybody.

    I am on a very economical basis here now. The management of this apartment house has agreed to let me live here by the week if I prefer not to pay monthly rent in advance after Nov. 15. Thus I could always leave here on short notice if you wanted me to come home promptly for any reason. Also I have found that the bus fare from Hollywood to Chicago is only $27.00. And I guess we could always scare up that amount to get me back to Ohio if necessary. That is a trip of three days and three nights on the bus. I would break the trip with a night somewhere else of course. Also the railroad rates have been reduced again.

    Bus fare to Santa Fe, New Mexico, is $13.50. I have always wanted to go there for health purposes. It is very high and very clear, but on account of the height it is very cold. And if I went there I would have to replenish my wardrobe quite extensively. They say there is deep snow there in November. Here the weather plods along, not very cold and not very warm, not very bright and not very dark. Just weather. It is by no means the ideal climate it is cracked up to be, but it is at least better than Ohio. There is a resort called Palm Springs three hours south of here by motor, where people always go when the rains set in here. It is in the desert and it is always boiling hot and sunny no matter what the Los Angeles weather is. I am invited to motor down there with my Argentine friends over this next Sunday, and I am very eager t see the place. It is within easy reach of Hollywood, less than half a day, but it always has invigorating weather. I will look it over and see what it is like.

        Max

Tuesday [November 14, 1933]

Dear Mother,

    In spite of handicaps, the play is still progressing wonderfully. Yesterday I finished the second act which was the toughest part to get over. The third act will be shorter and much easier than the others. Within the next two weeks I expect to have the whole thing finished and in shape to turn over to my agent. I also expect to have a new agent by that time. So cheer up. If I can get this play on in New York—agents handling it there too—we will clean up a lot of money. And if it should ever become a film too then we would make as much as you have lost, or think you have lost. In any case it will be a big selling point for me out here. As the agents in building me up can then say not only, "Here is his novel and here is his music," but also, "here is his play." And that is the main thing in talkies—dialogue. Brace up and give me a chance to get this over. Now will you or won't you brace up?

California this week is having the hottest weather for forty years. Just one damn surprise after another. It's a hundred degrees in Hollywood and hotter than that in the country.

Dudley Murphy says it is the biggest theatrical season in New York for years, that the town is full of hits, and everyone is packing the theaters. Kenyon Nicholson's new play—"Sailor Beware" has just sold for $35,000.00. There's a future in playwriting. There isn't any in dishwashing. So stop writing such nonsense. I'll get by but I have to do it in my own way. You'll get by too if you tried hard, and you'll have to do it in your way. I'm not coming back to Pioneer what you call "a failure," unless you go on getting sicker and sicker, and if you do then I won't care much about success anyway. So now you get your mind on success and off failure, and on gain and off loss. And pull with me toward accomplishment, and not pull by yourself toward doom and disaster.

Have Frances make you an eggnog and drink it to the success of my play.

   Max

I think you are quite right to stop tax payments on the store buildings. You could never sell them for even a tenth what they are worth, or were worth. And even if you were well you would not want to keep them and run them forever. You wouldn't lose them this year or next year if you stopped all taxes on them, and eventually if you could sell them you probably couldn't get much more for them than the accumulated taxes would have amounted to. So this is a good way to dispose of them eventually without the expense of tax payments in the meantime. Even when business in general does get going again it will be years or probably forever before small town buildings pick up value.

Thursday [about November 16, 1933]

Dear Mother,

    Since writing you yesterday I have spent another eight-hour day at my desk, hammering out what I think is one of the most amusing stage comedies in the past ten years. I expect to have it finished within a week now, and it will be a great feather in my cap. It might even get on in New York late this season if things work fast. But even if I could get a producer to take an option on it for next season I would get a lot of money for the option. So there is undoubtedly money in it for me this winter in either case. And I have discovered that it is much more important for a writer out here to have had a successful play than any number of books. I wrote you that Kenyon Nicholson's new play sold to the movies for $35,000.00. That was untrue. It sold for $75,000.00! Night before last a girl named Margaret Hawkins asked me to dinner. She is a great friend of K. [Kenyon] Nicholson's and she just learned that I was. She helped him on all his early plays, and she is very helpful in giving me advice here. She lives in the same block in another apartment building. She asked me how I knew Nicholson in the first place, and I said it was through his aunt and uncle, the Ann Arbor Wheelers, who used to be heads of the vocal dept. in the Ann Arbor School of Music. She said she knew about the Wheelers too, and they have lost every cent, and are absolutely destitute. I suppose Nicholson helps them. So will I help you if you'll give me another six months.

    The first of the week I am going to move downstairs into a small apartment in this building which is just now being vacated. It is only $30.00 a month, than which nothing is cheaper. I won't have any kitchen or stove down there, so will do no more cooking, but the savings of $20 a month on rent will more than balance the extra cost of eating out. It is just a good sized room and bath and closet. But it is big enough for me and a bed and a typewriter, and that's all I need these days. I am at the typewriter from morning till night. Dudley Murphy's film, The Emperor Jones, starring Paul Robeson opens here tomorrow at a gala premiere. Dudley is taking Charlie Chaplin to see it. As soon as it is over and that excitement dies down for Dudley I am going to meet all his friends. Something will come of that, I am sure. Mrs. Schulberg leaves tomorrow for New York to be away for two months, so I am definitely deserting her, as I have no confidence in her office staff working for me. I am full of confidence in our future. I have a strong faith in myself. If you will buck up and pull with me all will be well. But your letters since the Spritzer Rorick money became available have been more gloomy than before. That is very unreasonable. It makes me think that if the bonds all began to pay again you would feel still worse. What is the matter? It is terrible to lose a hundred dollars, and more terrible to lose a million dollars. But there is no amount of money in the world the loss of which is worth the agony you are putting yourself through. Your money might just as well have been "paper profit" all along. During the time when you had the most money of your life was very little different from what it was before you had that much money. And your daily life need not be frightfully much different now that there is not all that money. It was all in your head—the confidence that the mere existence of that money gave you. So now transfer that confidence to me. I am your best investment—not roads and bridges in the ends of the earth. I am off on a new rampage of productions, and I want you to show some faith in it. Brace up. You've got to be there in a front row seat at my play's opening in New York.

    Max

Saturday [November 18, 1933]

Dear Mother,

    The end of the week again, and practically the end of the play. I am delighted with it. It needs polishing and it is too long. It will have to be trimmed down here and there, though I hate to part with any of the wonderful lines. I have written you again and again that I am writing a play, but you never acknowledge the fact. However I once wrote you that I was writing a book, and you didn't believe in that either. However, the book was published on two continents, and publicized the world over. It didn't bring in the thousands of dollars it might have before the crash, but it brought in some comfortable hundreds which are coming in handy this winter. So, just as I once believed in the book, I now believe in the play—only more so. Because even a short run of a play makes more money than an enormous sale of a book. It is a play that should not need to be frightfully expensive to produce. It all takes place in one room, which saves cost of stage settings. I have had my mind all the time on the existence of staging, and I think it is a perfectly stageworthy vehicle.

    I don't like that you are so convinced that I can NEVER make any money. After all, you and Dad did not commence to make any money that you could really call MONEY until you were past thirty, and I am just that now. You both served long apprenticeships before the money began to roll in. Well, so have I served a long apprenticeship. It has been an expensive one but it will be a profitable one in the end. And when I cash in on it there will be more money than you made, I am sure. So, no more of this wailing about how I am going to be miserable all my life in Pioneer. I'm not going to spend my life in Pioneer. I'm going to get you out of there instead, if you will work hard to get yourself in shape to be got out. It half broke my heart when my book came out and Dad was not on hand to see it. And it would break my heart completely if my play should go in New York and you would not be able to attend the opening. So now you get a move on and get better.

    The first of the week I am moving not downstairs but upstairs into another apartment at $35.00. It has a kitchen and stove and ice box. So there I can still do my own cooking and still save $15.00 a month. It is just being vacated.

    Had a letter from Uncle A.E. today saying he had seen you again this week, and that he thought you seemed improved, though still exaggerating the difficulties. He said also that you had told him you had written me that you thought I should come home, but that I was not apparently going to and that it was probably just as well that I did not. If you ever did write me this I did not get the letter. Other people have advised me to come home, but all your letters have said not to. All you have to do is say the word, and you know I will come at the drop of a hat. And do not hesitate to say the word if ever you feel I could benefit you personally by coming. Only do not advise it as an economy gesture, for that would be a false economy in the end. If you think it is vital for me to come and open those safety deposit boxes in January, I will do so. Uncle A.E. does not seem to think it necessary or advisable that I should come home at present, and I count him a clear headed judge of these matters.

    Bright sun and warm weather are still here. I am all confidence once again. Not a cloud on the horizon except your illness. Can't you POSSIBLY snap out of it?

        Max

Thursday [about November 23, 1933]

Dearest Mother,

    Another blazing hot November morning, and the craziest part of it all is that the town has all its Christmas decorations out. Hollywood

Boulevard is lined for two miles with tinseled Christmas trees which look too beautiful at night, but too insane by day, when it is so hot you want to wear a bathing suit in the streets. I don't know why they do all this even before Thanksgiving. I guess they feel they have to make a big to-do over Christmas because nobody would believe it was Christmas in such weather if they didn't.

Most of this week is given over to my making copies and carbon copies of my play. I have to have a copy for Rosalie Stewart and a copy to send to Ina Claire to see if she likes it, and a copy for N.Y. producers, and a copy for the Copyright Bureau in Washington, and a copy for myself, etc. It is very tedious copying it over, even though with carbon paper I can make more than once copy at a time.

Spent yesterday at Dwight Taylor's again. I walked out to his house in Laurel Canyon, only about 2 miles, and I enjoyed the walk. Some of the songs I have already seem to fit into his libretto, and of course I will write more particularly for it too. I very much need a piano, and could rent one for $5.00 a month, but don't feel I can afford it at present.

I wrote you last week that you should not write me at all when you are in such a bad state of mind, but of course I did not mean it really seriously. I want to hear from you often and be in constant touch with you, so write soon.

I enclose a card from Marion Morehouse who is leading a luxurious existence in Africa with my friends, the Sebastians. Today I had a sweet card from Gertrude Stein, in Belley, France. Also a long letter from Muriel, still at Mabel Dodge's. She said Eddie Wassermann telephoned the other night, and told her all the news. Everyone seems to be doing exactly the same things as last year, and it sounds pretty gay if you think so. Lilyan Tashman is in N.Y. Also Gary Cooper and Joan Crawford and lots of other stars, on vacations.

I had another letter from Uncle A.E. today, advising me to be brave, and to stick by my guns here. He thinks that my accomplishing something here will do you more good than my return to Pioneer. I feel sure that is true. If ever you think differently be sure and tell me.

    Max

Max's next letter was handwritten on the back of a menu for the Hotel Vista de Arroyo, in Pasadena, California. The long list of viands included "Filet of Sole Poachee, White Wine Sauce, Ragout of Spring Lamb, Jardiniere, and Roast Stuffed Turkey, Celery Dressing, Cranberry Sauce." The menu was dated November 23, 1933 and Max's letter followed shortly after.

Friday [November 24, 1933]

    Dear Mother—I dined at this hotel at their dinner last night as a guest of the people who own it and run it. There is a young man out here who is a friend of Everett Marcy here, & also of Helen Bowersox in Toledo. He missed meeting me at that party there last summer but had heard a lot about me & wanted to meet me. So he did last night and he engineered this dinner party in Pasadena. We then went to the home of a woman detective story writer for the rest of the evening. Temperature still around 92 degrees.

    Have you no good work to report yet?

    Max

Thursday Nov. 30 [1933]

Dear Mother—

    This is Thanksgiving & bright & clear. Just like any other day for me—as I am letting no festivities interfere with my work. I am so terribly excited about my play and about the N.Y. Theater Guilds interest in it. I hope to have it all done over & ready to send to Philip

Moeller by Saturday—day after tomorrow. Had a letter from Kenyon Nicholson yesterday who said he too would do everything to market it for me in my absence in New York. He has made more than $100,000.00 this fall out of his new play. And the N.Y. theater is so prosperous this season that all the producers are eager to read new scripts. I think mine has every chance.

I worry, worry, worry about you. If you would just stop worrying, worrying, worrying about pieces of paper in tin boxes for a while, then I could worry less about you, and everything would be better all around. Still I give thanks today for lots of reasons. Hope you do too. And there will be more reasons soon. Believe me!

    Max

Max seldom needed to cope with money problems or to consider return on investments, stock purchases, or savings deposits. In January, 1933, Clara wrote to A.E.: "It's a pretty much charmed life for him--& he thinks it should be for me—but someone has to balance the budget & a budget to him has always been a Cinderella." Max took a different view of his financial interests and abilities. In late fall of the same year he told A.E , "It has been a family legend of thirty years standing that I have no head for business." He added that money meant nothing to him except as an expedient to some end, and that getting money for the mere sake of getting it was not one of his aims. What other people thought of him didn't mean a thing, Max wrote. As Clara's mental and emotional condition worsened, she seemed more determined to protect Max from knowledge of her financial situation, while at the same time she became increasingly despondent. A.E. found himself in the middle, bound by Clara's request to hide things from Max and bound simultaneously by the evident need to keep Max informed. They mutually agreed not to let Clara know what they learned from each other.

Sunday night [December 3, 1933]

Dear Uncle [A.E. Ewing]—

Have received both your letters. Thank you for the one in which you grant that I have sense! I may be lacking in "horse sense," but I can't help thinking I have some other variety just as good, and maybe superior!

Am encouraged that Mother got down town, even though she did not react well to the trip. Anyway, it was a start toward an "upturn," I hope.

Expect to ship my play off to New York tomorrow. Then we will hope for good luck.

Max wrote in his diary that he did, indeed, mail "The Golden Girls" to Phillip Moeller on December 4. He continued work on "Return Ticket," his second three-act play, written with Tallulah Bankhead in mind. On January 3 he hand delivered the second play to someone named Lovelace. He played tennis and attended movies for relaxation.

Dec. 11, 1933

Dear Max:

This is absolutely in confidence. You must not under any circumstances let your mother know I have written you about her letter just this morning received. Find my reply (copy) herewith. She asked me to please not write to you about it and it places me between two keen responsibilities,—that of being true to her confidences and of keeping nothing from you. She wrote a 3-page letter, and has evidently come to the conclusion that she will not now have an administrator. I will copy here some parts of her letter, and you can draw your own conclusions. The last line of her letter was "Please don't write Max." It pricks my conscience to do it, but you should know,—in case she has not already written you. One excuse is that something might happen to me,—who knows? She insists she is in for penalization because of tax evasions. Now here is the paragraph:

"I have a little metal trunk in my bedroom with valuable papers in it. I'll try to leave the key in Doddy's purse. It has a list of taxes, dates, etc. I have money in Toledo Trust for Max's life insurance for 4 years. I think it runs six. It's due in May. $117.35 last year (with dividend it was $192.36). I hope I can spare enough for the whole six years. Toledo Trust is bank & it's in his name with checkbook." ###### "I am sick enough to be naturally but it has to be some way. I am so dizzy. Just float around in the air,—like nothing I can describe. ##### I am not willing for Max to know this,—but I'll pass out of the picture if I can— then Max will have anything that's left & be less for you all to worry about. No one ever lived & suffered as I do."

Whatever this means, you can judge for yourself as well as I can. You can see how delicate a point is involved in my going directly against her request in letting you in on it. That's why I wish you to keep it to yourself, for I have written her that I would not write you. If I can lie about it, you must.

Love,

  A.E. Ewing

Dec. 13 [1933]

Hollywood

Dear Uncle

Just got your air mail letter. I must say I think both you and [Rev. Russell] Bready are miracles of patience and tact, the way you have to put up with such constant shifts and changes on Mother's part. I think your letter to her is a masterpiece. And I have just written to Bready that I think, as you do, that perhaps the wisest thing to do at the moment is to

LET THINGS SLIDE. Anything to get Mother's mind off the financial and get back a little judgment and balance, which can only return with the return of a little more strength of body. I think the Christmas season will take her mind off business a little. And I wish the administration might be postponed a few months. I might think if the administration were all over with, it might be a load off her mind. But I'm afraid she might break down completely while it was being gone through with. She would never relax and let other people handle it. She would have to be in on all of what was going on, and I don't think she's in any shape for that, even though it would be a relief in the end. Of course I think it must be done eventually. But not now, unless it seems imperative.

 I feel as if I were living on a psychological rollercoaster. Up one hour and down the next and never knowing what is around the next curve. But the mental strain seems to be a great mental stimulus, for I have just finished a second play which I think is better than the first. I have written Tallulah Bankhead (in N.Y.) about it, and she is interested. Had a wire from her today. The N.Y. Theater Guild is now considering my first one. Big money is unquestionably on the way. It is only a question of months. And with Mother we must play for time. Just keep her health up in the meantime, and keep her pacified, if possible. If either one of these plays is sold, and I feel sure that both will be, I can pay up all the taxes and everything else and never miss the money. I have found that the only way into movie money is via plays, not books. So I have written two plays, and they are both good. They have both been written under absolutely hellish conditions, because in addition to the worry about Pioneer matters, I have been suffering agonies with sinus trouble.

 THIS IS A SECRET IF THERE EVER WAS ONE. If you tell on me I'll tell on you, and oh dear, what I can tell on you & I spent Thanksgiving Day under ice packs and applications of cocaine, but since then I'm much better and the sinuses are "draining." I just escaped an operation by what my doctor calls a miracle. If Mother knew I had either a pain or a doctor bill she would throw a fit. So it's all a secret. I tell you this only so that you won't think I'm basking on a California bed of roses while Rome burns. The more trouble I have the worse I feel, the more I get done, for I just sit at my desk day and night and DO IT. No nonsense about the gay life of Hollywood, there isn't much of it anyway. As a matter of fact it's the hardest working factory town in the world, and the "stars" are nothing but slaves who begin their day's work every day at 8 A.M. So do I.

Max

Friday [December 15, 1933]

Dear Mother,

Had a very interesting post this morning form all sorts of people ranging from Alice de la Mar in New York to Marion Morehouse in Africa. But nothing from you. I get worried when there is nothing from you for this long a time. The people write me the most terrifying letters, about how you keep threatening suicide and the most hair-raising things. I can just hardly stand it, and I haven't a moment's peace of mind. If I even leave the building here for two or three hours I keep telephoning back to see if there is any message here. It has got me into a state of absolute panic, and if you have the slightest regard for my well-being you will make super human effort to curb yourself in these wild threats. People are all worked up over your condition, all the way to the Pacific Ocean. Do you really think it is worth it, spreading this agitation over such a large area, largely because some Florida road bonds have suspended paying their interest, and you are worried about paying your taxes? Even if every cent were gone forever it would not justify such a commotion. And as a matter of fact nothing is gone forever. Interest is suspended simply because of the tightness of the tax situation.

I am not saying that it is all delusional on your part. You are sick and run down, of course. But a lot of this hysteria is plainly self-induced by this incessant preoccupation with money, money, money. And you have simply got to stop it. Can't you change your attitude about money a little? For the most part it is pieces of paper, at best it is chunks of metal. It has a certain exchange value which people arbitrarily attach to it. But even when you had plenty of it to spare you never cared enough about the things you could exchange it for to exchange it for them. Money is one of the pleasanter decorations on the surface of life, but I should think anyone who had been as desperately sick as you have this fall would have reached an inkling that it is not very important in the long run. Money hasn't anything to do with the fundamental values of human living and I should think you would have come face to face enough with fundamental thinking this fall to half way realize this. To lose money is a misfortune. But it is one of the minor misfortunes. To completely lose one's health is a major misfortune. And if you lose your health just out of concern for having lost some money, that is supreme and inexcusable folly.

The necessary documents from the Register of Copyrights in Washington came today too, so now I can send the play there, and elsewhere and know that it is protected.

More anon.

Max

Saturday Dec. 16 [1933]

Hollywood

Dear Mother,

Glad to detect a ray of hope in your today's letter. I have signed card as per your orders. Find it enclosed. I wish I could make you see, as I see now, that this financial upheaval this fall was the greatest blessing in disguise that ever could have happened to me. For it has set me firmly on the track of great worldwide success. I have always been more or less on that track. But I never stuck exclusively to the track because there were so many attractive sideshows along the way. I knew I could always get on the track when I wanted to, but in the meantime I took an easy gait, looking in all directions. But this fall I have taken myself in charge and had an eye for nothing but PRODUCTION. And I have turned out two absolute knockout masterpieces. I wrote you yesterday that I expected ten thousand dollars out of them within a year. Well, I was only joking. I expect a lot more than that and I wouldn't be surprised if I sell my second play to the films within six weeks. It's sure to be a movie sooner or later, no matter what Tallulah does about it. I have two more days work on it, typing the third act over. I am turning it over to my agent here on Monday. I am not sending a copy to Tallulah until December 26th, because I do not want to risk its getting lost in the jam of Xmas mail. It is not just a manuscript. It is a piece of PROPERTY worth more than half a dozen bonds.

    Enclosed is a letter from Elizabeth Hull at the Merlin producing office, which came today. You see, the word is out on the rialto that I have written a play, and already the demand to see it has begun. No one knows why, but the theater has COME BACK this year with a bang, and producers are all eager to consider new scripts. And if they're good scripts, then it's only a matter of TIME.

    I already have a third play all mapped out in my mind. But I'm not going to start work on it until after Xmas, or I'll wear myself out. I have scarcely left my desk for weeks. Haven't been to Beverly Hills for more than a month. But the Beverly Hills crowd will gasp in astonishment when it sees my output in the interim. I was invited to a dinner party at Emily Hahn's last night, but I couldn't be annoyed.

I'm going to relax a little over the holidays if the news from Ohio permits.

My past misfortunes have turned out to be blessings in disguise too. For a year I was broken hearted over the injury to my finger. It seemed the worst blow that could possibly happen. But it was a godsend, for it got me off the idea of being a concert pianist. Piano playing today is a complete blind alley, and the greatest pianists are all broke. I thank God that I injured my finger. Now you thank him for this money scare. Calm down, little one, and GO TO SLEEP. And forget about that miserable little hundred thousand dollars. I am entirely willing for you or Dr. Bready to be A.E. Ewing's agent if he is definitely appointed administrator. I favor postponement of proceedings however until you are better and I have cleared up a few more matters here.

Tuesday [about December 20, 1933]

Dear Mother,

Just got your Friday letter. Can't tell very well from it just how you are feeling. But anyway I'm sorry it stays so cold in Ohio. It's still perfect here.

Everything is progressing. The play is finished, as far as the actual thinking is concerned. I still have to make a copy to send to Washington for copywriting before I start sending it out across the country. It is not safe otherwise. Rosalie Stewart does all her reading of new scripts over weekends, so she probably won't get around to reading it until over this next Sunday.

I am already at work in two new original story synopses for possible screen use. The three I wrote when I first came here, which Schulberg had and Stewart has now, are all comedies. Now I am writing two serious ones to see how they will fare. One I am basing more or less on Doris' situation of two years ago—a girl who suddenly gets an unforeseen chance to go and teach in another country. I am not making it Constantinople because I don't know enough about it. So I am sending her to Rome which I know fairly well. It is not actually Doris' story, but it uses her situation as a springboard into another story. I am fertile no end in ideas these days.

I did send the signed check back to you. Let me know that you receive it.

The reasons I am not living in Dudley Murphy's houses if that for one thing the big one is rented to and occupied by the Ralph Bellamys. And the beach house is 25 miles away without any means of conveyance to or from it, and no communications with the outside world. And though I am pretty good at walking, I cannot walk 25 miles to where I live whenever I need to come to the surface. Dudley himself is staying at The Garden of Allah, which is out towards Beverly Hills.

Too bad about Tod. I would like to see Fae, but I am afraid I have no friends there who would enjoy the trip there, and I am not considering going alone for the time being.

You'll be hearing from me. Keep your upper lip stiff!
    Max

Wednesday [December 21, 1933]

Hollywood

Dear Mother,

Am in a great excitement about my NEW play. I sent the first one to New York on Monday, and now I am well along in the first act of another, with Tallulah Bankhead in mind this time. She has been ill all fall, and the play she went East to do is finally being done without her, as she has to recuperate for another month or two. But after that she will be needing a play, and it might as well be mine. I have written her that I am preparing the role especially for her, and asking if she has any suggestions. I think it is a marvelous idea, and I am writing from morning to night in a real frenzy, hardly taking time out for meals—though I whip up a lot of eggnogs for myself through the day. If I can get Tallulah Bankhead and Ina Claire both interested in my output then all troubles are over. And I think I can. I think probably play writing is my calling, though it has taken me thirty years to find it out. I write excellent dialogue, and have an excellent sense of situation and character. And I have a wealth of material to draw from, from my life over the past ten years. I'll catch up with Noel Coward yet! I consider this winter as a complete recess from my life, a recess given over entirely to work, and producing something.

I enclose a note from Kenyon Nicholson, advising me to go to Hunter Lovelace as an agent, and I have done so. Lovelace is reading all my output this week, and I am to see him again Saturday. The Margaret H whom Nicholson speaks of in his postscript is Margaret Hawkins, who lives in the next building to me. She has read my finished play, which is called "THE GOLDEN GIRLS," and she thinks it is swell. She helped K. [Kenyon] Nicholson on his early plays.

Pull yourself together. We are getting somewhere fast, at last.
Max

In a short biography of Max written in 1951 for a college course, William John McAfee III summarized "The Golden Girls" as a three act play about the lives of three young women from an old Boston family during the 1920s. Max's other three-act play, "Return Ticket," featured characters similar to those in Going Somewhere. *Both plays, McAfee stated, were overdone, over loaded with puns, and much too obvious.*

Friday, Dec. 22 [1933]

To my Favorite Lady Worrier:

    I guess I'm no good as a mind doctor or faith healer. For the last ten days I have bombarded you with the cheerfulest kind of news, news about my recent work and the very promising stir it is creating on two seaboards. And what do I get today in reply, three days before Christmas? A sad little postcard telling me not to get excited about success, and adding that you can expect all the goods in the store to be stolen soon. I have never heard such rubbish in my life.

    If you would find it a relief to close the store for three months, or six months, or permanently, by all means do so. But it isn't going to be "stolen" in daylight. What a lot of drivel.

    I sent you a little Christmas present—a day book in which I wanted you to put down the dates of the good events that are sure to come in 1934. I suppose though that if you are left to follow your own impulses you will use it to put down in advance the date when you expect the store to be robbed, the car to blow up in flames, the roof to fall in, Spitzer-Rorick to close its doors again, the waters of Clear Lake to rise and inundate the cottages, Lansing to be razed by fire, the U.S. to turn communist and all insurance policies to be repudiated, Florida to sink into the Gulf of Mexico by way of tidal wave, the Stock Market to close by Roosevelt's orders and all stocks to be dumped into the Hudson River, and many other pleasant little fancies which you can work up at your own leisure. That is what you will do with the book if you persist in your present direction. I still hope though that there is a chance to get you on a reasonable track, and off this ludicrous sad go-around which you've been riding on all fall.

    I'm sorry your card to me shows no sign of pleasure in my work, no confidence in its worth, no hope, no gratification, no cheer, no nothing except just woe woe woe is me. I don't like your attitude. I don't like it at all. It is less conducive to sympathy than it is to toleration. For years you have been impatient with Doddy and berated her for her fear of staying alone. She is afraid to stay alone because she is afraid "something will happen." She doesn't know what it will be, she just thinks "something will happen." Well, if you are not careful, you will develop exactly the same trait. You are not afraid, as she is, to sit alone "in a great big house," but you have the same ungrounded and unreasonable fear of future catastrophes and vague dangerous bogey-men that have no reality whatever. So stop moping and counting your bogey men. Doddy has led a highly restricted life, and her fears, while they are childish, are at least excusable, because she knows so little about the outside world, and fears it just the way a child fears the dark. But you are a different kettle of fish, and you ought to know better, and show better sense. You may consider this a good sound scolding, and that is what it is. No more coddling of your delusions! I'm going to put you in a strait jacket and make you tow the mark. Stop inventing your future frights. What would you do if somebody cried "Boo!" at you right now? I hate to think!

It is 88 degrees hot here today. Boiling desert weather and quite perfect. Yet every night at 8, Santa Claus drives through the Boulevard in a "sleigh" pulled by silver reindeers. A steam engine puffs false snow into the air, and people stand on the sidewalks and sing "Jingle Bells." The court of the Chinese Theater has a dozen huge pine Xmas trees, covered with white powder snow and trying desperately to get a New England Xmas effect. It is quite pathetic the way the populace works to get the illusion of winter. Almost as hard as you work over your illusions of misery.

  Max

 The manuscript of the play Max wrote based on Doris's experiences, first called Margaret *and then* The Greatest Good, *is in the*

Yale University Beinecke collection. As A.E.'s letter states, he and Lotta gave it their blessing.

[About December 22, 1933]

Dear Uncle,

    I have just hastily written the enclosed story which I think contains a lot of good "movie material." The writing is slipshod and the typing careless, but I do not want to really polish it and "whip it into shape" until I receive an O.K. from you or Aunt Lotta. As you will discover when you read the story various episodes in it parallel similar ones in the life of a friend of ours! But I do not think the parallels are exact enough to cause any uneasiness anywhere. The second half of the story is pure fiction and complete invention. In the first part I have simply utilized the skeleton plot of an athletic girl who makes an inappropriate marriage, gets out of it, flounders around for a couple of years, and then goes unexpectedly abroad to new adventure. I feel she would probably feel highly gratified. The girl in the story is certainly presented in the most sympathetic possible light, and has a complete heart of gold!

    Events in actual life seldom follow in any dramatic order or climactic sequence, so I have made everything over to suit my purposes, added new people when I needed them, and made my own motives for everyone's acts. I have made the heroine as sympathetic as possible. Sometimes the people in the story are not sympathetic with her, but that is a device used to increase "audience sympathy." I think the story now moves along quite logically to a dramatic finish. As it now stands, I think it would provide a good movie "vehicle" for a star like Joan Crawford, or Barbara Stanwyck, or Elissa Landi, or especially Margaret Sullivan. Margaret is a new screen actress who has made only one starring film, "Only Yesterday." See it if you get a chance in order to visualize her in this story. Universal is looking for story material for her. I think she would be the best of them in this particular story, and it is with her in mind that I named the heroine Margaret.

If you thought it advisable I could sell the story under an assumed name, and no one but ourselves would ever need to know that any Ewings in existence had anything to do with it. Of course, when I say "sell the story," I mean TRY to sell it. There is no certainty that I could sell it, and even if I did, the film would probably not be made for more than a year, for all the important stars have two or three stories lined up in advance, and it takes several months to film each one. However I think this story has a chance. If you have any objections at all to its being filmed, be quick to say so, and there will be no spilt milk to worry about for anyone!

I don't know what the story could sell for. It would depend on the importance of the star it was bought for. Whatever price it sold for, I would have to pay my agent ten percent for selling it for me. After that I think it would be only fair to pay the next ten percent to Doris for the accommodation in having suggested the story! I don't have any idea how much that would be, but it ought to go quite a way toward another trip home—or maybe, more appropriately, a trip to ROME.

This is just one of a lot of stories that I am turning out. Nothing to do with "literature" of course. For original movie stories they want just a simple, present tense synopsis of what HAPPENS. Dialogue and all the rest of it are supplied later in a "screen treatment." It is all rather imbecilic, but I am trying hard to learn to be an imbecile—while here!
    Max

If you do O.K. the story please send it back to me for revision. If you don't you may destroy it.

Saturday [about December 23, 1933]

Dear Mother,

Was never more startled than to get your note this morning with check enclosed. Where did you ever get a hundred dollars! I was completely under the impression that for the immediate time being you were down to your bottom dollar, and that I was NEVER to expect ANOTHER CENT from any quarter except from my own efforts. Hence my recent Herculean efforts! If you have access to enough money that you can send me a hundred dollars just out of a clear sky, then you must stop this talk about not being able to buy a loaf of bread for Doddy's supper. If I hear of any more of that kind of talk I shall send this money back to you, for I really do not need it. I have hundreds of dollars already, enough to last me for months to come. This is just extra, and I have it in the bank for safe keeping. I may or may not rent a piano. I may just SPONGE on friends' pianos.

It is a comfort to know you got down town. Probably twice in one week was too much of a good thing after such a long seclusion. Don't go again for two weeks, and then go just ONCE.

I enclose letter from Phillip Moeller of the Theater Guild just to convince you that I am not talking hot air when I talk about my play. Please send his letter back to me in your next. Don't forget to do this. For I may need it to shake it in the face of agents here, by way of proving my N.Y. connections.

Max

Dec. 26, 1933

347 Charles Ave. SE [Grand Rapids]

Max Ewing
1825 Whitley Ave.
Hollywood, Calif.

Dear Max:

Synopsis of "The Greatest Good" came today and Lotta and I read it over from start to finish. We have no objections whatever to your using the material as you have. You have kept far enough away from real names and actual places to conceal the incidents which suggested the theme to all except those who may know the inside and who also know you and your intimate acquaintance with a back ground character. If it is ever put on the screen, not one person in ten million would catch the analogy. So far as I am concerned, go ahead and make the most of it possible.

I will let Lotta speak for herself. Both of us enjoyed the sketch, even in the rough—as you say it was—and if you can improve it by further study of the details, more power to you.

We are returning MS herewith.

Sincerely,

A.E. Ewing

Wednesday, Dec. 27 [1933]

Darling Mother,

Got your letter today with the twenty dollars. Thank you twenty thousand times, but you were very extravagant to send so much. I spent only fifty cents on you: but I want you to USE that day book to put down the happy dates of the coming year, and they are going to be pleasant, believe me. I'm sorry I wrote too soon that I wasn't hearing from you at Christmas. All the mail got delayed a day or two because of the Xmas rush.

I had as merry a Christmas as possible under all the circumstances. Went to Margaret Hawkins' dinner party in the middle of the day. And at night had supper with Paul Draper who is here for a month, headlining on the stage bill at the Chinese Theater. He is looking fine and is in high spirits over his good job. He was quite surprised to learn from me that

Muriel [Draper] had been here. He never knows quite where she is. And when she was here she complained to me that he hadn't written to her since she left N.Y. They adore each other as few people do, but they don't take much time off to write!

Christmas was warm and sunny, but today the clouds are out. I took a week off for Holiday celebrations, and today I am at work again on my new (third) play. Will write all week, and then relax again over the New Years weekend. I sent Tallulah my second play, which is safely copyrighted and registered and insured and everything. I ought to hear from her within a week or ten days. Today's mail brought another letter from the Merlin office in N.Y. begging me to send the second play to them if not the first one. There is great interest everywhere in everything I write, and it is all just a question of time now before everything is fine and dandy. As far as I'm concerned it's fine and dandy already. You are still lagging behind in spirit, but you'll catch up in the end.

I swear to God I'm not writing you cheerful news just to "buoy you up." That would be the meanest trick in the world, if I did not believe with all my heart that what I am saying to you is true. I believe everything I write to you. And you must too. You owe it to me to believe it. You owe a lot to me, and I don't mean you owe me any money. I don't give a hang about money. You owe me your support in a different sort of way, and you owe it to me to get strong and well and stop being so crestfallen. Forget your filthy lucre for a little while. From now on the filthy lucre is my problem. I assume the responsibility, and I will solve the problem. Get a new attitude about me and about yourself and about the NEW YEAR which is just about to begin, and EVERYTHING WILL BE ALL RIGHT.

      Max

Friday [December 29, 1933]

Dear Mother,

    This is to wish you a real Happy New Year. If only I could do something to make you realize that it is a happy new year, and if only these words might not fall on deaf ears. But I am very much afraid that they will. Everything I have written you all these weeks seems to have fallen on deaf ears, for you do not seem to accept it or to believe in it with any confidence. And I am very much discouraged—discouraged ONLY about you and your condition. About everything else I am more encouraged than I ever have been in my life. If ONLY you could just pull yourself together RIGHT NOW, when I am on the very brink of such success. These next three months should be the most exciting and gratifying of my whole life. But they will not be if you do not brace up and share them with me. I do not know whether the important development will be here or in New York. But I do know one thing—and that is that unless your condition changes rapidly for the better, I shall not be either here or in New York. I am returning to Pioneer next month, sometime late in January, unless you show marked improvement in every way by that time. And I want the word of your doctor and friends as well as your own to convince me.

    I mean this. I have reached the limit of my period of "watchful waiting" out here. And this difference between you being so miserable there and me being so comfortable here is too much, and it cannot go on. You may not realize it, but this illness of yours has been a terrific strain on me too. Ever since last August I have opened every letter with fear and trembling, and I jump at telegrams as if I had been shot. I received quite a lot of telegrams over the holidays, but the arrival of every one was like an electric shock. I have waited and waited, week after week, for some sign of improvement in your outlook, but you seem now just as unreasonably downcast as you did two months ago or three months ago.

I do not know what on God's earth I can do to change this attitude by returning to Pioneer, but I only know that I must return and see what I can do. My conscience will not let me stay away much longer. All I can do when I get there is to tell you over and over again what I have already written you over and over again—that nothing that has happened is of any ultimate importance at all. Even if all the money is gone it does not matter a damn. One dollar is as good as any other dollar, and plenty of new dollars are coming my way. I haven't a qualm in the world, or regret, except the regret that you take it so hard. When I sell one of my plays or stories to the movies I will automatically be offered a job at the studio to work on the "adaptations," but I am giving up such ideas to return to you. I would never draw a peaceful breath as long as I live if you just went on getting worse and worse, and I stayed on out here without doing anything about it. I repeat, I do not know what I can do. But I must return and try my darndest. My rent is paid here until after mid-January. After that I shall pack up, and take on a new job, working over you day and night, and laughing off these nonsensical worries with you. UNLESS, you take yourself in charge a little bit in the meantime, and show some results yourself. This letter is not prompted by any more "scare letters" from Pioneer friends. It is simply the expression of my own opinion, arrived at after weeks of nightmarish wondering and waiting and hoping and being disappointed. Your gloomy letters started last August, and since then there has scarcely been more than one or two rays of light in anything you have written. I have felt that you MUST snap out if it sooner or later, but you don't seem to without me so we'll see what you'll do WITH me.

Seeing you then very soon unless you show your spunk and get better. Max

The following letter was numbered page 2, and probably goes with the letter above. It clearly was written about the same time.

Paul Draper has just been in again, wanting me to come to see him in his show tonight, but I can't tonight because Rosalind Harrison is taking me to hear Stowitts lecture. The days and nights are fairly active this week.

Noel Sullivan wanted me to come and visit him and Langston Hughes over Christmas at Carmel-by-the-Sea, but I declined. A friend of mine here named Charles Crouch, has a family living in San Diego, and he invited me down there over the coming New Years weekend, but I have declined that. I am in such a state about you that I do not want to be out of reach if you need me—out of reach even for a weekend. Besides these particular weeks right now I have so many irons in the fire, in studios here, and in New York too, that I want to stay put and be constantly available for all sorts of communication. Tallulah Bankhead visited her father in Alabama over Xmas day, and she returns to N.Y. today which is just about when the play should arrive there. It has already been published in the New York Journal that Tallulah Bankhead is practically well and is eagerly looking forward to appearing in a new play by Max Ewing. Of course this report is not authentic for she had not seen the play when the report was published. It was only a report that leaked out into one of the many gossip columns which are syndicated from Hollywood. But it just goes to show that good omens are in the air.

Emily is in San Francisco with husband. On their way to Honolulu. Noel saw her and said she was flourishing.

All my N.Y. friends were very loyal about Christmas remembrances. My desk is piled high with greetings and telegrams. Everyone is excited over Muriel's forthcoming New Years Eve party, and everyone says I will be missed very much. The Sheldons sent a card showing Dorothy and Roy and their cat, Pouf, pushing hard against a half closed door—"keeping the wolf from the door!" All those people are broke, and they are all gay and brave and gallant and carrying on. Why must you be so difficult when you know damn well you could live good and well for the next three years without doing a single thing but draw out from Spitzer Rorick. Half my friends do not know what they will be drawing on in the next three months. You are the only one I know though who complains and grieves. Everyone else takes the sock between the eyes, staggers for a few minutes, and then goes on. You must too. No looking back. Look ahead. And let ME point the way.

  Max

Tuesday, Jan. 2 [1934]

Dear Clarissa,

  Just got your letter, with enclosed Pruddens check. I can't imagine what it means or where it came from, since everything we own is lost lost lost beyond recall. But anyway I have banked it. Seriously though, do not send me any more money unless you don't know what to do with it. For I don't know either. All I can do is bank it, and it will mean just that much more to bring back East with me, if I go back soon, as I wrote you last week I would do unless you take a sharp turn for the better. And I still mean it if nothing else can restore you to better health and better sense, then maybe my presence can. In any case I feel obligated to try it. If I don't do you any good then I will come away again.

  You have probably read about our big New Years rain. I seem to have struck a record breaking year out here in every way. September was the coldest on record in California. November was the hottest on record in California. And this was the heaviest and worst rain in 50 years! It poured cats and dogs for more than 48 hours without stopping, but it was the first hard rain in eight months. It caused a lot of damage, but it didn't cause me any, as I stayed in and let it rain. There was nothing else one could do. Paul Draper came around in his Cadillac (he is making loads of money suddenly) which he has rented for the length of his stay here, and took me out to dinner Sunday evening. We sailed through the streets as if we were in Venice. After dinner he drove me home, with water covering the streets and sidewalks. This was New Years Eve. Obviously I could not go out again, but some friends of mine came in, two boys named Tony Purdy and Richard Ames, friends of Jack Becket's [Becker's], and whom I met when I first came out here. Two other friends from San Diego came too. We saw the New Year in together while the deluge fell outside. Then when these boys were ready to go home, the problem was how to get them home. They telephoned for a taxi, but the taxi companies had stopped even answering their telephones because the demand was so great. And when they finally did answer they said they could not promise a taxi in less time than an hour and a half. So we settled down again to a long vigil. To walk ten steps in the rain would have meant getting drenched to the skin. In the end it proved impossible to get any taxi at all. So finally they had to send for a LIMOUSINE, the sort that drives people out from one town to another. I don't know what it cost them, but they had to get away, as it was now nearly four o'clock. I could not put up FOUR extra people for the night, though I did put up the two from San Diego. When Tony Purdy and Rick Ames got nearly home they found there had been a landslide and the road to their house was unpassable, so they had to get out and walk in mud KNEE DEEP. More than 8 inches of rain had fallen, if you can imagine such a thing. It is unheard-of out here.

 In spite of the rain, the Pasadena New Years Rose Tournament and Parade took place anyway, the most insane thing you could dream of. Dozens and dozens of great flower floats costing hundreds of thousands of dollars, plowed thru the drizzle, with girls in chiffon draperies all wringing wet riding on the floats, and thousands of people lined up in the streets under umbrellas! Everyone was drenched, but no one went in. I think all people are lunatics. It was quite a happy New Year for me in spite of the handicaps of the elements. It was dramatic anyway. Today is bright and fair again, but lots of bridges and things like that have been washed away.

Get rid of this notion that you are not "worthy" of me, and that your mind is "bad." It is NOT bad. But you have been bad to let yourself get so out of control. Now you take yourself in charge and let everything else go hang for a period of three months. At the end of that time I assure you we will be sitting pretty in every way. You do not need the store income for at least three months. And the mice can't eat the whole stock in that time either. If you would just sleep and eat and IMPROVE and BUILD UP for three months without giving a thought to our pasteboard and paper worries, everything would be all right. Won't you TRY?

    Max

5. Home Again

    A.E. Ewing received several messages from friends of his brother's family in Pioneer, Ohio, who were concerned about the state of Clara's health. In later correspondence A.E. reported that Clara had contemplated suicide and three times had to be "pulled from the cistern." A postcard written on Thursday, January 4, 1934 and mailed from Pioneer, said, "My dear Sir. Things not to good at home have sent for Max as the neighbors are frightened, [Clara is] quite determined to do something big, and looks dreadful. Wants to go to Toledo once more, chances are slim as the 'House Girl' & boy friend are tired of the performances. My endurance has left me. Can not stand any more. Felt sorry you did not come down, as there is a great deal to talk about, but M. [Max] is the one I think to straighten the kinks out. Hope you and yours are well. We are. Respectfully The 'Stove Woman.' She is determined not to see Max again." Russell H. Bready, Minister of the Methodist Episcopal Church serving southern Hillsdale County and northern Williams County, wrote to A.E. the next day. In his first paragraph he noted that "some of the Pioneer people had arisen on their hind legs and sent Max a wire saying that he must come at once and moreover they had his reply saying that he was starting and that he would arrive in Chicago Sunday." The third letter, received by A.E. on January 6, follows in its entirety.

[about January 5, 1934]

Mr. Ewing

Dear Sir—

    We have sent for Max and we received a wire that he will be here Sun—Mr. Touse will meet him—Mrs. E. [Clara] was determined to get rid of herself, and we could stand no more—She is determined not to ever see Max again—so we dare not give a hint of his coming for she will do something drastic—We think it advisable for you people to come, and be present when Max arrives—Use your own judgement, but I am afraid the shock will be too much for her—Please Mr. Ewing excuse pencil. I am invoicing & in a great hurry. Yours resp

  Mrs. F.E. Touse

P.S. We have no idea when he will reach Montpelier [Ohio]

Friday [January 5, 1934]

The California Limited
Santa Fe
en route

 Am on my way East. Expect to be on Pioneer Sunday. I don't know what to expect when I get there, but am hoping for the best. In any case, Uncle I hope you are planning to come to Pioneer for a day or two as soon after that as seems convenient. I will need plenty of legal advice and information. You may call it a professional job & give me a bill!

 Thanks for the O.K. of my Doris story. My Hollywood agent has it and I hope it sells.

 New Mexico is very rough!

  Max

A letter from The Theatre Guild, also written on January 5, eventually was forwarded to Max in Pioneer. The Guild rejected Max's "The Golden Girls." Similar rejections were received from Fox Film Corporation the next month and from Brandt & Brandt Dramatic Department in May. The latter returned both of Max's three-act plays.

Sunday [January 14, 1934]

Dear Uncle,

It's too early to say for sure, but I think we have some good results. Things are much calmer. Yesterday was a good day in every way, & both nights have been fairly quiet. Today there have been some flare ups, but short ones, & less lively than the first of the week. I think they are "tapering off." I think I can get Mother to go to church tonight, & that is quite a feat if I do it.

Will keep you posted. Things are not right by any means, but they are unquestionably better.
   Max

Tuesday [January 17, 1934]

Dear Uncle,

  Our patient is much better physically. She walks without wobbling and she had 3 nights sleep without drugs. Last night she was restless and needed her tablets again. Today all is fairly quiet. [Rev. Russell] Bready and Judge Holt and all that are now forgotten. Her March taxes are now the main difficulty!

  I think the will to live is still in her pretty strong for yesterday she thought she was catching cold. And you never saw such efforts as she made to avoid having the cold. She took cold tablets and smelled camphor for hours, and rubbed her throat with musterole & wrapped up in woolen clothes. All this to avoid a minor illness—and at the same time she talks about not wanting to live. But I guess her actions speaker louder than words—

  No further news today—
  Max

Friday [January 19, 1934]

Toledo Ohio

Dear Uncle,

This is to report a miracle. We have got Mother into a good sanitarium here in Toledo—against her will, of course, and without her knowing until we got her there.

Mrs. Grant and Mrs. Bowersox drove to Pioneer yesterday & saw what a condition Mother was in and realized that I could not put up with such a condition indefinitely at home. So we induced her to drive back to Toledo last night for a little visit. This morning she was in such bad shape that we just had to force the issue and take her to the hospital and leave her. She will probably rebel at first, but there she is, and there is nothing she can do about it. And we will get a little relief ourselves—and this is the best way I know of to handle such a difficult case. We will try a few weeks of this special care and see if she rallies. If she does not then I just don't know what to do next

You might write her a letter & tell her she is doing the right thing. Her address is

    The Toledo Sanitarium
    2102 Cherry St
    Toledo Ohio

Mother is under the impression that it is a free clinic. Of course it is not. Far from it!

You can write to me at Pioneer as usual.

    Max

Wednesday [January 24, 1934]

Pioneer

Dear Uncle,

This is to report that there is nothing much to report. I took Mother to the Toledo Sanitarium last Friday, and left her there. I have not seen her since, as it is against the doctor's orders for her to see relatives and friends at first. We would only stir her up and get her mind in its old track, while they are trying to get her on a new one.

I keep in communication with the nurse, of course, and she says Mother is eating well, three big meals a day, because she is given powerful stomach stimulant that makes her very hungry. Also she is sleeping a lot day and night. It may be due to bromides, but at least it prevents her from pacing and climbing around and wearing herself down that way.

Mother wants very much to get away and come home, but that is impossible, and we just have to ignore that desire. It is too bad that she is unhappy in the hospital, but the answer to that is that she is just as unhappy at home. As soon as she begins to feel considerably better she will be glad she is there and that she went there. I may see her this weekend, or certainly the first of the week. Meanwhile, the more letters she receives the better. I hope Aunt Lotta will write her too, at the sanitarium, at 2012 Cherry St. Toledo. I have got the license tags for the car, and it is in good working order for 1934. Next time I go to Toledo I will go in it. We are getting along very well here in Pioneer. The household is quiet and orderly, and I hope to get some work done. More later.

    Max

There are gaps in Max's correspondence between January 24 and February 16. In a message to Max written on February 8, A.E. recapitulated one of Max's recent letters. "We noted—with smiles for which you will have to excuse us—your string of tragic setbacks beginning with knee-deep snow, then zero weather, your building fire at store, selling ten cents worth of merchandise, spending it all to have the ashes removed, then having the ash man faint away, just when the town doctor had an undressed woman strapt down for a treatment (treat 'em rough, doc, treat 'em rough!) Then to cap it all, touch off the burglar alarm and arouse the town. What a time, what a time! That's 'comedy of errors' enough to engage a Shakespeare. As if that wasn't enuf for one day, 'to be cooked or not to be cooked' had to be fought out over a salmon's corpse. If experience makes the man you should soon be a giant. Don't ever count such time lost."

On February 3, 1934 Max sent Florine Stettheimer a postcard: "Dear Florine—I dreamed about 'Four Saints' last night, and I'm sure la Divinda Providencia has its eye on its success! Do send me an account of it anon. I'll be listening in Thursday night. I wish there were television so I could see your share in it. Max (PS Please give my congratulations and regrets to Virgil.) Front of p/c "La Divina Providencia" Four Saints in Three Acts *premiered at the Wadsworth Athenaeum in Hartford, Connecticut on February 7. 1934. Max's card makes it clear he knew about the opera, composed by Virgil Thompson with libretto by Gertrude Stein and featuring an all-Black cast. Florine Stettheimer designed the sets. Max's wish for television was a prophetic look into the far future.*

It's unlikely that Max went through this "*comedy of errors*" with the same sense of levity as his uncle.

Feb. 16 [1934]

Pioneer

Dear Uncle,

Enclosed are the papers which I trust are adequately signed up and ok. I hope all goes through all right. Hang on to the money at the Kent Bank until further notice. I think I'll wait and have you send it to me in New York. I'm going to have to make a trip to N.Y. sooner or later, even if only a brief one. And I don't want to put any more money in this bank at present. It is in a new upheaval of some sort again, and Herm

Higley was put out of it this week. The details are still obscure, and none too savory.

A new bank upheaval is all we need. The weather continues to hover around zero. No rain in sight, and so no water. I have had the flu all week, and so did not get to Toledo. Today Frances [Bollinger] has it. Only Doddy survives intact, and is up daily with the crack of dawn, overseeing this, managing and ordering and commanding that. She goes through every day like Hannibal crossing the Alps. Otherwise, we are arrived at a new low of depression, boredom, and discomfort. But we have practically reached the saturation point of all three, and each new mishap adds but little to the general total. It is like sub zero weather. Once it gets below zero it doesn't matter much whether it is five below or twenty below. The discomfort remains about the same. I expect to go to Toledo Monday if the walls don't cave in before then. I received Aunt Lotta's Valentine note. Also a card from Joe Brewer inviting me to dinner at Olivet last night, but I am forced to decline all bids into Michigan for the nonce.

I telephoned the sanitarium last night and the nurse said Mother had had a good week, but that the zero wave gave her a setback because she worried so about pipes.

Max

Feb 23 [1934]

Pioneer

Dear Uncle,

I am still snowbound, and unable to drive the old Studebaker over the ice and snow drifts. I am over my cold, but am only a coal stoker and snow shoveler these days. Frances went to Toledo yesterday, with a friend of hers, and went to see Mother. This is the first time Frances has seen her in over a month, and she brings home a very discouraging report. She thought Mother seemed no better and no different in any way and even thinner than before. I don't see how this can be possible, and I hope to get down there myself Monday. I am worried and at my wits end. The sanitarium is apparently doing her little of no good. It is impossible to bring her back into such a hell of a household as this one is at present, with no water, and zero weather. I don't know what to do about anything or anybody.

I telephone the sanitarium from time to time, and of course the nurse always tells me Mother is "doing nicely." But Frances says she certainly is not.

I am writing today to that man from Saginaw who wanted to buy the store, to tell him to come and buy it if he still wants it. For it is plain by now, that whether Mother gets well or not, she will not be well for weeks and months, and undoubtedly will never be well enough to be in business again.

The tax report blanks are here and I am going to fill them out and send them in myself, without her knowing it, as her deputy, for she is completely unable to cope with it.

I wish I knew what to do about the money on the closed bank in Toledo. The bank closed four or five years ago, and Dad and Mother had some nine thousand dollars in it. It looked as if the bank were closed for good and all, and Mother did not declare this money when filling her inheritance tax report. The bank is still closed but some arrangement has been made whereby depositors can sell their accounts for about 65 per cent of the value, against the time when the bank may sometime come back. I think it is better to have six thousand dollars in hand than a possible eventual nine thousand in the bush, and I would like to bring it to the surface, and pay the back inheritance tax, and get the money free to use it in case I need it, and I guess I'm going to have to need plenty. What step should I take about this? Would you do it now, or wait until these intangible taxes are paid?

The bank fracas here has calmed down, and the only result is the Higley is out, on account of some swindling he put over on an old bird more than ninety years old.

Is the $901.00 in G.R. ok and available now? If so, just hang on to it in the Kent bank. We will settle up for all your services when we meet next. You deserve more than just your expenses.

Doddy is up at the crack of dawn daily, so that she will have a longer day to worry through. When I came here I felt confident that the first month would be the hardest. But from the looks of things now, it's going to be progressively and increasingly harder and harder.
Max

March 5 [1934]

Pioneer

Dear Uncle,

Quite a lot of water has been flowing under the bridge since I wrote last—and also into the cistern. I spent three days in Toledo last week, and moved Mother from the sanitarium to the home of a nurse. This is a graduate nurse who takes care of three patients in her own home, which is a very attractive place overlooking park and Maumee River. She has had nervous patients like Mother before, and seems very efficient, and I'm sure Mother will like it there better, once she gets used to it. Of course she did not want to go. She wanted to come home. But that is still impossible, though I think she is better. The day Frances saw her was one of her "bad days" which she has occasionally, and also Mother undoubtedly was giving a species of "performance" for Frances
. . .

She still talks very unreasonably about her money troubles, but she talks in a far stronger voice and far more lucid way about them. Still, I was not satisfied with her progress under the doctor or the nurse where she was. She was getting hearty meals, but they were meals of a boarding house type, and not properly balanced. This new nurse understands more about food values than the other nurse. And I am changing doctors too, because the former doctor, Dr. Miller seemed peeved because we moved Mother out of the sanitarium in which he has an interest. He refused to cooperate with the new nurse, so I dismissed him. He is sort of a nut himself; for he has dealt with psychopathic cases so long he has almost got off his track himself.

So there is a whole new regime now, and I hope it will bring swifter results.

The Saginaw man writes that he will take the stock if sold at a sacrifice, but he will not take over the buildings and run the store. He would just clear it out, and leave the buildings empty. So that does not sound good.

I am going ahead and getting the Toledo bank matter straightened out. It should not take long or cost much. I was held up for weeks because of the fiendish weather, and could not even get to Bryan, but now it is warmer and I am going to do everything in sight, and then clear out. It is not as if my presence here gave any pleasure to anybody. My presence only antagonizes Mother in the state she is in. And Doddy hears nothing I say, and is interested, in nothing I say even if she hears it. She would much prefer someone who could discuss the local gossip and the food and the weather and the garbage and curtains and the grave digging and jelly and the underwear and the window-washing and stocking-darning and the motor accidents and all the other things she finds so fascinating.

Yesterday Jack [Pollock] and I drove into Toledo just for the day to lunch with Gilbert Seldes who came there to lecture from New York, and Joe Brewer who came from Olivet to see Gilbert. We lunched in Toledo, and then we all drove in a caravan to Pioneer where we had hamburger and coffee in the joint on road #20 near the cemetery. I did not bring them to the house, as I thought my grandmother would not be exactly hospitable. She is not in her best mood these days . . . the days continue to pass. I hardly see how they did it, poor things.

Max

Included with the March 5 letter was a business card for Ila May Hoy's "Private Convalescent Home: Special Care for the Aged and Invalids." The home was located in Toledo, Ohio. On the back of the card Max wrote: "This is Mother's address. I feel sure it would do her good to hear from you. Tell her anything—just gossip." A day or two later, Jack was gone.

Pioneer

Monday [March 12, 1934]

Dear Uncle,

Thinking things over, I believe I will have you send me the $901.00 from the Kent Bank, if it is in the form of a check which I can bank simply. I am getting very active these days about centralizing things, and I want to concentrate the various deposits as much as possible, and not have them scattered in little lots from Pioneer to Toledo, and from Montpelier to New York, and to Grand Rapids and back again. The bank is perfectly safe here, accounts and deposits are insured up to $2500.00, so I want to put the $901 on deposit here until further notice. Could you send it promptly without any bother to you? I am paying the taxes this week, and getting a release from the County Auditor on that Toledo bank account, and doing everything I can to get things squared away for a while, so that I can get away for a while. I can't bear things as they are much longer. Doddy was up at daybreak this morning raising hell because Frances was not up. She drove my friend Jack Pollock not only out of the house but out of the country. He has gone to Alaska!

I had a quite encouraging letter from Mother's new nurse, saying that Mother "minds" her, and rests well and eats well. But I had a letter from Mother saying that the nurse had just bought a new Buick on the money I had paid her (for less than two weeks care!) so that shows she is still off her track. I don't know what else is going to happen.

   Max

Friday [March 16, 1934]

Pioneer

Dear Uncle,

  This is to acknowledge the receipt of the check for $901.00 on the Old Kent Bank. It is now duly banked again in the old Pioneer Bank. I drew up a list of assets that could be readily turned into cash, and sent the list to Mother a few days ago, thinking it would reassure her. I had a reply from her today saying, "We have more money than I thought."

  She is writing to me often now in a good firm old time Clara Ewing handwriting, DEMANDING to come home, because it is costing so much to be where she is. She is unquestionably better. But for a while now, the better she gets the worse she is, if you follow me. For with returning strength of body and mind she will get increasingly willful and rebellious. When she first went to Toledo she was so weak she could not protest too much. Now she is able to protest good and proper.

  Aunt Lotta telephoned from Hillsdale today and asked me to come up there tonight, but I had other plans. She now plans to stay until

Sunday and come down then, and there is a plan on foot that we may drive in to see Toledo Sunday to see Mother. So she will probably have a lot of things to relate when she sees you. Thank you Sunday for the Eaglewing poem. Just how much significance is one to read into the letters of Eaglewing?

    Doddy is baking pies and pies today. She found a bottle of Mother's Milk of Magnesia in the cupboard yesterday, and she said she didn't know what we were going to do with all that Cream of Wheat. It goes on like that.

    Thank you for sending the check and for all the other efforts you have made.

              Max

P.S. George Town showed up yesterday, resembling a species of bear. I had never seen him, and he arrived before I was up, and facing such a strange apparition before breakfast gave me quite a turn. We talked over the mortgage. I said I would like to have it paid and squared away, because I was trying to get all the odds and ends tied up or untied, anyway off my mind. He said he would like to pay it but money was hard to get. I said I knew it. He said he would pay in May if he could. I said do your best. And he went away, leaving things just as they were before he came, except that I was now awake.

Thursday [March 22, 1934]

Pioneer

Dear Uncle AND AUNT:

    This is to inform you that Mother is home again. Lenore Bowersox and I brought her back from Toledo yesterday, on the doctor's suggestion. She was so much better he felt she would continue to improve faster here. She came home in good spirits, eats enormous meals, is crying for pancakes and sausage at this moment! She sleeps

fairly well, and rests often, and she does not discuss finance exclusively. She seems eager for outside stimulus but there isn't much here, as you know. I do wish you would write to her now. She is very thin and still weak, but she is quiet, and no longer frantic in any way. I only hope it keeps up as well as it has started now. She doesn't know what to do about the store, and God knows it stumps me too. I'm sorry I missed hooking up with Aunt Lotta, but I wish you could both come down again now. Could you?
     Max

Wednesday [March 26, 1934]

Pioneer

Dear Uncle,

  Thanks for your letter to Mother—But I am discouraged and without hope now. I wrote you that when she came home she was quiet in every way—but I now think it is the quiet of exhaustion rather than of improvement—the quiet that precedes the end. Her nerves are calm & her mind is clear, but she has such agonizing pain around her heart, and such upset digestion and constipation. And she is twice as thin as when you saw her last. I have a sneaking suspicion that the doctors advised her return home simply because they knew nothing could be done anywhere, and that she might as well be in congenial surroundings at least. I have been very brave and hopeful up to now—but today I am about giving out. She had to have a hyperdermic last night to ease the unbearable heart pain. She is still asleep, breathing heavily, and I don't know what to expect when she awakens. But I really don't believe that the end can be far off. She just hasn't a grain of strength left to rally with or revive with or so it seems. I would love to see you anytime—and don't be surprised if you get summoned on short notice.
  Max

The situation was too much for Frances Bollinger to handle & she has gone home. We have a practical nurse named Mrs. Kelly in the house who is doing all that can be done.

   Max

Friday [March 30, 1934]

Pioneer

Dear Uncle,

  Your letter was full of valuable suggestions which I may heed later. At present I am attending only to the more immediate issues of life and death. Yesterday we had all given up all hope. The Bready's were here, and Dr. Bready thought it was only a matter of hours. So did I. Mother just lay in an absolute stupor, and had been in one for nearly 48 hours. Last night the house was full of all the women of the neighborhood, who sat up with her in relays. Mrs. Bready, Mrs. Ferris, Mrs. Gilpin, Besse Durbin, as well as the nurse, Mrs. Kelly. But today she has revived a little, and while she is not perceptibly better, she is not perceptibly worse. She is surviving only on fruit juices, and has not had proper bowel elimination for a week. Poor Doddy is getting to be almost as great a problem as Mother. Night before last she wailed and walked the floor until I thought I would have to have a hypodermic given her. She was weak as a reed yesterday morning, and trembled from head to foot and could hardly stand on her feet, and her voice was as faint as possible. But two hours later, she was in the kitchen helping Mrs. Kelly do the WASHING. They are two unpredictable women, and when they seem down to their very last ounce of strength, some new flood of it always seems to appear from somewhere. Today Doddy is gathering up buckets of snow to melt and put into the reservoir!

After six weeks of maneuvering between Bryan and Toledo and Columbus, I at last got the Toledo Bank matter straightened out, and the final necessary documents of release arrived this morning. Now that account of approximately $10,000.00 is entirely cleared of encumbrance, and is in my name. It cannot be withdrawn of course, but it can be sold. The present prices are: bid 67—Ask 72. So I could easily get $6700.00, and I might get $7200.00. I brought the good news home to Mother, and at first she said she didn't believe it. Then she said Bryan would get after me, but I convinced her that Bryan knew all about it. Then she said it would not last long anyway! But finally she agreed that she was pleased over it, and that I did have a little business sense after all! She refused to smile at me, but I knew she felt some relief anyway.

The weather remains abominable—snow to the knees, slush to the ankles, and fierce winds that howl all night. It is the perfect setting for a nightmare, and that is what we have here constantly. I now take sedatives to get myself to sleep. I don't know how long it is all going to go on, or what to expect from one day to the next. At any rate, we are living just from one day to the next, and that is all we can do. Would love to see you any time, of course, but don't know what if anything specific that you could do. Will keep you posted at intervals.

Max

Tuesday [April 3, 1934]

Pioneer

Dear Uncle,

There is little to report except that everything is slowly but surely worse. There can be no doubt that the end is approaching—but there is no telling when it will come. Frances Bollinger has come back & is in charge of the kitchen. The nurse stays constantly with Mother, who is just about wasted away. It is so dreadful. I get thru the days somehow, I don't know how. Thank Aunt Alice [Ewing] for her letter & her offer, but I don't what she could do just now.

   Max

Thursday, I think [about April 5, 1934]

Pioneer

Dear Uncle,

  Got your letter. Am too disinterested in Lewis Valentine's proposal to reply to it.

  Sinus has let up, but my general condition seems downward. Am just swamped and bewildered by everything that got Mother down, and she understood it, while I don't. If it were not that I knew that their motive was that of indulgence and generosity, I would resent the fact that I was never brought up to know more about their affairs. I suppose it was my fault too. Or rather that it was no one's FAULT. But it is certainly my misfortune. It is exactly as if I were transplanted to China and alone had to build the Great Wall. I re-read the letters I wrote to Mother from California, and they sound like such childish drivel, bidding her to get her mind off these worries, and minimize them, when I understand now that she simply couldn't, and that they are enough to swamp a whole brain trust.

  Clara Sweet is helping me with various things, and wants me to go to Toledo and consult a friend of hers. I expect to go there tomorrow and stay until the first of the week again, maybe until Tuesday or Wednesday. Would like to see you soon after that. May telephone you if it becomes urgent. I wish you would write to Judge Holt, saying I have been ill and you have been busy, and that we will be delayed, for we certainly will.

  George Town paid off the mortgage at Hillsdale the other day. Wish you could have seen me in the courthouse. I was like a village idiot. Wasn't even sure what it meant to "discharge" it. Sounded like a pistol to me. But I bungled through, and was given more money than I expected.

Two people named Miller, man and wife, are going to stay with Doddy, for the house. Have found the deed, which Mother thoughtfully put back into Doddy's name by quit claim in January when she was half wild. My admiration for her mounts from day to day, and I so regret my frequent impatience with her during those winter days, when she seemed so unreasonable, but really was not. Still, again, it was not my fault. It was only my faulty understanding. How little of us understand another's processes.

I got the troublesome check cashed in Toledo and deposited it. Tried to sell some other stock, but was told I would have to have separate letters of administration for every variety of stock, that is seven or eight letters, and tax waivers too. These last will be troublesome, as some stocks had not been listed. I tried in Montpelier to cash some postal saving certificates, but they had not been signed, and correspondence between Montpelier, Washington and Pioneer, must go on indefinitely. It looks as if I would just have to be here for weeks or months, and Uncle A.E. I swear I can't. I just can't. This place is getting me down and I look like nothing I've ever seen.

Doddy rises at daybreak and is alert and gay and constantly active until late at night, rounding up junk men, mending old rags of carpet, doing incredible and maddening things in a very cheerful way. Frances prepares sporadic meals which I can't eat much of. I am beside myself with missing the old companionship of Dad and Mother which is all that ever tied me here, and with missing the abundant companionship of my New York friends, who are all so far away, and while they are sympathetic and solicitous they cannot possibly appreciate the ramifications of the situation here, and I cannot share anything with them. If there were only someone somewhere for me to really turn to and have around and have things in common with. But I am just as alone as a pyramid and as confused as a beetle. My whole past seems swept away in one swoop, the present seems unbearable, and the future impenetrable. Until now I always felt completely poised in the world, but I realize it was a poise born of security, and I now feel like a trapeze performer with the safety net taken away, or as if I were a balloon which has been swinging for years into extraordinary and enchanted regions but always controlled by a firm hand on the ground, and now have been let loose and deflated. All this is how I feel mentally, and physically I feel like a rung out rag. I don't see how I can get hold of myself here, and I don't see how I can get away, I don't see anything clearly, in short I don't see.

I had a letter from Doris today, first all winter, which was nice.

When you come down I hope you can stay awhile. I want to go into so many things with you, and I really need someone. Doddy is so old and so unaware, and Frances is so young and so unaware, and the neighbors are all so remote and unaware. I have no communication with anyone, I am up against a brick wall, and I am really questioning the universe for the first time, and my relation to anything in it. I seem to feel as if I have no identity at all.

Max

Sunday [April 8, 1934]

Pioneer

Dear A.E.,

Just another bulletin. I'm about losing track of bulletins & days & everything else. The days follow days & nights follow nights,--all dreadful, and not differing much from each other.

Today was a steady stream of callers—Theo Ferris from Jackson, Michigan, Clara Sweet from Toledo, a Mrs. Barger from Montpelier, Myrtle Shafer from West Unity, Ida Barkley, Gertrude Blount, etc. Mother recognized them all, and had a word of greeting for each of them, & then dozed again into uneasy troubled sleep. She takes more nourishment now than she did a week ago, but I'm not sure that is anything to rejoice over. She realized that yesterday was my birthday, & said she would like to get me some strawberries! I opened the store yesterday for the first time since she became critically sick. I told her last night that I had sold $24.00 worth of goods, & she hoped it was old goods.

There is no telling how long this situation may continue. It seems as if she just cannot live, and also just cannot die. She simply exists, suspended between life and death and we are powerless to help her toward either. I never knew of such a predicament.

Please thank Harriet [Ewing] for her note. There was also a sweet letter from Mattie MacDonald last week. You may begin to tell Doris again that she is a toad and a pigeon-toed pig again for never writing!

Spring seems to be really here today, but there doesn't seem to be anything to do about it.

Max

Sunday [April 15. 1934]

Pioneer

Dear Uncle—This is only to announce the continuation of the unbearable. It goes on & on & we stagger thru the days & nights somehow. Mother dies every day in everything but fact. Thursday it seemed final. There was an awful death bed scene—minister—neighbors—Doddy half-hysterical, etc. Then it was all over & all was as before. But it is getting to the place where almost no amount of morphine can quiet Mother. She takes twice as much as it would take to make [Primo] Carnera unconscious, but it doesn't affect her a bit. She has been talking constantly for the last 36 hours—mostly just "word salad' without much relation to anything. I have engaged two women here in the house but I'm afraid I'll have to engage a third. Two cannot handle it. And I don't know where we'll put a third one. In fact I don't much of anything at this time. I just exist in a stupor.

 M.E.

Wednesday [April 18, 1934]

The Battle Creek Sanitarium
Battle Creek, Michigan

Dear Uncle—

 As a last desperate resort I brought Mother up here yesterday. I don't know whether it will help any, but if she dies she will at least die in comfort and not in agony, which it would have been in Pioneer, for there was just nothing we could do there & I could not bear it a day longer. Josie Bloyd Riste who lives in Battle Creek came down to Pioneer to see us yesterday & reported various miraculous results gained at the sanitarium here in cases given up as hopeless elsewhere. I was so frantic I acted on the spur of the moment & got an ambulance for Mother & sent her here. We followed after the ambulance. She stood the trip all right & today is having thorough examinations. No one seems very hopeful, but there is a small chance. If it fails I will know I have done everything possible. If you or Aunt Lotta could come here, Mother is in room 275.

 I am staying at Mrs. Riste's. She lives at 499 Capital Ave. Telephone 8857. Also she runs the Neumode Hosiery Shop opposite the Post Tavern in the Bank Bldg.

 Until further notice.

  Max

Friday [April 20, 1934]

The Battle Creek Sanitarium
Battle Creek, Michigan

Dear Uncle—

Got your letter today. Nothing much for me to add. There is little hope expressed here, practically none. It is only a matter of keeping Mother comfortable. That is being done. The days here are just as sad but not as ghastly as at Pioneer.

Max

Clara passed away in the sanitarium on Sunday night, April 22, 1934. Her body was returned to Pioneer and her funeral was held the following Wednesday, with Rev. Bready officiating. The next day Max wrote to Muriel Draper, "Mother died last night at the Battle Creek Sanitarium. Please tell my friends. I can't write. I can scarcely even sit up. I don't know how I can get through these next weeks, and I don't know how I got through the past month. I need you." She responded by telegram: "DEAREST MAX ALL MY DEEPEST LOVE AND SYMPATHY COME BACK AS SOON AS YOU CAN WE ALL MISS AND NEED YOU MURIEL." A few days later Max, still in Toledo, answered, "I got your wire but I am too ill to make the trip. I am flat in bed here at a friend's house with a sort of nervous collapse and a heart trouble and bronchial trouble and sinus trouble and I have no strength to even lift a suitcase. I don't know how I can get well at all. The winter has been such a strain I am down to the last of my endurance, and my mother was the whole strength on which my life has been built. Without her and my father all the props of my existence are gone, and I am stranded."

[Postcard to A.E., mailed May 8, 1934]

Just got your letter after writing you one. Nothing much to add only to say come on down as soon as you can. I hope Aunt Lotta is better. I am glad that Doris may come home. I so need some one to take charge of me & say "Do this" or "Do that" for I can do nothing.

    Max

Saturday night [May 12, 1934]

Dear Uncle,

It is increasingly evident that I am just floundering and apt to continue to do so unless or until I get help. It is undoubtedly difficult for you to understand my position. What is ABC to you is blank wall to me. It is as if you were told to get on a concert stage immediately and give a concert without any more preparation than thirty days. I am like a babe in arms, literally. I don't know what any of this situation means, or what to do about it. I know it looks bigger than it perhaps is because I am not well, and because I am so dominated by now by Mother's dreads. But all the same I am helpless, and I really should not sign a single paper without legal advice. I would prefer yours. Could you possibly break with Grand Rapids for awhile and come right down here and see me through—through trips to Bryan and Toledo and Angola, I'll go really nuts if things keep up like this. My will is paralyzed and I cannot go ahead with things all alone here any more than this, and these first weeks are pure panic. No one can possibly realize how I have been shielded from all such matters, or what my predicament is like at present. My coming to Grand Rapids would not solve anything, though it is sweet of all of you to ask me. Please thank Aunt Lotta for her kind letter. But I simply must have some guidance through a technical tangled maze. The auto problems are tangible enough. I am not able to drive to G.R. alone, or I would come for you. If you can come south by train I could meet you at Bryan.

    I did not go to Toledo with Clara Sweet, because my mind changes every minute and I cannot face decisions. It seemed foolish to go there for a Saturday and Sunday when I have business to do and could not do it those days. I may go later. I just don't know one day what I am going to do the next, and usually it is nothing, in the end, for I am not myself, and do not know what to do. I know I sound like a helpless fool, but that is exactly what I am in the situation I am placed in. I hate to impose on your life which I know is harassed enough these days, but I am so fantastically alone without a person to lean on or turn to in any direction. My props are out from under me, the wind is out of my sails, and alone in the night my thoughts hits up against the very end of reason. The neighbors tell me I am beginning exactly as Mother began, and that I am in danger of falling exactly into her trap. I realize that I am. Aunt Lotta writes that you are all like reeds for me to lean on. But, my dears I am clutching at even straws. Strange as it seems, you Grand Rapiders are the only family I have, and though you may be reeds you appear as mighty as bulwarks to me. On my own ground I can hold my own,—but my own ground is a protected and in these times useless little plot of ground which everyone can get along without. I am in most ways a useless creature, and through no fault of my own. But here I am, anyway, eating (a little), sleeping (not much), and wondering and wondering and wondering. I hope you can come down and turn a good strong long light on my affairs for me.

    Max

    Max's mental and emotional condition continued to worsen. On Saturday, May 19, A.E. visited him in Pioneer. The next day, in a letter to Doris, A.E. summarized his meeting with Max in the next letter.

Yesterday I just devoted myself as a 'mike' for Max to talk at and into. He is nine tenths beside himself and can hardly get up steam enuf to move about the house. He won't read nor turn on the radio, nor write, nor go anywhere. I staid over for the express purpose of being company for him. He is so 'shot' that he complains of being afraid if left alone. I can't begin to tell you the pitiful plight he is in. He is as near like Clara was as any two peas you ever saw. However, have talked my tongue loose trying to get his mind running in a different channel, but it has seemed hopeless because he would invariably repeat his negative appraisement of himself and his inability to cope with the situation, and then I would have to try a new tack. We talked from yesterday morning until 11 last night, and occasionally he would seem to be more like himself. We discussed religion and philosophy and he shows an inclination to take an interest in Christian Science and I have encouraged him to go strong on it. I believe I noticed a change about 9:45 last night. I had suggested in the fore noon that if he wished to drive out in the country it wouldn't offend me, but he didn't respond to it at all. Last night he surprised me by saying that he might feel better if he would take more exercise. He was strictly right, but why he should mention it at that time of night, I don't know unless some angel was giving him absent treatment. I called his bluff by challenging him to a two mile walk and he called mine by accepting it pronto. We hit the road running west and walked a full mile plumb in the face of the crescent moon and under a heaven of gleaming bright stars. We turned around and walked right back to starting point, sat down and talked for another half hour and went to bed. I slept like a log and I believe he slept better than usual. Anyway, he has actually seemed better today. Not once has he opened the subject of his despair or his hopeless condition. He has kept away from that topic better by far than he has for the five days I've been here. I do not call him well by any means. He looks like a fish that has lain in the hot sands for two days.

May 25, 1934

Pioneer

Friday

Dear Uncle,

 I have had both your letters. I should have written you sooner, but hardly know what to say except to say thank you a thousand times. I do genuinely thank you and want to repay you with more than that. I went to a Christian Science practitioner at Wauseon [Ohio]. And I wish I could tell you I felt better, but I do not. The present emptiness of my days and the past emptiness of my heart keep gnawing at me. I am still here. Frances is still here. I don't know where to go if I go. But will of course keep you informed. I salute you for being so gallant. I feel little deserving of your solicitude. Let me know anything you think I should do next.

    With love,
    Max

On May 26 Jack Pollock arrived from Portland, Oregon for his final visit to Pioneer.

[About May 28, 1934]

Dear Joe [Brewer],

 Thanks for your note. It was too bad we missed connections. I had been in Lansing on business that day. You ask how I am now. Frankly I am worried about myself. I am in a state of absolute paralysis of will. Everything I have to do now is so absolutely unrelated to anything in my past, and everything in my past is now so cut away, that I am simply at bay, and more alone than any human being, in this godforsaken town. There is no one to entrust business to, so I cannot get away, and it is equally true that I cannot stay, and remain sane, and I mean sane. I am in the verge of I don't know what kind of cracking up, and I am tempted to go to a psychiatrist, but there isn't any within hailing distance.

My Grand Rapids relatives keep asking me to come up there, but it doesn't seem like any solution. My mind simply cannot accept what has happened, and instead of pitching into a thousand new duties, it cannot select even one to pitch into. The days pass and I deeper into a state of coma. At first I thought it was just natural reaction to grief and nervous shock, but it gets more so each day, and I begin to lose all recognition of myself or my identity.

I do hope to see you before the summer passes. When is your school out, and where will you be then? New York sounds very eventful, but it is all like a dream to me, and the immediate situation here is like a trance, and there seems to be no reality at all.

Max

On May 24, the Ewing store was sold to Gurth Repp of Williams County, Ohio. Max made his last diary entry on May 30: "at May Stumps with Jack. The Stump family resided in Williams County. As the spring of 1934 progressed, Max's diary entries had become increasingly erratic and brief. His next letter, written to Muriel Draper two days before his death,

Pioneer

June 14 [1934]

Dear Muriel,

What a wonderful letter. You are so generous and genuine and brave and true and good, and I want to learn to be like you. I have basked in your light for so long, and I have been deluded into thinking I was part of the light. I know now that I never was. But I still cling so to the illusion. And more than anything I would like to go with you to Russia. How magnificent that you can go. You have thought for me and felt for me so long, I haven't needed to think or feel, and have done neither, ever. Now that I must learn to I do not know how to go about it. Jack is here, ready to do anything and everything for me. Yesterday I did "let him down," and sent him away, and then drove away after him and got him again. He may rescue me from what looks like a condition worse than death. He will not let the people here do what they think they must do with me unless it is taken out of his hands by some member of my family. Muriel, you have often called me heartless, or a stone image or things like that. Without a single grain of feeling of any kind. I have put people through absolute hell. Especially my own people. I have never done a single true or genuine or heartfelt of even slightly admirable thing in my life. I have been more selfish and despicable than anyone can imagine. This realization has come all at once, and has overturned my faculties. The property angle is secondary. It has become a real mental crisis. Ellery's [Larsson] condition that time was nothing compared to mine. I feel a profound sense of guilt, and I want to come out of it. But I will do what I can. I need your constant presence. But it is there and Jack's is here. I will try to appreciate what he does, though. I have never appreciated what anyone else ever did. I need strength, reassurance, Muriel. You must help cast out the devils. Humility does not come naturally to me, nor forthrightness, nor any other good qualities. I must work for them, I suppose. The first steps are the hardest. I do not wonder I seem a stranger to you. I am a stranger to myself. I despise myself and I want to find a new way.

Effort and atrophy are equally unacceptable. Dear Muriel, how I need you. I need you.

Max

Jack added at the bottom of Max's letter this postscript:

"We both know Max when But the Max of to-day is so different & very difficult for Im no Brother or any thing altho I treat him like a two year old Bro. or have But now its so different & he has changed so. I shall do all I can & try to git him their with you awhile But it does seem quite hopeless at time for he make it so difficult. He seem [sic] so normal some times & then again so very far from me or any one at times. Love, <u>Jack</u>

6. Here and There: Jack Pollock's Letters to Max

On June 1, 1934 A.E. composed a letter to Mrs. J. R. Stump of Montpelier, Ohio, expressing his opinion that Max "was between the 'can'ts.' He can't stay in Pioneer and can't get away from there. He can't live in his own house and can't live in any other. He can't be happy outside New York and he can't be happy in New York." Max did not have the will to move in any direction, yet he dreaded remaining in Pioneer. Jack Pollock, a professional boxer, had been with Max off and on for at least two years, including a short visit in Hollywood in 1933. Aware of Max's torment, Jack joined him in Pioneer two times, once in March and again in June. During the latter visit, Jack provided the impetus to get Max on the move. Although very different in background, personality, and aspirations, the two men had formed a deep attachment. Max first mentions the boxer in his letter dated May 27, 1933, where he refers to him as his "physical trainer," but it is clear from Jack's correspondence that they had befriended each other in New York City no later than 1932. Jack's first letter dates to about the time of Max's arrival in California around August 1, 1933. Although Max stopped in San Francisco on his way to Hollywood, he and Jack apparently were unable to meet at that time. Jack's letters are seldom dated, and all but one of the envelopes were discarded along the way. Unless there are clear contextual clues, the order of the letters relies on guesswork, although the letterhead that he picked up at various hotels helps in grouping them.

Jack was a traveler. He was able to go from one end of the country to the other with very little cash on hand, primarily by hitchhiking and hopping freight trains. From the context of Max's letters and Jack's we know that the boxer was in New York City in 1932, met Max in Florida in March of that year, boxed awhile in Texas, and then relocated to Chicago before landing at the Hotel Federal in San

Francisco, where he roomed at the time of Max's arrival on the west coast. He next settled in Burley, Idaho.

[after August 1, 1933]

Hotel Federal
1087 Market St at Seventh St
San Francisco, Calif.

Hi Ho Max,

    No matter if we did miss connections in Frisco Ill no doubt see you later in Hollywood. Max I have a Broken right. I Broke it in San Diego my last fight. I have no money although Im stoping here at this Hotel. Im fighting Tony Palini in Reno Wednesday of next week it's a Bussiness fight & Im using a phony name because I have to make enough to exist & tony & I are good friends. Don't say anything to any one pal for Ill pick up 100.00 Bucks is a Hundred Bucks these day's. I have got connected with a swell boy since my last letter to you pal & if you could have spared 15.00 Id have sent it right back to you for Im O.K. now Max. boy its Been tough as Hell at times But I can take it I don't squack [squawk] But its going to take me a year to pick up the meals I have missed. Oh Well What the Hell its all in my life. I don't stop to think any more Max for if I did id no doubt jump out some window But I can still take it & really hope I don't ever weaken.

    You are swell Max. I mean it. Cant express my regards for you But really Id give my right arm Before Id let you get stranded like I have Been at times. I'm pretty sure you may never come to that but one never know's & if at any time you need 5 or 10 in the future as long as I have a little Break why Max Ill punch you silly if you don't write to me.

    I must go to the gym & loosen up.
        Love,
        Jack

[August, 1933]

Hotel Federal
1087 Market St at Seventh St
San Francisco, Calif.

Dear Max,

Just a line my boy. "Well" the promoter here got wise my right hand was Broke & so I don't Battle the Semi Final. I went to him & gave him a song & dance about Being flat (which is nothing unusual with me.) & he gave me a four round battle well up toward the top on the card so I am dam glad it happened for I won't have to Box 6 rds with my left hand now for I doubt very much if I could have K.Od the boy. In this four rounder Im not going to try to kill my self you can bet on that to K.O. this Boy But in the Semi I would have had to work hard as Hell.

I suppose you are quite tanned up by now. Well Max I look like a white man almost for Im not tanned up much.

In case you hear of a job such as a wet nurse to some Baby. Say 20 years old or something on that order let me know & ill accept the position at once.

I must rest after this coming week & under go some more dam treatment.

I Box 6 Rds to-day in the gym & after the work out and my shower why I politely stuck around the gym & got tight as a tick. A friend Had a gallon of wine & Boy did we get tight. Im perfectly sober now Max but Oh boy what a Bun I had on this after noon.

Well Max I suppose you spent quite a lot of money coming across. "Not Bragging" now! But I can make the same trip from Hollywood to N.Y. on 10.00 Bucks & have enough left when I hit N.Y. to kinda look around. Don't think Im going to do it for Im not. I just turned down a chance to go Back & Box in N.Y. this winter. But not for me.

I must Bore the Hell out of you with so many letters. If I do say so.

Cherrio

Jack

In March, 1931 Jack Pollock lost by a knockout to Eddie Hanlon. The match was held in Oakland, California, which Jack listed as his hometown. On March 30, April 10, and April 24 three years year, Jack boxed in Dallas, Texas. He won two of the bouts by knockout and lost one by a knockout. His hometown was listed as New York City. In the following letter, Jack acknowledges owing $25 to a hotel manager in Dallas. Jack also is credited with five fights between 1928 and 1931. Of these he won four, two by knockout, and lost one, again by a knockout. The record for these fights shows Kansas City, Missouri as his hometown. There is no proof these various records belong to the same Jack Pollock, but the dates fit. Jack also fought under the name Jack Shirley. A Jack Shirley boxed in 23 matches between 1920 and 1933, winning eight, losing nine, and having six draws. This Jack Shirley listed his hometown as Sacramento, California. He presented Muriel Draper with a ticket for his bout with John Brodhead on April 12, 1933. Whether he fought as Jack Shirley or Jack Pollock isn't recorded.

[August, 1933]

Hotel Federal
1087 Market St at Seventh St
San Francisco, Calif.

Dear Max,

"Well"! "Well"! my boy it looks as tho the Boy's up here haven't forgotten me. After I wrote you the last letter the Promoter & my manager & I went to the gym & the promoter told me I wasn't Boxing for him Monday night for the Boy that was supposed to fight me run out Max. In other words he took a powder & wont fight me because he says Im to good.

What a laugh my manager got out of that for pal my right hand is on the fritz & Im not well & far from condition. After all I have the respect of these pug's up here for they remember how I put the Boy's on ice up Here two & half yrs ago.

Max I only Box once this coming week in Reno. I Box Here for Schuler a week from to-morrow so it look's like I won't get to come down after my Reno Battle. I'll be seeing you some time any way punk & in the mean time watch your step don't stay out late & drink nothing stronger than Tea & watch the Hollywood <u>Dames</u> above all things.

Its to dam bad Max that I cant write a Book for Gee I have so much experience in so many different lines that its Hell to be dumb But we all cant have everything so Im not kicking But dam glad I have you for a friend.

I have a friend that may come up here soon & in case he does he will go to work here & Ill grab off His straight eight [automobile] & drive down & see you & remember the quart of Champayne for Im politely going to get on a Hell of a <u>drunk.</u>

How do you like Hollywood By now. You know Max your Big Shot friends respect you so much & have you way up in the air on a throng [throne] all By yourself that in case you ever fall down & go Boom every one would Be oh so sorry. But Max nothing surprises me any more.& I do so want to see you make good but in case its me that does on up then Boy you are as welcome as the flowers in may. I don't know why Im writing this way pal But you did so much for me that Ill never forget it & I for one certainly wont criticize you in case you do Blow up.

After all from the looks of this letter one would think I was married to you & here we are a couple of regular Boy's. Well Im positive no one will see this that's why Im writing this way.

I wrote the manager of the Hotel in Dallas the other day. Id told him Id pay him off this coming week after my fight. Yes I still owe the old Boy 25.00 smackers But he will get it. Can you Imagine in all those Heavyweights I didn't even make expenses. But one thing I can take it for I dam near lost my eye twice But never a squack. I can certainly take it Max.

My regards to you & every one Back in N.Y. & I do hope we don't get grey before we must.

   Cherrio

    Jack

Tony Poloni and Billy Donahue had two matches in September, 1933, one on the 6th and second on the 27th. Tony lost the first bout and won the second. Both were held in San Francisco. Jack probably is training Tony for the first match in the next letter.

[August, 1933]

Hotel Federal
1087 Market St at Seventh St
San Francisco, Calif.

Dear Max,

I rec'd Your card here in Frisco. Glad to hear from you. I enjoyed my stay in Reno although I worked hard while there. I didn't go around much for Schuler sent me up to train with Paloni [Poloni] & get him in shape & pal I did all I could. Tony is in swell shape But really this will be one of the toughest fights for some time. I don't know who will win I really cant say But pal Im for Paloni all the way. He is a swell kid. It seems as tho you are having a delightfully time in Dear old Hollywood. Max get ready for a Bawling out for really you don't ever get to Be to Big a shot but what this lad will Ball you out when necessary. "Now the Bawling Out!" Max I appreciate the Signature of Love and the end of your card & I feel delighted that you feel that way about this old horse of the ring. But please Don't address cards that way for some one might misconstrue the meaning of the word if they didn't know what friends we are & then you know Id politely have to punch the Hell out of some one. In the future just address them Friend or pal "O.K. Max Old boy!"

Im in a spot! "Max" I also Box Wensday But not a ten rounder "No! Not even six." A 4 rounder & Boy I have a tough punching young strong Boy from Oakland. Lewis is his name pal & here is the dope some wise Baloney's are trying to put the skids under me in the racket & I must hang this boy on ice inside of 4 rds or it looks like Im done. Max Ill say this much to you right now if I lose pal Ill write a farewell letter & Ill wish you the Best of everything always & forever & then Ill fade on out of the picture probably change my name & get a job some where & never again tie on the gloves. It's a great life if one dosent weaken. Well Max I can still take it But God! It makes a man wonder if its all worth while A Broken right hand & Im sick more or less. I must win or else. Gee Pal it's a funny life after all the way I have lived it. Your life may Be Boresome at times. Well Pal mine isn't.

I want a nice long letter from you in answer to this Max for it may Be the last I ever get from you. Who knows?

Well Cherrio Pal. I shant hang any more crape until after the Battle. I do hope for the Best & Im sure I have you with me.

My regards to everyone we know in N.Y. just in case I don't get this boy out with my left hand. Also your friends & Kay Francis in Hollywood.

In regards to [Maxie] Rosenbloom I met him once in N.Y. in Grupps gym in 1928 have seen him a number of times Max But Max as for him knowing me I don't suppose he remembers. I was training with Jack Renault at the time in N.Y. You see Im a small shot anymore & never was a very Big Shot for I just never was lucky about getting a good manager to Back me up with money & every young fighters need it & then again I got mixed up & married the kid that turned out to be a quitter & it kinda did me up Max for I loved her & you saw me in N.Y. & met me when I was at my worst I had lost all confidence in myself & gee you were swell & always's will Be to me for Max you helped me so much But now I often think if the life I have lived is worth while.

Im not Blue or meloncolly or any thing such Im just writing the truth Max & I want to sign this thing off Before it gets to Be a Book.

<u>Love Always</u>
<u>Jack</u>

P.S. Answer at once by airmail. I must hear from you Before this Battle.

Jack

In October Jack unexpectedly dropped in on Max for an early morning visit at the Hollywood Roosevelt Hotel, where Max was staying. It evidently was a short get-together. Max wrote to Muriel Draper, "... Jack Pollock showed up suddenly and unannounced from Reno. He stayed three days and then went off to some indefinite destination in Idaho. It was all about what you are no judge of." The next group of letters was written shortly after Jack's visit.

Jack left San Francisco permanently, returning to Hollywood to see Max once more before heading north and settling in Idaho for a few months. *Burley is in southern Idaho, just off today's Interstate 86 and about 70 miles from Pocatello. Occasionally he boxed under the alias "Jack Shirley."*

[October, 1933]

Hollywood Roosevelt Hotel
Hollywood, California

Jack Shirley
Burley Idaho
Gen. Del.

Dear Max,

    It seems we have Both taken the old saying "Go West young man"! "Go West." To heart and are carrying it out.

    Max so much has happened since I left Hollywood the morn I said adios to you that I shant tell you all But give you a rough estimate of the trip & what not. I left L.A. by paying my way to San Fernando which was 50 cents & I got a ride on a truck to Bakersfield & then that night about midnight I got another ride on to a little town near Stockton & I worked & helped this chap I rode with unload & made a Buck after I Hitch Hiked on to Roseville where I mailed you a card telling you to write me in Salt Lake City. I took the freight out of Roseville & Hit Reno. But I came in through Reno & rode to Ogden, Utah & then I hitched 42 miles to Salt lake & spent the night in Salt lake & looked her over the following day. Well I didn't like the lay of things in Salt lake so I came to Pocatello, Idaho. I looked over Pocatello But it's a rail town & union so pal I put that town behind me. I spent my last 15 cents in Pocatello so it could not Be long Before this kid had to stop & take the town in Hand I decided to stop in Burley "well" that [is] about what I have done. I was thinking about this town & of course Id Began tightening up the Belt By notches & this town or any other look good when a man has taken up the last notch in the old Belt. Max I did take this town in & it has also taken me in phony name & al. Ill confess there is one man in this town that I layed all my cards out in front of & he know's who I really am Max and is for me 100% per cent. He is Ross Youmans the Big Banker in this town & is the captain of the National Guards & that is How I happened to connect with him through this Guard. Well Pal I am writing you from the office here in the armory for this also the place where I hang my hat. I have a cot & Blankets & all of that & I'm the one an only that sleep's in the joint or ever has. In return I have taken over coaching of these young Boy's of the guard in Boxing. I have a Hell of a swell gang of Boy's I do not charge any thing for that was captain Youman's & my agreement But the Boy's know Im flat & there fore they see that I eat quite regular. I worked one Hour & made 50 cents one morn since I have Been here But out side of that Im flat <u>completely.</u> Ill no doubt work into something Max for it really gets cold up in this part of the country & I want a job & a few thing's.

  Well Max Im through with the fight racket & the past life absolutely for Its only made dam near a tramp out of me & now I shall devote my time to the future in other lines. What ever I can get into is O.K. By me. Just so its square. I shall keep in touch with you Max & as you know I lost my coat in Florida last year. Get me a camel Hair top coat size 40 Max & send it to me. They are very cheap say 15 or 18 Bucks & Pal Im pretty sure you will Max for I need it. I cant say when Ill be able to pay you Back But we never know what the future Holds so stick Behind me Max until I get straightened out. Your Pal Always.
  Jack Pollock   Jack Shirley

Don't let anyone know where I have gone or a dam thing pal for Im starting out new & all is Behind But <u>you!</u>

[October, 1933]

Hilton Hotels
Dallas, Abilene, El Paso, Marlin, Lubbock, Plainview, San Angelo, Waco

Jack Shirley
Burley Idaho
Gen Del.

Im out of circulation from now on altho I may see you in 1934

Dear Max,

Rec'd. Letter & card O.K. & Boy do I wish Id have Been a usher & got to Bounce Lincoln Kirsten [Kirstein] out. Gee Max Id have wrecked that Jew really & truly. You may send more such clippings & I hope you send plenty.

Max about the coat! Yes I need one the worst way soon. Any time with in the next month & you will get your royalties next month so march Down & go shopping for me size, 40. Not a wolly [wooly] one like I had in N.Y. No not near as expensive as that one but a slick camel hair. I have a <u>COT</u> here in the armory Pal & it [is] O.K. a nice COT and 4 army Blankets to keep warm.

Burley is population 3,300 people that's without the cemeteries although half the town's Dead But they just haven't gotten around to Bury it yet. No Max really this is a nice little town & I have met some very nice people. The cream of this town & pal Ill hole up here no doubt this winter so Ill need the coat as soon as you can see your way clear. O.K.

Max you know me & you also know that I have taken plenty in my time especially from the girl that was my wife. You called me a gentle men while I was their. You were right Max only lots of other people don't think so Because I never tell them a dam thing. Im just not interested that's all. Why I Became so attached to you is more than I can explain But without a doubt you are the Best person I have ever known in my life or shall ever meet for really Max Im out of circulation from now on Because the past with the Vivian girl that ruined me & wore my name when she did it. Don't think Im squaking Pal for Im not it was just fate & to Hell with it. Im man enough to take even that.

 I like this little town very much Max & I do hope to get lined out soon with a job! Say about 10 a week & Board & room. Ill get that job about a month from now for the winter This Bankers name is Ross Youmans & a fellow thats graduated in the school of hard knocks Pal & a real fellow. Yes I have Been to dinner at his home & he has a very nice wife & a daughter 5 years old. At present Im coaching Boxing here in the Armory 3 nights a week we plan on running Boxing exhibitions this winter & also a dance twice a week. At present Im just coaching Boxing & that's all & we have this armory under the Bank in the Basement Its quite a nice place But in two weeks we move to a Basement of a first floor of one of the largest Bldg in town & we will have the armory in the Basement & use the 1st floor for Boxing Show's & Dancing & any other little racket that will make us some money.

 You don't have to apologize about me not meeting so & so while I was their & that you were sorry every one was ill. Max I came to see you & Pal Im glad I did for you are you & all I wanted to see so knock off the apologies it isn't necessary & if I live to be a thousand I could never spend a happier week end. Send Muriel my love also Max & gee I certainly would not like those drum's dancing in my Dining room. Poor Annadella [Winslow]. Gee Max Id have sworn she could take it. Perhaps she will show up soon.

 My regards to everyone & loads of luck to you.

  Sincerely Always Jack

[Before October 15, 1933]

Hollywood Roosevelt Hotel
Hollywood, California

Dear Max,

    Saturday in a farming town is quite the thing as you can imagine. That is if you can imagine all of the native sons of the soil coming to town & stocking up with Groceries & having at least one whole Dime left to raise Hell with! Generally they buy a Bag of peanuts & a bottle of pop & see which can Whoop the longest & really they have had a wonderful time & are then ready to go Back to said farm & top Beets & Dig potatoes as those two are the main crop's raised here. Yes pal I can take it But at what price. You may read in the papers where I passed out from Boredom this coming winter. At least do not Be surprised if such a pleasant thing happened. I do wish to hell I had the money to get to Africa for really old top Id at least scare me up some excitement with the black natives their. But their isn't a whole lot of chance doing any thing such here for as I mentioned in my last letter half the towns dead But really don't know it. I think Id welcome Indians playing in the dining room (providing a had a dining room) for at least I could toss those Babies out on their ears if I became to Bored with them But here I haven't even got that to look forward to for these farm Boys know Im a fighter & therefore Im supreme!

    Write Muriel [Draper] & tell her we should get the Indians & my farmers together & if she can sincerely do some dancing in Venice this season why my Glorious Punk Kid I for one would think the season a hugh success. Of course you must get a nice job in the movie colony & I shall include that in the season. Max did you sign a contract yet & if so how did your story about the big Cattle society matron of Cheyenne go.

Its to dam Bad Im so dumb for pal if I could write a Book God what a Book it would Be.

I go to work this coming week & really my Boy if I make 20 Bucks a week Ill Be way up in money. It Gives me the shivers to think of the coming winter for Ill no doubt hibernate such as a Bear does up here in these mountains of Idaho. Im mailing you a Roosevelt Hotel letter But to heck with clerk's on duty Max for you pay your rent you know so to Hell with em.

Say did Joe [Brewer] get the College yet. If so pal Ill think it over & see if I should brighten up my mentality at his joint this year if not this then the next. What a hell of a dignified President of a College little Joe would make. Max Give me his address & Ill write the Boy a letter & politely inform him that I shall put in my request for a job as his protector for those rough big foot Ball players are liable to try to take advantage of little Joe!

Im the Big Bouncer at the town dance Hall to night. I go to work & keep the peace & lets hope one of these Bozo gets tight & tough from eating sour apples Max for Im a little stale & need to excercize my left hook. Ill make 2.50 to-night. Gee I don't hardly know what to do with so much money all at once. I had an offer today to go over there 50 miles & Box the top spot this Thursday night coming But Max I hung my Gloves up in frisco & I shall not take them down even tho I need the (75.00) seventy-five Bucks. Six rounds pal But I do so want to exist a little while longer & I know I couldn't go the pace & I might really get hurt so no more Boxing for me. It seems every one will Be working like hell for the next 4 or 5 weeks here so we don't start Boxing until a month & half from now.

What did Mother say about the car can you have it or not. Let me know for really my punk kid I might welcome a trip Back their. Its only a short hop for me & really it wouldn't take very long. You know that so far as traveling minus a ticket Im a champ a thousand miles or two hardly warms me up.

 Well Cherrio Max I shall now shave & wash my ears & Be ready for the towns wrestling match which is known as a dance.
     Cherrio Jack.

[no date]

    Hollywood Roosevelt Hotel
    Hollywood, California

Dear Max,

 Have Been working pal for the past two day's & then again I make 5.00 bucks on a wensday & sat. night at the dance. Im the floor Manager! In N.Y. Latin Im the strong arm boy who throws them out Max! I want you to shop around for a size 40 Camel Hair Coat or a good looking Black over coat & let me know how cheap I can get it for. Boy it really gets cold up here in this man's country & Im needing it as soon as I can get the money. I also want you to go to a first class drug store & get me a Bottle of Mallophene. Its made by the Mallinraft Chemical Co Max & the Bottle contains 50 pills for the kidneys & Bladder so get it pronto & mail it to me air mail if possible & Ill have a nice pay check Sat. night & the following Sat I hope to send enough so you can get me the coat for this coming winter. If you can cut your living expenses enough to spend 3.50 & get me that bottle why Ill see you get it Back. I cant get it here & another thing this is a small town & what people don't know don't bother them.

 Im tired Max. I went to work at 7:30 AM & its now 11:PM & I just got in Im working on a potato truck & Im really working. I have handled so dam many spuds in the past two day's that I doubt very much if Ill ever care to eat one again. When I left Hollywood I knew more or less I could get in most any town I cared to stop in But I never thought

Id get in such a small unsophisticated town as I have here in Burley. Max Im really Happy around here & I now have gotten lined out 100 per cent as far as making a living.

 I do hope you could have some of my luck & get set in some thing worth while their. You will I feel pretty sure Max. Keep a stiff upper lip all the time.

 I must get to Bed Max for 7:00 comes pretty quick to me for Boy I do like my sleep.
    Cherrio
     Jack

Jack Shirley
Gen. Del.
Burley Idaho

[after October 2, 1933]

|**The Plaza**|**The Hutchins**|
|Harlington, Texas|San Antonio, Texas|

Dear Max,

 Boy what an experience [the October 1 earthquake]. Im positive Id have left the Hotel as quick as I possible could have. Max Ill now finish this letter pal for one of the Boy's up stairs in the Bank came down at 11:00 AM this morn when I started this & told me that I was wanted to go to work so down I goes & to work. I was Bucking potoatoes on to a truck all after noon its now 6:00 PM & I have just finished washing up & everything & now Ill try to finish this letter. I made $1.75 this after noon & boy did I work I work to-morrow & make $1.50 and then to-morrow night Im official Bouncer at the Palm Gardens opening dance. The other joint is folding up pal so of course I used diplomacy & got me a job at this new joint. They named it Palm Gardens & Max that draw's a laugh for it only gets about 40 Below Zero up here in winter.

Max now wait a minute a joke is a joke But Im pretty sure the <u>pest</u> named <u>Vista</u> didn't send her love to this old war horse.

Its certainly tough about your Mother & all. Gee Max I never remember my Mom But you can Bet your neck if I had one & she Became ill Id come from Africa to her even tho I didn't have a dime. That how Id feel about it .

"Max" Gee! I wish their was some way Muriel & I could get our farmers & Indians to-gether for the season would Be complete with out a doubt.

After the earth quake Ill say this much you sure had plenty of guts to go to the spiritualist séance and take such a Beating off the dead Indian chiefs & from ten trumpets. What a Beating you must have taken But even so I suppose the shower you had while there was rather welcomed.

We have a rodeo here the 13 & 14 no doubt But what Ill get a job out at this point doing something & of course Ill let you know about everything. Its too Bad I cant afford to have you with me in some of my experiences Max for you would really enjoy it.

Please send me 5 more pictures of my self in front of the Jean Harlow & Noah Berry Max for I do like that one very much. Get them made off the proof & send them on as soon as you can. Your picture is swell. Gee punk why the hell did they make you so good looking & with so many Brains & cheat me out of Both. Gee Pal I can take it & Ill do my Best not to weaken Before Xmas. You think of everything.

Well Max I must go & put the feed Bag on so Cheerio
    Jack of Burley

[about October 15, 1933]

Hollywood Roosevelt Hotel
Hollywood, California

Dearest Boy,

Max you certainly seemed very low in regards to your coming job. Please! Keep your chin up & you will get what you want sooner or later. Any way if worst comes to worst & no more money is available why you let the old man know & Ill see you up here in god's country with me pal & you know the old man well enough to know we wont go hungry & I will have a warm place to sleep. Hollywood weather must Be terrible Max & it certainly cant Begin to compare with this weather up here.

Gee! I hope Muriel is great Max & from your letter it seems she is O.K. Its to damn bad the Dumb squaw was along to spoil you two dishing the dirt & all. Im positive you Both were Bursting over with new's. its to dam Bad that you & I or Muriel couldn't Be worth 5 or 6 million for Max we would do so much good with it really & truly instead of marrying some dumb Indian just Because it seemed to Be the popular thing to do. I have never met the dame but Im positive I would not like her for she seems to me as the same type of person as Lincoln Kirsten & God knows I hate that Jew.

With out a doubt Gary Cooper seems to Be the most sensible in Hollywood.

Im sure Ill recieve the extra snapshots from you.

So you pull the sincerely dancing stuff on me. You get a Break Because you are so far from me pal But really if I could get a hold of you Id politely wrap you around a telephone post so you would look like a pretzel.

Max Im enclosing a snap shot of one the toughest mugs out of Butte Montana. Yes he is a puncher or used to Be But he picked me off as a regular guy & I got him a job last week although he is on the loose & hideing out from a few jobs on Banks in South Dakota & North Dakota. Max! really he is O.K. But he is one tough nut when he has work to do But with me he is regular.

I worked all last week & made my self 25.00 Max but I payed out money to some of the Boys here & I didn't work yesterday & to-day friend & today I had a tooth pulled & it cost me a Buck & half then I went to a doctor & got a treatment & payed him five Bucks & made arrangements for further treatment & I Bought a shirt & work shirt & one suit of heavy underwear & two suits of shorts & razor Blades & socks so you can see the old man hasn't much money left. I want you to Be sure & send me that Bottle of Mallophene Max for Boy I need it. I tried to get it here Sat. But Hell the suckers don't know what the score is let alone Mallophene.

Ross & I went to the show last night (the Banker) & He invited me out to shoot pheasant next Sunday. I went to the rodeo yesterday & it wasn't anything to write home about.

Well my Boy keep me posted on every thing & if it gets unbearable why you come up here to old Jack pal & we will get along.
    Cherrio,
    Jack

[about October 15, 1933]

The Plaza   **The Hutchins**
Harlington, Texas   San Antonio, Texas

Jack Shirley
In Burely Idaho
Gen. Del.

Dear Max,

Oh what a sternious week end. I was a Bouncer Sat night at the Dance (if one can call it that) & I got to Bounce one guy that weighed about 220 But pal he kinda knows me so I didn't get to unlimber my left hook for as soon as I grabbed him why he was plenty peaceable & marched right out.

Max Im kinda Balmy I guess for I mailed you a letter yesterday (Sunday) morning & I did forget to put a stamp on it. Just now I was over to the large P.O. (one storie Bldg) here & talked to the clerk that sorts mail & he told me their was a loose stamp in his mail & he put it on my letter to you & sent it on to you.

What a Break. Im ahead of the Govt. 3 cents But I still owe you 3 cents from Florida.

Max as soon as I get a head a little Ill no doubt send you a letter & have you mail their in order to get my stuff trunk & everything in Hollywood & have you send it on to me. I don't want Helen or anyone to know where Im at & pal I do worry the Hell out of them By letting them think Im in Hollywood & God knows they have done enough damage to me so let them worry for that out fit has sure slowed a good man down when they slowed me down But Max Ill come Back Im pretty sure "No" not as a fighter thats out But as something else for I must Max & I do so want to put my kid nephew up as he will get a chance in this old world.

I haven't written anyone Max not even my Sis out side of you But I must & shall do this morn. I don't even write all my fair lady friends or anything & Im pretty sure they are all Broken hearted. Pal I cant help it for I haven't made But one lady friend since I left N.Y. & that's my little squaw in texas Im pretty sure she will live without me writing so to heck with it.

While you are going around the different partys & meeting the cream of Hollywood why not give this kid a thought once in awhile Max for I need it. I can take it as you know & I do hope Ill always Be able to do so. We have a rodeo coming up here the 13-24 of this month. You know Cowboys & every thing that goes with it. I met the champion trick roper yester day at the Ball game. He is running the show & is advance man for the troop. At least we have a couple day's excitement in Dear old Burley

"Well" Max write more often for I thrive on your letters up here in the sticks.

Your as long as I can take it. <u>Jack</u>

[no date]

National Hotel
Burley, Idaho

Dear Max,

Boy you must Be Nervous, "<u>Yes</u>!" Nervous "No!" Nervose to say the least.

Well Pal Im out of jail Got out last Friday. I gave the damn county 4 Bucks for I still had too day's to do on account of the girl friends was having her show at the large (about as Big as the one in Pioneer) Burley Theatre. "Well"! out of jail & I helped her run the show off & it was a hugh success to say the least. Boy if you don't think I have almost caused a riot then you are all wet for pal a jail Bird is a disgrace out in this spud pickers town & me helping my girl friend run off her show & then again just as soon as I got out I went down to the Bank to Ross Youmans & the president & the other chap that works their almost tore the joint up getting to shake hands with me. Of course Sat. I was Manager of the Dance & Boy I know who my friends are here & right off the Bat I throw three guys out. Oh Max! How I love a good fight But the lice Bastards are certainly low as they ever come. The Mugg I started out with in Boxing & double crossed me left town as soon as he heard I was out. It's a dam good thing for if Id have got holt of him they would not doubt have hung me with a new rope up at Boise.

Max. I cant afford to stay here really for these Bastards will frame me Bowlegged & I know it now just as they did Before so if you see me in Ohio do not be surprised.

Gee pal you asked for an ear full & I do think I have complied with your request. Havent I? I don't know how long I will stick Max But to tell you the truth Im going to get holdt of 10 slugs & then travel really & truly for I don't care for jails especially when I haven't done anything . I do know this if these lice were men & acted like men & fought as a man does then really I wouldn't care if I got a few day's in the jail house once in awhile pal But as I have said Before they are lice.

Perhaps one of these day's with your help I may write a Book as such & really Max with my vast experience around this old U.S.A. I should Be able to put out something worth while.

I shall expect to hear from you soon.

My regards to your Mother & Grand Mother.

Love,

Jack

[November 25, 1933]

National Hotel
Burely, Idaho

Dear Max,

Of all things you would write & tell me how wonderfully warm it is their & here us poor souls with our knees knocking & what have you with our teeth chattering to-gether so bad. Really old topper—this lad can take it.

Im glad to hear your play is completed. As for having to wait until you return to N.Y. to produce it "<u>Well</u>" I do hope it's a sensation & those <u>Calif</u> producers will then have to crawl to Max in order to get it. After all I shouldn't Be so terrible hard on the Californians for they did send me greetings last year. "Oh!" what a life it is as I have Been lucky enough to live it or perhaps I should say as I had guts to live it.

I cant tell you for sure if I shall get to come & see you see you for Xmas. But Max Ill do my Best.

You may look over this program Im enclosing to you my dear & say By the By after all Burley has its own Opera & what nots such as dancing instructors & Boy how I know about women, "Well" Max Believe it or not we are great pals & outside of that I shant say more. We also have Bouncers for our dance. Im the kid in that spot. Now just what do you think of Burely. I know what you think of Shirley, But you have never told me just what you thought of Burley.

In case I come down it will no doubt Be a pleasure to sleep standing up in a folding Bed providing you are Beside me.

I am writing Muriel & sending her one these programs also.

As for making the little doggies get along. Yes my punk kid I can also do that.

If you weren't so regular Id never write to you as I do Max. But after all you are you & say I may have to marry the girl for she thinks she is pregnant. Now isn't that some thing. Oh Hell if they ever get me to marry again after the way the one sister turned out on me Im darn sure it will have to be a shot gun wedding. I quit the job of Manager at the old fashioned dances last night Because the guy that runs the joint pulled a cheap trick & I suppose he did expect to get away with it But Max I have quite a lot of that foolish stuff called pride & confidence in myself & I told him to politely go to hell & quit. Thanks to you for my confidence & pride. I shall never forget 1932 in N.Y.

At last we move into our new joint next week.

My jobs at present are building a fire in a little wood stove everyday for my dancing instructor which is $1.00 a month managing the Palm gardens twice a week which is $5.00 a week & training 7 boys at 2.50 a month each one which is 17.50 for the month. Say 50.00 a month this lad is getting along.

                Cheerio Pal. Jack

[December 25, 1933]

National Hotel
Burley, Idaho

Dear Max,

    Merry Xmas & Happy New Year & what nots. I do sincerely hope this coming year is Bright success for you in every way Max.

    This is quite an odd Xmas for me to say the least. My girl is sick in Bed with a cold & I have Been with her all evening & I really haven't taken a drink. Hope you are doing some Better.

    In regards to the past Tuesday night when I planned to kick Hell out of two national guards why Ross the Captain asked me to lay off & so I did.

    We run our first fight show here the 5th of Jan, Max & I have Been quite Busy to say the least.

    I mailed Eddie Wasserman & Muriel Draper & your self Xmas cards & of course I sent some to my folks & other friends. Xmas cards was all I could stand pal & perhaps Im lucky to be able to stand those But it wont Be long Before Ill have the Do Ra Me I do hope.

    I do wish I could have made it Xmas Max But just couldn't so Ill see you in 1934.

    Will pay you your money I owe you after this show is over

    What is new with the Dramatic Genius. You may get to Be a Great Great Big Shot Pal But to me you are always my punk in just lots of way's.

                Cherrio

                      Jack

Not long after the start of the New Year and Max's return to Pioneer, Jack also appeared there. His stay was brief, however, as Doddy's eccentricities were too much for the boxer. By March 8 he was out of Ohio and on his way to Alaska, according to Max's letter of that date. Jack scribbled a note to Max while en route. Jack never made it to Alaska.

[about March 8, 1934]

Dear Max,

Cedar Rapids Iowa 11:30 Wensday night. Do I travel or Do I travel.

I had to Buy a ticket to Elkhart Indiana Cost <u>2.87</u>. I didn't have to But waited till 4PM & no freight so I Bought a ticket & got out of Elkhart that evening.

Max write me in care of my Girl at Burley Idaho & I keep on as is I shall soon Be their. I just quit the crack train on the North Western Because my feet got to dam cold.

I haven't had people to tell about the Stein opera But you can Bet dough Ill have all the spud pickers having it happily with a spoon Before I hit Alaska.

My regards to Francis [Frances Bollinger] & tell her I still wish her luck

I shall dash off a note to Flora & then <u>1:30</u> to Omaha.
    Cherrio

        Jack

[no date]

Dear Max,

Well! I'm still out of Jail& trying to kick up a fight so I can give my girl a few Bucks to get to Ventura Calif & study awhile & I shall take the rest & go north to Alaska if theirs any left. Havent got a fight scared up yet But hope to soon.

My regards to Dotty [Doddy] & Francis [Frances Bollinger] & I suppose by now Nellie [Gilpin] thinks I have kids all over the country. I have never stopped to check up.

I think I shall drop little Joe Brewer a letter.

Have you managed to get back to N.Y. yet or not. When you do tell <u>every</u> <u>Body</u> Im getting on O.K. even tho Im among the spud pickers.

I shall manage my dance here Sat. night & boy the spud pickers Better watch out or Ill loop a left hook around some ones skull.

How's your Mother Max. & just what do you plan on doing.

Alaska looks good to me Max. & I shall hit Seattle & go north next month. I did have a tough trip Max. It cost me dam near all the money I had. I spent over $13.00 Bucks coming back.

This is some world the way I live it some time. But I do make it well fish [?]

    Cherrio
      Jack

Jack Pollock
Gen. Del.
Burley, Idaho

Jack next turned up in Twin Falls, Idaho, about 40 miles west of Burley.

[no date]

Tourist Hotel
257 Main Avenue East
Twin Falls, Idaho

Dear Dear Max,

I have changed places & its for the Best Im pretty sure.

Write me Jacko Pollock twin falls Idaho Gen. Del.

Max you remember me telling you about Dean [Hartwell] writing me while their in regards to the fight racket. Well Pal they muss it up in swell shape while Im away & there fore Im damned if I work & worry with this spud pickers again so Im going Back in the ring myself Ill fight soon max & Ill meet the Heavy weights out in this country.

I really cant tell you when Ill get to Alaska pal But Before very long Im pretty sure. The first 75.00 Bucks I make Ill give to my girl so she can get out of Burley.

Gee I saw a marvelous show this after noon Francis Lederer & Elissa Landi in a man of two worlds. Have you seen it? If not then go & since I have seen it I have changed my mind in regards to teaching an Eskimo to fight. After all fighting is plenty tough for a white man let alone for me to Bring one of those poor savages out into what we call civilization & he would also have to Buck what known as civilization to us & also the fight racket. Hell Max a hop head wouldn't do such a thing. I know I don't live up to conventions But an Eskimo in the Garden would Be to much. I wrote Joe Brewer a letter also Francis & yourself so Im pretty Busy considering Im training also so Ill pick up a few Buck's. Yes & my girl friend at Burley & Dean Heartwell [Hartwell] & my father. I also had lamb chops for Dinner. Really max I don't think Ill eat Beef for quite awhile it reminds me to much of Dotty [Doddy].

Have you gone Back to the city yet. Let me know all the dirt when you do.
    Cherrio
        Jack Pollock

[no date]

Tourist Hotel
257 Main Avenue East
Twin Falls, Idaho

Dear Max,

Im right in the middle starting to-night of an amateur Boxing tournament that Im helping Bill Child's put over. I have Been so Busy & done so much work to-day that really Max don't feel slighted if I don't write much for its now one o-clock & we had fight after fight from 8 till 12 mid night & still have two more day's to go. But we are going to have to extend it until its finals are ran off Sat night & that will make three more nights of it. We advertised for only three nights Wens. Thur. & Fri. But Hell pal these spud pickers really want to Become fighters & you can Bet money I have my foot right in the middle of it. Ill fight right soon also Max & I hope I can get Back down to my old form when I was Exquisite & Decorative & such & such.

I do claim that I prefer to fight the entire Mormon population in preference to living at Pioneer Ohio. I do love a fight & thanks again to you & Muriel for I shant ever forget 1932.

My regards to Dotty [Doddy] & Francis [Frances Bollinger] Max & I do hope your mother is lots Better when you receive this.

Cherrio

J. Pollock
Gen Del.
Twin Falls
Idaho

[April 2, 1934]

Tourist Hotel
257 Main Avenue East
Twin Falls, Idaho

Dear Max,

Boy how my poor old heart goes out to you Max sooner or later we all must go But its terrible hard when they are so close to you.

You once asked me if you could publish my letters in case any thing happened to me. Yes!! Max you are free to do with them as you choose in case any thing ever stops this boy. I know of nothing outside of Dotty [Doddy] I cant take.

The weather is wonderful here. It snowed some yesterday (Easter) But dear Boy it really isn't near zero & hasn't Been.

My girl had her show again last week & made a few Bucks & me Im O.K. have 2 girl classes and one man's class & also a Boxing class & then Im also training. Expect to fight a week from this Thursday But really wouldn't Bet on it.

No Im not Exquisite yet!

Well pal I know every spud picker worth while here even the Mayor.

   Cherrio,

  Love Jack

In his next letter and the one following, Jack reveals that he is going to "come into my dough." Although he doesn't specify the source of that money, he makes it sound as if it would be substantial, possibly an inheritance. There is no evidence that anything came of it. Perhaps it reflected more hope than reality or a desire to get Max out of his depression.

[April 21 1934]

Tourist Hotel
257 Main Avenue East
Twin Falls, Idaho

Dear Max,

    I am in Seattle & have Been away from Dear old Idaho for about a week.

    My plans are to go from here to some where at sea for Im trying to line up & get out to sea. Its pretty tough so far But Hell I know what it is to hit tough spots & its really just one more tough spot to me. How's your mother Max. I suppose I have a letter from you at twin falls But I left town over a week ago & went to Boise & then to port land & at last a port town Seattle & I hope my next jump is China. Id just as soon travel this old world as I have traveled the U.S.A.

    Max I suppose you will wonder why I don't go Back into the Marines until I come into my dough & then live as I want to Well pal I don't care to have some spud picker tell me what to do in the out fit for we also have spud pickers in their & Im not fighting any more I wouldn't Be able to pull strings for Id have to Soldier & so no thanks.
Jack Pollock
Gen. Del.
Seattle, Wash.

Cherrio Love

    Jack

P.S. Max old Boy send me $10.00 Bucks & put it down on what I owe you for its going to take a few extra Dollars to get a job & out to sea.
    Love Jack

Pioneer Ohio
Monday

[around the end of April, 1934]

Tourist Hotel
257 Main Avenue East
Twin Falls, Idaho

Dear Max,

 I dare say you frighten me with such a letter. Max please it isn't all that Bad. Life is tough as hell at times Max But a man must Be a man & just as tough as the job calls for. You have a hard assignment & have had for months But Max you have done swell much Better than any one I know of so pull your self together & finish your job.

 You know you have my sympathy & all of that Max & more & God if I could settle the estate for you & pay the taxes & sell the store & decide what to do with the house Id Be only two glad to do it for you. Max I cant so you must go on & on for a few months & then I expect to step into your life with some change in it for you.

 I Dare say this post script worries me & again it makes me feel that I am a good friend & Im wanted by you. Max this life isn't unbearable if one is Broke & that is what I presume you are referring to. No its just the beginning for you Max. It will Be some time yet Before I can get my Dough & then really take it easy. But pal Im not going to starve until I do get it.

 This letter you write gives me room for lots of thought Max & I do think I can think straight in a pinch & that is really what this case of yours puts me in.

 Here is what I have in mind Max. Get out on the Admiral line as soon as the dam strike is over. I stand a very good chance & know positively that Ill get to work as soon as the dam longshoremans strike is over. It is tying up all Boat traffic here on this coast. Get on the Boat as a seaman which pay's $55.00 month & Board & Bunk & meet you in N. Y. & by that time Ill have an A.B. [Able Bodied Seaman] ticket & Be able to ship on any line & take you with me & Break you in on the job & travel the seas until I can come Back & get my money & then a home in Southern france & peace Max. this may sound very terrible or very wonderful or some such but the job on the Boat is quite a bit of work Max But still one is travelling from Port to Port and also different parts of this old world & really life isn't so Bad if one cant get to operas & entertain all the Big shots. Max my Boy this life is now up to you & I shall do everything I can for you. On the other hand if you want me their with you I will gladly return to you at Pioneer. Max you will have Dotty [Doddy] in her home & we can close the house & go to the cabin at the lake to live & straighten out the estate & sell the store & Decide what to do with the home in town & after all I guess its Best for me to return to you their until you can settle the estate & all for you wont Be able to join me at sea. Not until you at least have the estate settled.

 I hope I have made myself clear Max. so send me 20 or 25 Dollars & Ill return to you & we will manage some how Max. I know Pioneer is quite a Bore Max But you & I do get along nicely so Pal that's O.K. By me & you & I will see it on through.

 I left Seattle for I couldn't land any thing. I worked a couple day's here & picked up 12 Bucks. My girl friend is here with me pal & we are living with friends of hers. She is leaving to-morrow Max and she is quite Broke the same as I But we aren't going to quit. I wouldn't ask you for the money if I had some myself But my Capital is 65 cents at present so Max send me an air mail letter & money as soon as soon as receive this & Ill see you real soon.

 Max my mama is indisposed she is lieing on the sofa in P.J. she sends her Best regards Max & now Ill sign this off.
    Love Max Jack

A.E. Ewing dated the following letter as May 1. It is clear from the context that Jack had not yet learned that Max's mother had died on April 22.

[about May 1, 1934]

Tourist Hotel
257 Main Avenue East
Twin Falls, Idaho

My Dear Max,

    I recd two whole letters from you to-day. Gee But my mail has a terrible time keeping up with me when I travel so far. Max you know By now that I can & do put miles and towns Behind me when I want to. Im glad you feel as tho you have done everything possible for your Mother. I know from experience what a terrible strain you have Been under all this year of 34 & part of 33. Max of course its to Bad about your Mother But Ill say this there is all kinds of Brave & courageous people in this old worn world But you Boy are as Brave as any fighter that ever crawled through the ropes or any cop that ever shot it out as man to man with a thug as any Body. Max your courage tops mine for I would pass out if I had to stand Dotty [Doddy] as you have had to do and also your Mother being ill as She has Been & is! "Well" you are a 100% in my estimation & I feel as you do about the experience we went through their. It will Bring us lots closer & I can safely say that I shall always want you for my own favorite friend.

    I recd a letter from Francis [Frances Bollinger] But I shall give her some of her own medicine & wait a month Before I answer.

    Well! Max I have put Idaho behind me & at present Im not lined out with any thing definite But will as soon as I get enough cash to Buy a job. This is a funny world the way I live any More But I suppose lots of people would think it terrible tough But Max even tho I see the rough spots & manage to pass over them I hardly give them a thought for no matter how tough it gets I know I can stand it & get a laugh out of it sooner or later.

After receiving your letters I have softened up to the extent that I am sorry I asked you for any money Max. Just forget it & Ill get By as long as I can get around & I do hope there is nothing waiting to trip me up. Boy you have all my love sympathy & everything it takes & I do hope you make out O.K.

Jack

Yes Im more or less exquisite I weigh 178

    Cherrio

    Jack

About the same time Muriel Draper wrote Max, "Jack is the loyal and helpful angel we knew him to be, and if you let him down by not responding to his help, I will never forgive you. Tell him I am hunting for that 'couple of bucks,' and will come straight out and marry him as soon as I find them. Thank him for his letter, and for being there when you need him so much."

In the middle of June A.E. received a telegram that must have caused him a sleepless night: "MAX EWING WAS DROWNED IN THE RIVER THIS PM WIRE INSTRUCTIONS VIA WESTERN UNION –FJ HITCHCOCK CORONER." The wire was dated 9:34 p.m., June 16, 1934 less than six hours after the young man plunged into the Chenango River at Binghamton, New York. Possibly Max had been planning his suicide for some time. At the very least he contemplated it. He had one dollar in his wallet when firemen pulled his body out of the water 30 minutes later.

The Ewings' friend and neighbor, Frank Touse wrote on June 16: "But we still have Max to think about and he is more Crazy than his mother ever was don't eat half enough. Going to drown himself tried to get Jack to shoot him, etc etc. . . ."

Two days after Max's death Jack wrote his side of the story in a letter to Besse Durbin, a resident of Pioneer and another friend of the family.

June 18, 1934

Dear Bessie,

I'm in N.Y. Arrived this morning. Bessie I'll try to right this letter But oh its going to be hard. After we left Pioneer we hit Cleveland and took route 20 up near Buffalo & then took route two & then 17 to Binghamton & stopped for a sandwich about 4 oclock Sat afternoon. I drove all the time & all day Sat. Max was his old self & were going to try to have Muriel come back with us to Pioneer. He was swell just a great kid all day& he ordered his sandwich & I ordered mine & I closed my eyes & he went out and although I saw him go for I opened them (eyes) after I got worried & went to look for him & couldn't find him But I wasn't really worried for he had been so swell. I ate my sandwich and he hadn't come back so I scraped his up in a napkin & took it to the car & drove the car over to the Crown filling station & went back to the restaurant and told the boys & I had the car to the station to tell the boy that was with me that I started back Bessie & one boy hollered to me & I came back & he told me some Body just jumped in the river. I go to the river & it just happened But lots of people were there. I got hold of the police officer in charge & he just did it not long before & they had Police searching for him all ready What a shock I was out on my feet I have Been hit hard before But nothing hit me like that I came too my self when a Lieut & another Big Police man tried to take me away. I would not go. They tried to handcuff me & take me But they couldn't I threw them around like Baby's. Then they were going to gang me so I said Id go. They took me to Headquarters & what a day they grilled and grilled me over & over & then they found Max & they told me it was a local boy that my friend must have hid from me. Oh I felt so much Better God & then they Brought his coat in & threw it at my feet I don't know yet why Im alive then they took me to the morgue where Max was. I don't know what happened I came to with a nurse working on me they took me back to Headquarters & grilled me some more I was about dead all ready I don't know yet why Im alive then the coroner & still I never got loose I didn't Care then if they shot me or not for Ill not kill myself But Im Not Nothing like you knew me Oh Bessie I failed that Boy I loved. I threatened him & Bluffed him But God I wouldn't hit him ever Oh I tried everything But force altho I used force to take him out of Pioneer & failed Bessie they turned me loose & they took charge of Every thing. I told them Ill stay their until his uncle came But Bessie I couldn't Id have killed myself I got so drunk & they took care of me on the train But I passed out Bessie Im at Muriels home She isn't here until this morning She be back I have never known fear until to night Bessie I got to thinking if Max can go crazy perhaps I will to & God I'm afraid Oh Bessie I have Been Brave & could laugh & Be gay But the more Im afraid to death some thing will happen to me Oh Bessie I never hurt him & haven't done anything But try God I may Break for this is awful But Bessie if I do anything you will know how far I have sliped & I want to be the gay Happy Boy you knew. I need Muriel so & yet Im afraid it May Break her too. Bessie why does things happen like that. Im afraid my mind will go for we can stand so much & No more. Bessie right to me Have Francis write Oh God this is awful Jack

In an undated note Jack admonished Muriel, "Here is a Boy you may think you know But Im pretty sure you don't know. Max Ewing has

never had an affair with Man Woman or Child. A Boy 31 years old that has with out a doubt Been every thing I am not. I was Ill in 1932 if you will refresh your memory & Max Ewing & I must say your self helped to pull me out of it. Now their has came a time in my life where Im doing the Best I know how to pull Max back to Par & its such a difficult job that I dont think I can stick much longer."

Jack Pollock
% Muriel Draper
312 E 53St
New York City

Id come back But God Bessie Id die if I did

A week or two after his nephew's death, A.E. wrote to Duncan McD. Johnston, the mayor Twin Falls, Idaho, asking for information about Jack. He received this reply: "The party in question, Mr. Jack Shirley, was a prize fighter, at least he got into the ring once and was knocked out in about 47 seconds, and in my estimation is a very undesirable character and we don't like his brand of bed bugs in our jail; but in all seriousness, I am sure that any business dealings you may have with the party in question will be very disastrous to you or your clients."

Max was buried with his parents at Floral Grove Cemetery in Brady Township, not far from Pioneer. Doddy passed away exactly a month after her grandson's death. Jack Pollock continued his journey to New York, where he stayed with Muriel Draper, returned briefly to Pioneer, and then headed to the Northwest once again. Clara Sweet wrote A.E. that she hoped "[Jack] might accidentally lose his footing" and slip into the ocean. Perhaps he did. He left no trace after making a brief appearance in Portland, Oregon.

The week following Max's suicide, Doris visited Binghamton. She wrote a long letter to Muriel, summarizing her emotions and her findings. Among her observations were this: ". . . There was an old, old woman with a young, young child who were the only witnesses. We met them. They were walking there & saw this young fellow with, what she termed a 'duster' on, walk down the street, climb the fence railing (?) and as the bank is very steep with rank grass & shale, he ran down to the waters edge and right on out into the water. He thru off his coat & hat as he went in & called out something (ah Muriel what could it have been?) but she couldn't hear clearly enough to understand." Carl Van Vechten shared with Muriel his conclusions about Max:

No date.

    Thinking everything over, dearest Madraper, I am almost convinced that Max's act was the result of a realization on his part that he was (at least partially) insane, a fear that you would recognize this, and an inability to face the (probable) consequences. If he were insane, and Jack Pollock's report of his reaction to burned carrots is pretty good evidence, he is thriced blessed for doing what he did. Think of all that he and we have avoided! Whether or no he was insane, I think it must have been <u>fear</u> insanity that drove him to this walk into the river. I am haunted by the whole story: more even today than I was last night, and perhaps I shall never forget it. But I dont think you have any reason to reproach yourself. Had you acted differently, you might have precipitated something worse.

    my love to you always,

    Thursday   Carl

    As early as July 16, 1934, just a month after Max's death, Carl Van Vechten suggested to A.E. that preserving Max's library, photographs, and manuscripts would be "a slight memorial to his charming soul." Max's friend, Warren Bower, in 1942 inquired of Van Vechten why the papers were going to Yale rather than to the University of Michigan.

Appendix A: Fragments of Undated Correspondence

The following letters may be fragments of several letters or they may be complete. In any event, they are undated, although the last one, from Doris to Carl Van Vechten, dates to about 1943, the year the Max Ewing collection was sent to Yale University. "Manikin pis" is a reference to small statue a fountain of that name in Brussels.

Max to unidentified correspondents

May or June, 1929

In Europe I always felt you around a corner, but in Madison Avenue this fall I felt you one day around the corner and the next in Tibet. And unreasonably, I'm sure, but my sensitiveness to you is unreasonable. My indifference to everyone else in New York is so complete that it leaves the whole range of susceptibility concentrated in my reactions to you, the apparition of your image in the top means to me simply you, the apparition of your image in the top balcony of Carnegie Hall, is of greater importance than the appearance of Mengelberg on the platform, and so on through every spot in town., so that if you go off an inch, the whole city goes off completely.

And Peter Jack has returned to Ann Arbor, a broken man! He is leaving Ann Arbor at the end of this term, and had hoped to teach at Columbia next year, but he says now he could not bear it to be here, since he could never be of any importance in the life of Muriel, and he could not stand to be in the same city and be insignificant to her. So he broke down and said he was returning to England where he could remember her and speak of her for the rest of his life.

Two more messages have arrived from Carl begging me to hurry and join them in Berlin. No amount of telling him I can't come seems to convince him. Since inheriting his brother's fortune, I think he has forgotten all about financial limitations! Roy Sheldon is making a head of A'Lelia Walker, the colored heiress, and she said to Dorothy the other day, "Mrs Sheldon, of course you know so many rich people a little fortune like mine wouldn't seem much to you, but all the same it does keep me occupied taking care of fifty-five thousand dollars every mouth." Dorothy tried to act cool and unimpressed, but she came to me afterward and laughed and we nearly died at the idea of A'Lelia having troubles. As a matter of fact she has troubles, and she tells Dorothy how wretched and miserable she is. She is wretched because the man she loves leaves her for another woman, and she still loves her last husband from whom she is separated, and she has no child, and she has to live on a diet which she hates, and she hates her business and its responsibilities, and she regrets the fact that she can't run it as well as her mother did and that her profits are less each year, and because she is so prominent in her race and is so conspicuous, she has to be careful how she behaves, since she is considered "an example," she has to bother with charities which bore her to death, and she hates her house on the Hudson but she can't sell it because her mother's will forbids it, and in short life is almost unbearable. And there you are.

The Finale of the Follies is called "Ghosts At the Waldorf," showing a ball there in its heyday in the Nineties, with people like Lillian Russell, Maude Adams, Anna Held, etc. represented in attendance.

[before 1931]

More than a hundred people were there. It is nothing but one damn farewell to Europe after another. The steamship lines report a decreased business, but it doesn't seem to affect any of the people one knows. Muriel looked marvelous at her party in a new evening dress of blue silk lace, very well made with a short train. I had never seen it and asked her where she got it. She bought it yesterday ready-made at Klein's for

$2.99. Two ninety-nine. She was so astonished she bought four dresses on the spot, all very attractive, and all four cost less than $15.00

But Mary got impatient and capricious and came today. She rented a limousine and drove up like the Queen of Sheba. Sister, the colored slavey and her husband will never get over it! Mary is in New York for two weeks, alone, without her sister Aggie, and in her highest spirits. She adored the house and explored every inch of it. She climbed to all floors, sat down on all the chairs and all the beds, looked into all the mirrors, and even tried out the plumbing in the bathroom! She need not hesitate to look into any mirrors for she looks, even at closest range, like a woman of twenty-five. Slim and smart as nothing on earth, with her hair golden yellow this season! She said over and over how sensible she thought it was for Muriel to take a house where she could lock her own door. And then she ended up by saying "of course, Muriel, you are still the craziest woman I know!"

I am always moved by the thought of myself sitting up there in that room at the Wisdoms in Madison Court, worshipping Mary from leagues away and hungrily reading Carl's pages about her and wondering what the great world was like. Well it is like this. And very pleasant too.

Muriel's reaction to California is of course her own and exaggerated. But it is the natural one, given her particular conception of living. She has always lived at such a white heat, and so much in the center of constant activity that she is unable to endure stagnation of any kind around her. If nothing is going on she stirs something up. Her greatest gift is for being a storm center of action. And naturally she is exasperated by a land where stagnation is the rule, and which has grown entirely out of peoples' desire for inactivity. People go to southern California because they want to sit under palm trees for the rest of their lives. To be sure this is a semblance of activity. Los Angeles gets bigger all the time, but it simply means that more and more people are collecting in one place to sit down and stagnate. And the thing that Muriel finds upsetting about it is that the country itself is so grandiose and so magnificent scenically, but that the life that goes on there is so insignificant and so at war with the natural surroundings. She finds New York thrilling and exciting because all the young life comes here to DO something, no matter what it is, and she finds southern California depressing because people go there and do nothing or after they have done something somewhere else. So of course such a dynamo as Muriel is affected by the tropical lethargy of the place. The Hollywood thing, of course is something else again.

 Friday night I went with him and Muriel and Eddie Wasserman, and a niece of Carl's named Douane [Duane] Van Vechten from Chicago, to Alelia Walker's party which was SOMETHING. She lives in this absurd apartment far uptown, amid much silken splendor, with divan-like beds hung from ceiling to floor with red, green and yellow taffetas, with elaborate canopies, and hundreds of satin cushions. Her own bed is very white and frilly with a white lace umbrella over it that conceals a reading lamp! Japanese prints and Indian embroideries hang around, and all sorts of odd trappings. This apartment is just a small place she uses when she is not in her big town house or at her country estate on the Hudson! After her party she took the best of it on to the opening of a new night club in Harlem, called VO&DE&O, which was sumptuous, and noisy, and crowded with a very well spangled, well-jeweled people. Alelia became bored and finally went away home, leaving her guests behind her, like Queen Victoria in a temper.

 The visit to Mrs. Van Rensselaer was delightful. Her house too is beyond anything, old-fashioned New York of the nineties and earlier, with enormous rooms filled with fearful and wonderful old furniture and paintings in Tenth Street. We had tea, and the old lady sat in a state like a gay wrinkled Empress of France, smoking more cigarettes than could be counted. She was one of the great characters of old New York, and knew George Eliot and the Brownings and the Hawthornes and everyone in that period. She used to entertain all celebrities visiting New York, but nearly all her generation has died out, and she is left living and very much alive. Lloyd Morris wants to start a revival of her salon, and have all the most brilliant of the young generation go there often next winter. And he is flattering enough to want me and Glenway [Westcott] as the nucleus of the group if we are here. Of course, Lloyd's enthusiasm over and confidence in me is beyond all bounds. He is determined that I must write a novel more or less under his guidance, and he has even gone so far as to speak to the Viking Press and Harpers about it, and they are already making steps toward rival bids for it, on the strength of his recommendation. He wants me to write an amusing story of contemporary New York with candle-holders procured from ancient Chinese temples, and everything exotic and gorgeous, tho' the Raymonds are not particularly brilliant. Dick Hammond was there, and a lot of people including Eva Gauthier. I told her I had had enthusiastic reports about her Toledo concert, and she agreed that everyone was enthusiastic, and that she had enjoyed it, except that she is always bored to sign in the morning. She is sailing soon, going to spend Easter in Spain. In Seville, Easter is particularly beautiful in the cathedral there. She then goes on to Paris and Berlin, and she says that Berlin is just the place for me to go now, and hopes she will see me there in August. The Raymonds are about to sail. Esther sails in May, and says I must sail. Edith sails in April. I saw Alfred Lowden today, the boy with whom I met Vadim Uraneff through whom I met Muriel. He (Alfred) sails in three weeks. Seymour Blair sails today. Marion Putnam and her husband sail in May and have their reservations. Jane is getting hers.

    Alice de la Mar sails when Esther does and has taken the apartment above Esther's in Paris. Alice has become now one of the four richest women in the world. She has so many millions she doesn't know what to do. She pays all the Fifth Avenue traffic cops twenty five dollars a week to let her go down the Avenue when the traffic says stop, because she can't be annoyed by looking to see whether a red or a green light is ahead of her.

Max to an unidentified correspondent

[1932]

We were all discussing Lloyd Morris's novel which is just out, called "This Circle of Flesh." He has put everybody into it under fictitious names, and indulged his spite and venom to the full. He hates Muriel because he is so envious of her, and he has written the most disgusting things about her under the name Mildred Fentress. Rita Romilly called him up and condemned him for this, but he said while everyone would think he meant Muriel, he actually meant several people at once, including Isadora Duncan. So after setting in everyone's mind that the Mildred character is Muriel, he proceeds to attribute Isadora's love life to her, which seems a little too much—particularly on account of Smudge and Paul. Esther appears in the book too as the mistress of a gangster. Carl is in it and referred to as a "fat old auntie" and as "a public monument to forgotten statesmen." It is incredible, the whole thing, and I imagine that what friends remain devoted to Lloyd after this will be enough. He and George Davis can go to the South Seas with everyone's satisfaction. Eddie Wassermann is also in the book and described as "a pretentious ass who lives on to collect celebrities and give them cocktails."

He wanted to go to Harlem where he has never been, but I discouraged him. Harlem is a dead city and I never go there anymore. The depression has put an end to nearly everything. Except parties. Everybody gives parties all the time like mad.

Prices seem to be going down and down. I bought handsome silk socks this weekend in 42nd st for ten cents a pair. In perfect condition, very good quality. Underwear 15 cents.

A Salon somewhat in the grand style, although the grand style intensely modernized and made more intimate, is what Mrs. Muriel Draper's afternoon teas have become, since her return from a long sojourn in London. People call one another by their nicknames at Mrs. Draper's or by their first names with an added "darling," if one of the parties to an oral interchange is a woman.

Mrs. Draper is simply amazing, fascinating. At my first tea in her studio I felt exactly like the man in advertisement who has not devoted fifteen minutes a day to the classics.

Mrs. Draper lives and acts and talks with an expression of intensity entirely outside of my experience. Only once in my life have I witnessed anything like it before and that was when, as a small boy, sitting in the balcony of the Benson Opera House in Shawnee, Oklahoma, I saw Sarah Bernhardt in the role of Camille. Mme. Bernhardt would give—and Mrs. Draper can give—an expression of emotional intensity to a commonplace of speech like "Won't you sit down?" or "lemon or cream?" greater in degree than I was able to feel when my first sweetheart gave me the air, my grandmother died, or I became a father.

When Mrs. Draper said that Marcel Duchamp had stopped painting and that she did not know why, but she knew somehow he would never paint again, and that she could burst into tears whenever she thought about it, my heart pounded, my mouth gasped, my head swam. Would anyone in the world, I asked myself, show such anxiety and solicitude if I should give up writing–or, indeed, if I should give up living?

Doris Ewing to Carl Van Vechten
[about 1943]

John and Clara stowed away, before the thirties a neat $250,000. Just before John's death I believe, the depression sliced out a hundred thousand, more or less. That left Clara feeling destitute, as she would not touch the principle. She developed a financial persecution and never reported for inheritance or national income tax. When she died, Max discovered that there was compound interest, etc. on both father and mother. And that confounded him! He then damned himself for so criticizing and blaming his mother for losing her balance over money affairs and promptly proceeded to go into a button-holed barrel role, and considered himself destitute. As I have written, he would buy a penny's worth of this and nickel of that, sugar, matches, sausage … Jack KNEW he had money coming (everyone in Pioneer knew that) so that is why he was so tenderly considerate. He wanted Max to buy a kingdom in France, where the TWO of them could live happily ever after.

Whatever Max had had while alive, after the deaths of the whole family, the estate which was divided between four heirs, totaled around $72,000.00 or less, if anything, not more. And that $72,000 was in stocks and bonds which when cashed lost heavily from the time of the investment, etc. So that it really wasn't $72,000.00.

Max and I held hands like Siamese twins.

Max's French teacher, who STARTED him on his High Road, was Mildred Henry. He thought a very great deal of her.

May the united of all of us who loved–and LOVE—Max, keep alive the Max we loved!

Bessie told me that Max usually called her Blossom (tactfully refraining from Cherry) and his pet names for me were Pet, Toad, Dump and Dove.

As for Pioneer, Mrs. Josephine [Doddy] Bartoe was Max's grandmother. She died a week after he did. She damned Jack in everything but Portuguese, to the very end. She was superb.

I've seen Doddy throw one of Clara's unworthy cakes out the back door.

Does anyone ever hear or see of Jack [Pollock]? Is he behind bars or tippling under them? Or rippling his swabodas? Such a manikin pis, that one. Wish he were set up in a square in Brussells right now.

The Ewings haven't any more sense than a baby bunny in clover and our financial apple cart is all topside like hell and probably always will be. Whatever Max had, was due to his mother—she had the financial vision and sense and John patience and perseverance.

Films of the Venetian sets as well as photos, clippings and albums of Venice etc. Maybe I'm just aging and sour, but this naked SEX assortments, doesn't seem likely to ban addition to any gallery or museum. However, that is up to you or his artist models. Of course there are fig leaves!

Carlo, where in such-a-such are Max's personal belongings, i.e. the paintings of Muriel and those others show the photographs? Where is that lovely batik which I would adore? Where are the "sculptures"? SOMEBODY had them as a loan or else. The furniture of his that was sold at auction or rummage, was cheap and horrid, except for the piano. It would seem that whoever had them would have come forward after Max's death and declare them—or doesn't it?

Yes, they owned a cottage at Clear Lake, Indiana. A very nice little place where Max wrote most of Going Somewhere.

In fact, you must understand that he was just crazier than any two god-damned fools out of an asylum could be. With the exception of Clara Sweet, this frustrated bee-stinging Bessie, Theo (who married early and left town) and his immediate circle of "intimates" and

DODDY—God rest her raging soul—were about all the friends who Max counted on in Pioneer. If they listened to him at all, as some did out of morbid curiosity they were all spotty afterwards, like strawberries and crabs, with indigestion afterwards.

Pioneer is, or was when I knew it and visited there, a tiny village of about a thousand. Must be more now. It had the usual CORNERS, i.e., two main thoroughfares on which were located the "café" where Clara used to treat us to chicken-Sunday-dinners on Saturday when she was too tired to go home and cook. There were two large department stores, Ewing's and Hadley's, a corner apart. Frankly, Ewings catered to the farmers and had an excellent trade. They sold EVERYTHING from linoleum to shoe laces. At one time they had an extra-super department for Milady, millenary and costumes. Clara had several clerks then and two "trimmers." It was there that Max got his early inspiration and training for costume designing. He played among bits of brocades, velvets, satins, and calico, etc. They never actually closed the store. During the big buying seasons, one of them would sleep down there, so as not to miss a penny sale. They were open nights as long as there was business, none was too petty. Clara and John knew every costumer and their family, for miles around. They actually used to drive thirty miles to buy from Clara and John. I suppose their personal interest and advice was high powered salesmanship before the guy who wrote about it, wrote about it. Now alas, the store is a beer parlour and nothing could be more cruel or ironic, as John and Clara were total non-elbow raisers.

I judge from memory that the whole town is about ten to fifteen blocks through each way. Max's home was a block and a half from the store, so Clara could conceivably sell a corset and run home to jam gooseberries. Their house was one of those built early in 1910 or there abouts. Much, too much, golden oak, pillars between the "front" room and the library. God knows what if anything they were ever called. The dining room was filled with glass front dish cupboards, some nice dishes and glassware. Some Limoges saddled with Kresge! Or early Pioneer. The table was nearly always left "set" to facilitate manners and methods. Of course when no one was there they ate in the kitchen, as no two hardly ever sat down and ate at the same time.

And when Max or company was present, they literally put on hotel fare, so that several choices could be made and they stood at your back while you ate waiting to refill. Max *always* got the choice cuts, jernts etc, company next, John next, and then Clara and Doddy would slam it out. Doddy spent hours of meal times rocking furiously in a chair on the front porch, because Clara insisted on her taking the last piece of pie.

They quarreled constantly yet, let Clara or Doddy have pain and either would heave out in the middle of the stormiest night to care for the other. Clara loved dressing Doddy up in finery and Doddy made a character worth looking at and remembering. That magnificent head of heavy white hair, and ivory-clear skin and fine dynamic brown eyes. She sat like a queen though she walked bent from hard work in the garden etc. and her hands were gnarled. She must have suffered from rheumatism for the last few times I saw her particularly the year, the week before she was "taken to her bed" and died, she used a cane. She punctuated every hiss of profanity, such as held me in awe, between her teeth, with jabs of the cane at the carpet. This was through the Jack-damnation period. Doddy by the way lived across the town from Max's, in a sweet little old house, clean and orderly and jammed with her collection of things over a LONG period of years. She had a very thriving little garden, which would make some of the present victory gardens look like back alleys. Her cupboards and cookie jars were always filled with "eatables." For a lady who was forever feeding others, she was the slightest bit, looked so frail. When she was pleased or laughed she was charming, her face lighting with dimples of good humor! If only Max had had some of her or his mother's dynamic qualities as I have. He was composite lad, that one, a heart of honey dripped from mauve narcissus.

Jack brought the name of the Rouses to the front, the local jeweler who held down a counter of Tiffany's counter parts, as Jack slept on their front porch for several nights and arranged some tidy loans from them, which Clara finally had to settle from the estate.

But it was hard for Pioneeronians to pass the house and see the shades drawn in daylight and lights on all night, all with MUCH REVELRY and WHOOPLA just before the sun rose! That coupled with the fact that Max wouldn't leave house for more than five minutes or so and then returned hurriedly and in panic. When he bought food it was a penny's worth of matches or sugar etc. or *one* steak, with Jack and Frances in the house. Clara [Sweet] insisted that Max died of starvation as well as of other things. Said all of the food went to Jack. Frances told her that she didn't get enough to eat there.

The house was refinished but I KNOW that it is haunted. Literally. Ask Muriel. She will understand, though I can't! Father, mother and I lived there most of the summer following the last funeral in the family, i.e., Doddy. The walls exuded currents that invariably raised a family of gooseflesh all over me! I couldn't sleep nights even with lights turned on and I am not *scared* or susceptible (to ghosts!) Perhaps my head was turned because my heart was jammed and torn with the sequence of events, the unfolding tragedies of an entire family, a family so near and dear to me. I used to spend vacations with Max when he was learning to sit up! He was an adorable, golden, curly haired baby. Then they lived in a large white colonial house over near Doddy's, one in which the Masters live now, Paul's aunt and uncle. There was a recessed porch that was then an oddity to me, for in all my experience, were built out from the house. This house, incidentally, was next to the Grand Stand, where the band played Wednesdays, I believe. He was naturally beloved by his teachers and tolerated or ignored by most of the kids.

Well, the man IS IN the barn right this minute nailing up the boxes and tying up one package that wouldn't fit into either box.

John is the kind of car owner who dusted off the car after every trip. He rarely if ever used it in rain, unless caught out in it, and not any more than direly necessary, like going after Max or taking him back, to meet trains.

Max had a fur collared coat and a DERBY hat that opened even the sleepy eyes of the ticket agent. I believe that the car was a Paige, Graham-Paige. No, that was the last one. Notice that John's caution prompted him to block the tire on the far side so that Max in his driver's capacity couldn't start the car rolling! The only long trip that I can remember, they had in their car was driving to New York.

Once or twice he came to the Wilderness, but he was babied so much by Doddy and Clara and Mary Wortley, one of the trimmers who lived with them at times, and other females who wanted someone to nurse or mother.

There was an old fashioned pump-organ in the 'front' room in which and on what Max and I would spend hours, doodling away. It used to drive Grandpere NUTS because we were always giggling and talking about SUCH things that no one quarter-brained would bother about. It was the beginning of our strange-creature land with mumping can opener and liliput. We used up reams of paper illustrating, which was easy as we had no competitors!

GOING SOMEWHERE is filled with beings, BORNED from Strange creature land. His first copies more than the final, I mean the ones he wrote at Clear Lake, when he started doing it just for amusement.

Mary____, another little old wizened lady, who cleaned for Clara, was another subject for tantalizing. Mary belonged to one of those Seven Day Adventist or Mennonite groups, which abound around the country-side. Dunkers I believe was the name. Anyway, she abhorred happiness, gaiety was displeasing to the Lord and looked upon card playing, dancing and singing as a king-sized *vice*, which is of course where Max and I shined. We never danced, sang or played as many cards as when we HOPED Mary would be around!

Incidentally, it was such a rare sight that I can say that I never saw Clara lie down and sit down for more than the necessary moment it took to read the Toledo Blade or business magazines of industry and energy. Well, it was like the national war debt, endless!

Max and I used to attend the carnivals and 'lectures,' which ever dared pitch its tent in the Meadows. I saw Uncle Tom's Cabin and Julius Caesar once that would stop any Broadway production ever given!

Max used to play the piano for the movies, in the days when they were STILLS. The kind where the girl stands at the garden gate and sings a song (a tinted Gibson girl) and the next flash would bring on the Hero. When the flickers came on Max would delight in the fire-scenes and galloping horses etc. We both felt very superior to the usual crowd, because we had seen better pictures!

I wonder where Muriel and the Robesons etc. ate? Max, Muriel, Larry Elseworth (?) and Taylor [Gordon] and I once tried to get a dinner in a Spanish restaurant and they refused to serve us. If I remember Muriel got so hot under the collar that she encouraged Taylor to bring suit which he won.

She [Muriel] still claims that Jack ran off with Max to New York to 'save him' from the sanitarium where Dr. Brady and Dr. Solier had made arrangements to stay unless it was to his benefit, and going to NY and getting out of Pioneer was definitely to his advantage. Jack may have been informed about the sanitarium. He admitted to Bessie that he 'overheard' the doctors in the 'bug house' in Bryan [Ohio] (Max sat out in the car REFUSING to move, for fear they would keep him there) talking about Max and making the arrangements to collect him bag and baggage on this certain afternoon. I do know that Dr. Brady told Father that Max's case was hopeless. That men his 'age and <u>kin</u>' always went that way and that it was simply a matter of making it easy and safe–for whom god knows. Max would never have harmed an ant. Bessie asked if I didn't think that Christian Science would have helped Max and I said no because 'it' went back too far, I mean what ailed him went back too deeply and I am coming to conclude, to the erotic sex-and-otherwise, life of the Andersons. Certainly the Ewings are they damndest, plodding, middle-of-the-roadest pioneers our country has seen. Several of the older folks I talked with said that it was all Doddy, with her temper and the fight between her and Clara to dominate Max.

    And this is strictly Bessie's experience and viewpoints. That Max literally lived at their house, while Jack was there (holding hands with her on every occasion) and in a passion of exasperation and worry over the way Doddy worried and bothered him and his mother. She said that Clara came running to her once and just threw herself literally in Bessies arms, more literally I mean, her lap and wept and wept, that Doddy was driving her MAD and get her out of the house. She claims that Doddy SCOLDED with every breath she drew.

    It seems that Clara, after John's death (and I'm not sure whether while Max was there or not) gave out a lot of clothing to a very poor family who lived across the street from Doddy. And that either Doddy or Clara, not clear, went across on the coldest day, when the family was piling off to church and literally hauled the clothes they had given, off of the backs of the mother and children. There is something nutsy there, unless it is a phase that was a result of her present state of mind and pain. You knew didn't you, that she died of cancer of the brain? Her suffering had been excruciating. This dear old gent, Mr. Masters, Paul's uncle, who was eighty-four and had lived in Pioneer for 72 years, said that if John could have lived, <u>none</u> of the ensuing tragedies would have happened. That John had the poise and BALANCE and wouldn't have lost his reason over the loss of their money, as Clara did—would have worked and slaved with <u>HITLERIAN</u> fanaticism, to earn and save every little penny. And I am inclined to believe him.

I knew that John used to sing a great deal as a young man. Belonged to a Glee Club that toured around the country. He used to indulge on one of those long whistle-tooters, flute or pipe.

No one but his kind could have acted as backdrop to Clara's high colored personality. He was very religious in the accepted sense and the tragedy lies perhaps in his early death. He was modest and unassuming and in awe where ever Max was concerned. Max was a swan among barnyard fowl, temperamentally not socially.

Young Fred Hadley, of Hadley Dry Goods Store, told me that he thought Max was a peach and that he and his brothers liked Max very much. He said that the day <u>before</u> Max left Pioneer, he came and talked very rational to him about what to do with the store: would Fred be interested in buying and at least what would he advise etc. He said that at the oddest moment through the day or night, that he and Jack would come down to the store, set the lights ablaze and open up for business until they cleared enough for pocket money!

The Meyers have bought and redecorated the Ewing house for a FUNERAL HOME! The house is a rectangle with four gables as stodgy as cocked pancakes over four sleepy eyed attic windows. How can ghosts walk in a house with so little apparent imagination present???

Carlo, really, goose pimples ran like electric shock all over me. Bessie mentioned them and showed me hers, two neurotic old women. But when we got back to the house (hers) she said that as long as I FELT that way too, she wanted to tell me what she hadn't dare tell anyone, that she KNEW the house was haunted! Nonsense of course but we were both in a psychological state of nonsense by this time. She said that the houses' two tenants, one from Cleveland and the other Toledo both disliked the house and one family left because of noises and strange skin tingling experience they felt!

The family from Cleveland claims that the little toy piano of Max's (Clara Sweet had given it to the little girl of the renter family) tinkled, all by itself in the closet one evening. I suggested mice or the vibrations of the water pump downstairs, but Bessie's scorned the idea. She said that she knew Max was psychic and that they had always worked the "weegie" [Ouija] board to find out when she would receive letters or do certain things.

She was the one who, in Bessies opinion, earned the house and lot, because of Doddy's temper. Said Doddy would spit tea and crackers clear across the dining room table!

Appendix B: Allusions to People, Places, and Miscellaneous Items

Berenice **Abbott**, 1898-1991; photographer and author, Max was one of her subjects.

Abysinnia [Abyssinia]; former name of Ethiopia.

Maude **Adams**, 1872-1953; American stage actor; her birth name was Maude Ewing Kiskadden.

Adrian, 1903-1959; costume designer who was born as Adrian Adolph Greenberg and was also known as Gilbert Adrian.

Edgar Holt **Ailes**, 1905-1981; attorney and resident of Detroit and Grosse Pointe, Michigan.

Algonquin Hotel, located at 59 West 44th Street in New York City, the hotel opened in 1902.

Aunt **Alice**, 1874-1969; wife of Frank B. Ewing, the brother of John C. and A.E. Ewing.

Delicia **Allen**, a character in the novel *Miss Delicia Allen* by Mary Johnston [1870-1936], published about the same time as *Going Somewhere*.

May **Allison**, 1890-1989; she had a short career as an actor on the silent screen, then became editor of *Photoplay* magazine.

Ambassador Hotel, 132 West 45th Street in New York City.

Richard "Rick" Sheridan **Ames**, writer and film critic.

James **Amster**, 1908-1986; an interior decorator based in New York City; Leonard's brother.

[Nathaniel] Leonard **Amster**, 1905-1987; writer for *New Yorker*, *The Nation*, and other periodicals; James's brother.

Donald **Angus**, @1900- ?; an actor, set designer, and friend of Carl Van Vechten's during the mid-1920s; Max sets Donald's death date in a diary entry, but the date is not confirmed.

George **Anthiel**, 1900-1959; concert pianist and composer; his wife, Beshky [Boski], 1902-1978, was a native of Hungary.

Elsie **Arden**, 1883-1945; singer and vocal teacher in New York City.

The **Arensbergs**, Walter Conrad Arensberg, 1878-1974, writer, and his wife, Mary, 1883-1964.

Michael **Arlen**, 1895-1956; novelist, born in Bulgaria as Dikran Kuyumjan; settled in England.

Merle **Armitage**, 1893-1975; set and costume designer in the New York theater and later an impresario.

The **Askews**, [Ralph] Kirk, 1903-1974, managed the New York branch of British-based Durlacher Brothers Gallery; he and his wife, Constance Askew, 1903-1984, held salons that attracted many of New York's leading artists and authors.

Mary Bancroft **Badger**, 1903-1997; worked for Elizabeth Hawes, an American clothing designer; she and her husband, Sherwin Campbell Badger [1901-1972], were divorced in 1932; Mary married Swiss financier Jean Rufenacht in 1935; she later became a reporter, and during World War II she was a spy for the United States; Max refers to her as the "social register lady" [March 8, 1933].

Mrs. Max **Baer**, wife of Maximillian Adelbert Baer [1909-1959], heavyweight champion in 1934, he also appeared in films, such as *The Prizefighter and the Lady*.

Jon [John] L. **Balderston**, 1889-1954; playwright and screenwriter.

Ballets Russes, started by Serge Diaghilev in 1909 and officially organized two years later, Diaghilev managed the group until his death in 1929.

Bernie [Bernard] **Bandler**, 1904-1993; editor and essayist.

Tallulah Brockman **Bankhead**, 1902-1968, film actor, her romantic interests were bisexual.

William Brockman **Bankhead**, 1874-1940; Tallulah's father was a member of the House of Representatives from 1917 to 1940 and was Speaker of the House the last five years; William's brother, John Hollis Bankhead [1872-1946], was a U.S. Senator.

Mrs. Angelia **Barger**, @1861- ?; resident of Montpelier, Williams County, Ohio.

Ida B **Barkley**, 1861-1946; a resident of Williams County, Ohio.

Natalie Clifford **Barney**, 1876-1972; American playwright, poet, novelist, and lesbian; she spent most of her adult life in Paris.

Mrs. Lionel [Irene Fenwick] **Barrymore**, 1877-1936; Irene was a film actor and the second wife of actor Lionel Barrymore [1878-1954].

Clarissa "Clara" **Barto** [Bartoe], 1869-1934; John Caleb Ewing's wife and Max's mother.

Cecil **Beaton**, 1904-1980; photographer and film and theater set designer.

John "Jack" **Becker**, @1890 to @1980; Jack owned an art gallery in New York City. [Max consistently cites Jack Becket, but he apparently is referring to Jack Becker.]

Noah Nicholas **Beery**, Sr. 1882-1946; character actor in early films.

Ralph **Bellamy**, 1904-1991; star of stage, film and television.

Mrs. **Belmont,** probably English-born Eleanor Robson Belmont, 1879-1979; a one-time actor in the early 1900s, she became a supporter of the Metropolitan Opera Association; she married August Belmont, Jr., who died in 1924.

Constance **Bennett,** 1904-1965; film star.

Richard **Bennett,** 1872-1944; Vaudeville performer and stage and screen actor, film actors Barbara, Constance and Joan were his daughters.

Bergdof Goodman, a prestigious New York department store, located at 745 Fifth Avenue.

Sarah **Bernhardt,** 1844-1923; actor on stage and in films.

Frank, @1903- ?, and Clair [Claire], @1899-1993, **Bishop**; Frank was a concert pianist, and Clair was an author of children's books.

Seymour **Blair,** 1889-1975; a Chicago real estate agent.

Gertrude **Blount,** @1911- ?; a resident of Williams County, Ohio.

Josephine Mary **Bloyd**; see Jacob Norman **Riste**.

Frances **Bollinger,** 1875-1961; resident of Pioneer, Ohio and friend of the Ewings.

Black Bottom, a dance that originated in New Orleans and made its way to New York City and across the country when it became a fad in the mid-1920s, it eventually replaced the Charleston.

Arthur Cleveland **Blumenthal,** 1885-1957; financier and husband of Peggy Fears.

Frances Rose **Bollinger,** 1875-1961; resident of Williams County, Ohio and housekeeper for Clara Ewing.

Lucius Messenger **Boomer,** 1878-1947; manager of the Waldorf Astoria Hotel.

Booth Theater, located at 222 West 45th Street in New York City.

Aleksandr Porfirevich **Borodin**, 1834-1887; Russian-born composer.

W. [Warren] **Bower[s]**, 1891-1976; he taught English at New York University.

Helen **Bowersox,** 1896-@1986; the daughter of Charles A. 1846-1921 and Laura Bowersox @1855-?; Helen was a resident of Pioneer, Ohio, but later relocated to Toledo; her father, Charles Alexander Bowersox [1846-1921], wrote a history of Williams County.

Lenore **Bowersox**, 1886-?; a native of Pioneer, Ohio and later a resident of Toledo; one-time housekeeper for Clara Ewing; Charles A. Bowersox was her father-in-law.

Zelma Corning **Brandt**, 1891-1990; a literary agent and crusader for social issues.

Mrs. [Mary] Russell **Bready,** @1878-1938; wife of Rev. Russell Bready, her birth name was Mary Elizabeth Richards.

Russell Herbert **Bready,** 1876-1938; Minister of four Methodist Episcopal Churches in the Williams County/Hillsdale County area; married Mary Elizabeth Richards.

Joe [Joseph] Hillyer **Brewer**, 1898-1990; appointed President of Olivet College in January, 1934. Joe's father, Joseph Henry Brewer, was President of the National Bank of Grand Rapids, Michigan, the family also owned a printing business in Grand Rapids. Prior to becoming president of Olivet College. In 1928 Joe formed the publishing firm of Putnam & Brewer, which later was sold to Harcourt, Brace.

Fannie **Brice**, 1891-1951; born Fannie Borach, she became a comic star of radio and film.

Broken Bow, John and Clara Ewing purchased municipal bonds issued by Broken Bow, Oklahoma.

Romaine **Brooks**, 1874-1970; artist who was born Beatrice Romaine Goddard, married briefly [1903-1904] to John Ellington Brooks, a pianist; John was gay and Romaine was a lesbian; among her many works was a portrait of Muriel Draper, done in 1936.

Elizabeth Barrett **Browning**, 1806-1861; British poet, born as Elizabeth Moulton.

Nancy **Bryant**; no information beyond Max's description of her as a fortune teller.

Fanny Amanda **Butcher**, 1888-1987; literary editor of the *Chicago Tribune*, married Richard Drummond Bokum.

Nicholas Murray **Butler**, 1862-1947; president of Columbia University from 1901 to 1945.

Dr. **Cameron**; one of the physicians attending John Ewing.

Carmania; a passenger ship of the Cunard Lines.

Carmen; opera written in 1875 by Georges Bizet [1838-1875].

Primo **Carnera;** 1906-1967; Italian born prize fighter who lost his world heavyweight title to Max Baer in 1934.

Tullio **Carminati**, 1894-1971; Italian-born film actor.

Jean **Carr**, @1906- ?; Max noted that Jean was a "young English pianist;" no further information.

Albert **Carroll**, 1895-1956; stage performer; appeared in "Grand Street Follies."

Earl **Carroll**, 1893-1948; theatrical producer and director.

Marco **Carson**, 1905-1986; born in Georgia, but lived in Atlantic City, New Jersey about the time *Going Somewhere* was published.

Miss [Susan B.] **Carstairs**, 1901-1978; wife of Carroll Carstairs [1888-1948], an American art dealer.

Eve [Eva] **Casanova;** Broadway performer in the 1920s and 1930s; she was one of Lou Tellegen's six wives.

Lina **Cavlieri**, 1874-1944; Italian born operatic soprano; she and Bob Sheriff Chanler were married briefly.

Mr. Lord [Samuel] **Certauld** [Courtauld], 1876-1947; an industrialist and art collector, Lord Courtauld came from a wealthy British family and helped start the Courtauld Institute of Art in London.

Princess Paul **Chachavadze;** Nina Georgievna, Princess Romanova, 1901-1974; wife of Prince Paul Chachavadze, 1899-1971; members of the Russian Romanov royal family.

Robert "Sheriff" Winthrop **Chanler**, 1872-1930; an American-born artist, his work was exhibited at the 1913 New York Armory show; he was married for a short time to Lina Cavlieri, his second wife.

Charlie **Chaplin**, 1889-1977; early film actor, well known for his role as "The Little Tramp."

Ilka **Chase**, 1900-1978; American-born film and stage actor and writer.

Childs Restaurant; one of the first national restaurant chains in the United States.

Walter Percy **Chrysler**, Jr., 1909-1954; son of the founder of the Chrysler Corporation.

Ina **Claire**, 1892-1958; film actor.

Alma **Clayburgh**, @1882-1958; wife of Albert C. Clayburgh [@1865-?].

"Dick" Richard **Clemmer,** 1902-1995; his wife, Wilma, lived from 1916-2010.

Clover Club, located in Hollywood on Sunset Boulevard.

Club Deauville, a nightclub on Park Avenue in Manhattan.

Gifford Alexander **Cochran**, 1906-1978; in his letter of March 27, 1933, Max wrote "Gifford Cochran is a Cochran who married Ganna Walska;" Max may have been thinking of Alexander Smith Cochran [1874-1929], an American manufacturer and philanthropist, who was briefly married to Ganna Walska [1887-1984], but they were divorced in 1922; Gifford Cochran was a Hollywood film producer, and apparently Max confused the two.

Jean **Cocteau**, 1889-1963; French poet, writer, artist, and film maker.

Charles **Cogswell**, 1874-1933; resident of Pioneer, Ohio.

John S. **Cohen**, Jr.; movie critic for the *New York Sun*.

Sibyl, Lady **Colefax [Colfax],** 1874-1950; English interior decorator and cousin of Winston Churchill.

Colombo, the passenger ship *Cristoforo Columbo*.

Betty **Compson,** 1897-1974; actor from both the silent and talking film eras.

Donald **Coney**, 1901-1973; in 1920 Donald was a newspaper reporter in Jackson, Michigan; by 1930 he and his wife were residing in Chapel Hill, North Carolina, where Donald was Assistant Librarian at Duke University; he died in Berkeley, California.

Lawrence @1898- 1982 and Roberta **Conrad** @1891- ?; Lawrence, a Michigan native, was a teacher at a private school in St. Louis, Missouri around 1930.

Gary **Cooper,** 1901-1961; Hollywood film star, born as Frank James.

Aaron **Copeland**, 1900-1990; American composer.

George **Copeland,** 1882-1971; American pianist.

Katherine **Cornell**, 1898-1974; film star.

Ricardo **Cortez**, 1899-1977; actor who starred in such films as *Illicit.*

Miguel **Covarrubias**, 1902-1957; a Mexican artist, well known for his caricatures of celebrities and book illustrations.

Lucy **Cotton,** 1891-1948; silent film actor.

Noel **Coward**, 1899-1973; English-born actor, playwright, and composer.

Dan **Cox**; apparently a Hollywood agent.

Dotty [Dorothy] Maude **Crawford**, 1885-1976; write and actor.

Joan **Crawford**, 1908-1977; film star, born as Lucille Fay Le Seuer; Douglas Fairbanks Jr. was her first husband.

The **Crawfords**; Max probably was referring to Joan Crawford and her husband.

Rene **Crevel**, 1900-1935; an artist who was born and died in Paris, France.

Crillon, a restaurant located at 116 East 48th Street in Manhattan.

Charles **Crouch**, @1876-1952; a San Diego attorney.

George **Cukor**, 1899-1983; director of many successful films.

Marguerite **d'Alvarez**, 1886-1953; operatic mezz-soprano.

Walter Johannes **Damrrosch**, 1862-1950; Director of the New York Symphony from 1903 to 1927; born in Poland.

Mary **Dangerfield**; evidently from England.

Marion **Davies**, 1897-1961; a film actor who was born as Marion Cecilia Douras; she was known as William Randolph Hearst's paramour and lived with him at San Simeon, California and elsewhere for about 30 years.

Charles Gates **Dawes**, 1865-1951; lawyer, financier, and Vice President of the United States under Calvin Coolidge from 1925 to 1929.

Mercedes **de Acosta**, 1892-1968; lesbian, poet, playwright, and set and costume designer.

Duke **de Arcos**; possibly the Spanish Minister to the United States in the early 1900s.

Baroness **d'Erlanger**; probably Myrtle Farquharson [1897-1941], who married Baron d'Erlanger [1896-1934].

DeGrasse; this transatlantic passenger liner of the French Line made its first voyage in late summer of 1924 carrying just under 500 passengers.

Alice Antoinette **de la Mar** [de Lamar], 18951983; the daughter of Joseph Raford de Lamar and Nellie Virginia Sands, Alice in 1918 became "the richest young heiress in America," she was a well-known patron of the arts and supporter of social and environmental causes; her mansion in Miami, called Stonebrook, was built on 11 acres that included a mature trees, a brook, gazebo, stone bridges, inground pool with an underground swimming tunnel, fieldstone terraces, perennial gardens, wild flowers, meadows, and well-maintained lawns.

Henry **Dell**; manager of the Castle Harbor Hotel in Bermuda.

Ray **de Mare**; no information.

Countess **de Noailles** [Anna-Elizabeth de Brancovan], 1876-1933; member of a noble Romanian family; she became a 'stylish and fashionable" poet.

Emmy **Destinn**, 1878-1930; Czechoslovakian-born opera singer, given the name Emmy Kittel at birth, she later adopted the name of her vocal teacher, Marie Loewes-Destinn.

Chick **Devlin**, 1909- ?; middleweight boxer; he also fought under the name Jack Devlin.

Spivvy [Spivy] **Devoe**, [Le Voe]; see Spivey's.

Thomas E. **Dewey**, 1902-1971; Thomas Dewey attended the University of Michigan the same years as Max, but was a class ahead; he later became governor of New York and presidential candidate in 1948.

Miss **De Witt**; no information.

Serge Pavlovich **Diaghilef**, [Diaghilev], 1872-1929; Russian impresario who founded and ran the Ballets Russes from 1909 to his death in 1929.

Marlene **Dietrich**, 1901-1992; German-born film star, known as a bisexual.

Countess Dorothy **di Frasse [Frasso]**, @1888-1954; hosted parties for Hollywood stars and others.

Mabel Ganson **Dodge** Luhan, 1879-1962; writer, married to Edwin Dodge, a wealthy New England businessman; Tony Luhan, a Native American; Maurice Sterne, and Carl Evans.

Donohue; probably Billy Donohue, a middleweight boxer, who had bouts in the San Francisco area in 1933; among his opponents was Tony Poloni.

Norman **Douglas**, 1868-1952; English author.

Tom **Douglas**, 1896-1978; film actor in the 1920s and 1930s.

Muriel Sanders **Draper**, 1886-1952; born in the United States as Muriel Gurden Sanders, she moved to London with her husband, Paul Draper [1886-1925], who was a concert singer; after Paul's death, Muriel and her two children, Paul II and Ruth, settled in New York City, where she became an interior decorator; she also was a writer and lecturer, and befriended many artists and authors.

Paul **Draper**, 1909-1996; the son of Muriel and Paul Draper, Paul II was a dancer.

Marcel **Duchamp**, 1887-1968; an artist, considered to be the father of the Dada movement and of post-modernism.

Isadora **Duncan**, 1878-1927; considered one of the founders of modern dance; named Dora Angela Duncan at birth, she died when her long scarf became entangled in the car's rear wheel, strangling her and breaking her neck.

Mary **Dunkers**; no information; according to Doris, she was a housecleaner for John and Clara.

Mme. **Durand**; no information.

Besse **Durbin** Harrell; 1891-1964; resident of Pioneer, Ohio, where she was switchboard operator and friend of the Ewings; her husband's name was Joseph.

Jeanne **Eagles,** 1894-1929; actor.

Elektra; Max's pet cat and the name of an opera written in 1909 by Richard Strauss [1864-1949].

Mischa **Elman**, 1891-1967; Russian-born violinist.

Larry **Elseworth**; no information.

Hotel **Elysee**, New York City hotel built in the 1920s on East 54th Street.

The Emperor Jones; a drama written in 1921 by Eugene O'Neill [1888-1953].

Edward Paul **England** III; social director at the Waldorf Astoria Hotel in Manhattan.

John **Erskine,** 1879-1951; educator, author, and musician.

Hobe [Hob] **Erwin**; interior decorator in New York City, later joined MGM as set director; he worked on such films as *Gone With the Wind* and *Dinner at Eight.*

Donald **Evans,** 1884-1921; American poet and author of "Sonnets from the Patagonian," 1914, which probably inspired Max to write "Sonnets from the Paranomasian," published ten years later.

Walker **Evans,** 1903-1975; photographer, writer, and translator.

Alvin Enoch [A. E.] **Ewing,** 1864-1945; a brother of John Ewing; A.E. married Carlotta Walkley Bailey.

Alice **Ewing,** 1874-1969; born as Alice Raymond, she married Frank Ewing, John's brother.

Burke **Ewing,** 1894-1974; oldest child of A.E. and Carlotta; he married Marjorie Elizabeth Kelley.

Doris Isabel **Ewing,** 1898-1998; the daughter of A.E. and Carlotta.

Frances B. **Ewing,** 1908-1975; the daughter of Frank Ewing, Frances was Max's cousin.

Marjorie Elizabeth Kelley **Ewing,** 1897-1964; Burke Ewing's wife.

John Caleb **Ewing,** 1867-1932; married Clara Barto; their only child was Max Ewing.

Harriet Edwards **Ewing,** 1898-1989; wife of Walkley Ewing.

Lotta [Carlotta] **Ewing,** 1870-1971; wife of Alvin E. Ewing [A.E.], brother of John Ewing.

Frances **Ewing,** 1908-1975; daughter of Frank and Alice Ewing.

Frank **Ewing,** 1901-1993; another of John Ewing's brothers; he married Alice Raymond.

Walkley **Ewing**, 1901-1993; A. E. and Carlotta's youngest child; he married Harriet Edwards.

Douglas **Fairbanks**, Jr., 1909-2000; following in the footsteps of his famous father, Douglas, Jr. was a film star in the 1920s and 1930s; he was Joan Crawford's first husband.

Michael **Farmer**; 1902-1975; a native of Ireland, he married Gloria Swanson in 1930; they were divorced in 1934.

Geraldine **Farrar**, 1882-1967; operatic soprano, who starred in a 1915 film version of *Carmen*; she was the wife of silent film actor, Lou Tellegen, from whom she was divorced, also was known as the lover of Crown Prince Wilhelm of Germany.

Larry **Fay**, 1888-1933; bootlegger and racketeer in New York City, Fay was murdered by Edward Maloney on January 3, 1933.

Peggy [Margaret] **Fears**, 1903-1994; Ziegfeld Follies showgirl and movie actor, she married Alfred C. Blumenthal.

Fellsmere: John and Clara owned municipal bonds issued by this Florida community.

Irene **Fenwick**; see Mrs. Lionel Barrymore.

Mrs. **Ferris** and Theo **Ferris**; John and Clara Ewing's friends from Jackson, Michigan.

Fieldston, New York; a wealthy neighborhood in Bronx.

Lettie Belle **Finkel**; an acquaintance of Max's and Clara's, Lettie lived in New York City and Hollywood; Max may be referring to Bella Finkel Muni [1898-1971], wife of stage and screen star Paul Muni [1895-1967].

Arthur Annesley Ronald **Firbank**, 1886-1926; English author.

The **Foujitas**: Leonard Tsugoharu Foujita, 1886-1978, and his wife; Leonard, a painter, was born in Japan.

Paul E. **Flato**, 1900-1999; jewelry designer on Fifth Avenue in New York City; he designed jewelry for many of the movie stars of the 1930s.

Hotel **Foyot**; a chic Parisian hotel with a popular restaurant.

Kay **Francis**, @1903-1968; film actor whose real name was Katherine Edwina Gibbs, her birth year varies from 1899 to 1911; she married Kenneth Mackenna.

Elaine **Freeman**; no information.

Donald **Friede**, 1901-1965; literary agent and editor for such firms as World Publishing and Doubleday.

Kenneth **Friede**,1910-1982; no additional information.

Furness Steamship Lines; founded by British-born Christopher Furness, 1852-1912.

Clark **Gable**, 1901-1960; Hollywood film star.

Lewis **Galantiere**, 1895-1977; wrote *Antigone* and other dramas for the stage.

Mary **Garden**, 1874-1967; Scottish-born operatic soprano.

Garden of Allah, an apartment complex on Sunset Boulevard in Los Angeles.

Garyflappers; a Gary Cooper fan club started by Max Ewing and patterned after the Gerryflappers.

Eva **Gauthier**, 1885-1958; mezzo-soprano who helped introduce jazz and oriental music to main-stream America.

Gerryflappers; the name given to fans of Geraldine Farrar, that is "flappers" who admired the operatic soprano.

George **Gershwin**, 1898-1937; pianist and composer.

Nellie M. **Gilpin**, 1889-1965; resident of Pioneer, Ohio.

John **Glenn**, [@1903- ?]; dancer.

Rube **Goldberg,** 1883-1970; cartoonist best known for his elaborate—and imaginary—contraptions that performed simple tasks.

Mrs. Sam **Goldwyn**; wife of Samuel Goldwyn of MGM.

Sam **Goldwyn**, @1879-1974; a native of Poland, he was the "G" in MGM.

Doddy [Josephine] Anderson Barto **Gonter** [Gonther], 1844-1934; Clara's mother, born in Wayne County, Ohio, Doddy lived in Pioneer since 1865; Clara resided in Doddy's house during the winter following her husband's death; Doddy died in Pioneer on July 16, 1934; her first husband, William Barto, was born in 1840 and died in Pioneer in 1873; Doddy married Adam Gonter five years after William's death.

Bonnie and Eugene **Goosens,** 1893-1962; Eugene, a native of England and an orchestra conductor; he was knighted and became Sir Goosens.

Taylor **Gordon**, 1893-1971; Black musician, singer, and performer; he was part of the Harlem Renaissance.

George **Gould**, of Beverly Hills, California; no additional information.

The **Gouldings**; no information.

Grand Street Follies, in 1928 the Follies presented a "topical review in two acts" at the Booth Theater in New York City; Max composed the music, including "Just a Little Love Song;" Albert Carroll and James Cagney were among the players; the *Follies* ran each year from 1924 to 1929.

Mrs. **Grant**; resident of Pioneer; no additional information.

Grupp's Gym; owned and operated at 2582 West 116th Street in New York City by William "Billy Grupp" [1879- ?] and used primarily as a place for boxers to train; Grupp was born in Germany.

Florette Seligman **Guggenheim**, @1871-1937; wife of Benjamin Guggenheim [1865-1912], who was lost aboard the *Titanic*.

Irene Rothschild **Guggenheim**, 1868-1954; husband of Solomon Robert Guggenheim.

Solomon Robert **Guggenheim**, 1861-1949; art collector whose legacy provided funds for the Guggenheim Museum of Art in New York City; the brother of Benjamin Guggenheim.

Texas **Guinan**, 1884-1933; born as Mary Louise Cecilia Guinan in Waco, Texas, she gave her name to the New York City speakeasy that she owned and operated.

Jesse F. **Hadley**, @1844-1917; Clara Barto worked at Hadley's store in Pioneer before she married John Ewing; he had a son named Frank.

Emily **Hahn**, 1905-1997; world traveler and author.

Andy **Haigh**, 1895-1973; a native of Michigan and music teacher.

Dorothy **Hall**, 1906-1953l film actor.

The Rody **Halls;** no information.

Tom **Hall;** no information.

Dick **Hammond**; no information.

Natalie Hays **Hammond**, 1904-1985; artist.

Adlai Ewing **Harbeck**, 1908-1991; a book illustrator and Max's distant cousin.

Jean **Harlow**, 1911-1938; film star who successfully made the transition from silents to talkies; born as Harlean Carpenter; she adopted her mother's name, Jean Harlow; the film star first married Charles McGrew [1904-?] when she was only 16; she next married Paul Bern [Levy], who a few months after their divorce killed himself [September 5, 1932]; Harlow's third marriage was to Harold Rosson [1895-1988], from whom she also was divorced. [One reference cites Bern as Harlow's husband's name, and another gives Levy.]

Rosalind E. **Harrison,** 1902-1980; a native of Michigan and later resident of New York City, Rosalind died in California.

Marsden **Hartley,** 1877-1943; American artist.

Baroness [Barono] Lili **Hatvany,** 1890-1967; playwright born in Germany; she also wrote plays under the name Christa Winslow.

Margaret **Hawkins**; no information.

Elizabeth **Hawes,** 1903-1971; American clothes designer.

Mrs. William Randolph **Hearst,** Jr.; her husband [1908-1993] was the son of the newspaper magnate, William Randolph Hearst [1864-1951]; William II was married three times, and Max probably is referring to the first one, a woman by the name of Alma Walker [1906-1979].

Dean Rulon **Heartwell** [Hartwell], 1896-1970; he and his wife, Nina, were residents of Burley, Idaho.

Jascha **Heifetz,** 1901-1987; Russian-born violinist.

Helen Anna **Held,** 1872-1918; Polish-born stage actor; she worked closely with Florenz Ziegfield.

Frieda **Hempel,** 1885-1955; a native of Germany, she was an opera singer and screen actor.

Mildred F. **Henry,** 1889-1975; Doris states that Mildred was Max's high school French teacher; later she taught French at Florida State College for Women in Tallahassee. In the 1940s she wrote to Carl Van Vechten that she often was a guest at the Ewing home in Pioneer.

Herm **Higley**, @1873-?; bank president and resident of Cambria Township in Hillsdale County, north of Pioneer; he was a friend of the Ewings.

Betsy **Hildreth;** no information.

Martin Thomas **Hodson,** 1855-1933; resident of Williams County, Ohio and owner of a store in the same building as John and Clara's first place of business.

Edith, @1897- ?, and Samuel Goodman **Hoffenstein**, 1890-1947; Samuel wrote humorous verse and prose and also was a screen writer.

Warren L. **Hogue**, @1862- ?; resident of Williams County, Ohio, and a physician.

Hollywood Roosevelt Hotel; 7000 Hollywood Boulevard; named for Theodore Roosevelt, the hotel opened in 1927; the first Academy Awards Ceremony was held here on May 19, 1929.

William **Holt**, 1865-1941; a judge in Williams County.

Libby **Holman,** 1905-1971; torch singer and social activist; she was a bisexual and led a "tabloid life."

Louise **Homer,** 1871-1947; born Louise Dilworth Beatty, she married the director Sidney Homer; Louise sang contralto in operas.

Miriam **Hopkins,** 1902-1972; film actor and wife of the author Austin Parker [1893-1938].

Hound and Horn, a literary magazine founded in 1927 by Lincoln Kirstein of Harvard University.

Ila May **Hoy**, @1895-1938; a nurse and Clara's caregiver in early 1934.

Langston **Hughes**, 1902-1967; novelist.

Elizabeth **Hull;** associated with the film industry; no additional information.

William **Hurlbut**, 1883-1957; playwright and screenwriter whose work included *Bride of Frankenstein* and *Lilies of the Field*.

David **Hutton**, 1901- ?; married Aimée Semple McPherson in 1931 and divorced her three years later.

Il Trovatore; opera written in 1852 by Giuseppe Verdi [1813-1901].

Imlac; a character in *Rasselas, Prince of Abyssinia*, by Dr. Samuel Johnson [1709-1784]; apparently used occasionally by Max Ewing as a pseudonym.

Indiphodi; a book of dramatic poems by the German author Gerhart Hauptmann [1862-1936].

Samuel **Insull**, 1859-1938; born in London, England, Insull became Thomas Edison's private secretary; he helped found General Electric Corporation and became very wealthy; he had lost everything by April 1932, when Chicago Consolidated went into receivership.

Peter **Jack,** born about 1896; Scottish-born, Jack around 1930 was a member of the faculty of the University of Michigan.

Elsie **Janis**, 1859-1956; born with the last name of Bierbauer. Elsie was a writer, actor, and composer.

Lady **Jean-Paul**; no information.

Diana **Jenkins**; no information.

[Lydia] Fae Masters **Johnson,** @1886-1935; the daughter of Clara Ewing's sister, Viola, and Viola's husband, Frank Masters; Fae and her husband, Junius Johnson [1882-1943], resided in California.

Dr. **Jones**; one of Clara Ewing's physicians; no additional information.

Robert Edmond **Jones**, 1887-1954; designer of stage sets.

Billy [William] **Justema**, 1905-1987; an artist who in 1933 painted Max's portrait.

Otto **Kahn**, 1867-1934; banker and financier.

Gertrude **Kappel**, 1884-1971; German-born soprano who appeared at the Metropolitan and other operatic settings.

Clyde **Kelly**; Max refers to him as an aspiring singer; no additional information.

Mrs. **Kelly**; a resident of Pioneer, Ohio, Mrs. Kelly assisted Clara Ewing in her household duties.

Mrs. **Kesler**, 1903-2004; resident of Pioneer.

Sarah **King**, [Sallie Marsh]; sister of Julia Hoyt.

Lincoln **Kirstein**, writer and impresario who helped establish the New York Ballet Company and the School of American Ballet; founded the literary magazine *Hound and Horn* at Harvard University in 1927.

Mr. and Mrs. **Knopf;** Alfred A. Knopf, 1892-1984, founder of the publishing company that issued Max's novel *Going Somewhere* in late 1932; his wife, Blanche Wolf [1894-1966]; became president of the firm.

Koo Koo, [Minnie Woolsey], 1880- ?; known as the Bird Girl because of her bird-like appearance, Minnie was a public figure in the mid-1930s; she had a non-speaking role in the 1932 film *Freaks*.

Fraulein Maria **Kopp**, @1888- ?; born in Switzerland, she lived in the same building as Max at 19 West 31st Street in Manhattan.

Elissa **Landi**, 1904-1948; born in Italy as Elizabeth-Marie Kuhnelt, Elissa acted on stage and in film, including *Man of Two Worlds* in 1934.

Lawrence **Langner**, 1890-1962; Welsh-born playwright, author and producer; married to Armina Marshall.

Ellery **Larsson** [Raymond Edward Francis Larsson], 1901-1991; Catholic poet, popular in the 1920s and 1930s.

Spivy **La Voe**; see Spivy's.

Mary **Lawton**; no information.

Georgette **Le Blanc**, 1875-1941; opera singer, known for her liaisons with Margaret Anderson [1886-1973]; also famous for her "scandalous" love affair with the author Maurice Maeterlinck before his divorce.

Francis **Lederer**, 1899-2000; born in Germany, Francis became a star in both silent and talking films.

Lorelei **Lee**, character in *Gentlemen Prefer Blondes*, a novel written in 1925 by Anita Loos [1881-1981] and turned into a stage production the next year.

Eva **Le Galliene**, 1899-1991; stage and film actor and lesbian.

Edgar F. **Leo**, 1877-?; a stock broker, Edgar was the husband of Rita Wellman; he took his own life some time before April 26, 1933.

Jimmy **Leopold;** no information.

Julien **Levy**, 1906-1981; Julien and his wife, Joella, owned a gallery that offered exhibits of modern paintings, photographs, drawings, and books at 602 Madison Avenue in New York City.

Libby-Owens [later Libby Owens Ford]; a glass manufacturing company in which the Ewings owned stock; its headquarters were in Toledo, Ohio.

Beatrice **Lillie**, 1894-1989; actor and singer, born in Canada as Constance Sylvia Munston.

Lindbergh baby, 1930-1932; Charles Lindbergh Jr., son of Charles [1902-1974] and Anne Morrow Lindbergh [1906-2001], who was kidnapped from the family home in Hopewell, New Jersey and held for ransom; his remains were found on May 12, 1932; Bruno Hauptmann, born in 1899, was convicted of the crime and executed in 1936.

Lorna **Lindsley**, 1889-1956; reporter and author of books on current events.

Little French Girl, a novel written in 1924 by Anne Douglas Sedgwick [1873-1935] and made into a movie the next year.

Beatrice **Locher**, 1903-1980; married to Bobby [Robert] Locher [@1889- ?], who was a decorator, designer, and magazine illustrator; Robert designed the cover for *Going Somewhere*.

Albert **Lockwood**, @1871- ?; Albert was on the faculty of the University of Michigan School of Music and head of the Piano Department.

Anita **Loos**, 1893-1981; author of *Gentlemen Prefer Blondes*, *Gigi*, and other scripts for stage and screen.

Mindred **Lord**, 1903-1955; writer, also known as Mindred Loeb.

Florence **Louchheim**, 1881-1976; her husband, Joseph Harry Louchheim, was a New York stockbroker.

Alfred **Lowden**, @1903- ?; no further information.

Ernest **Lubitsch**, 1892-1947; German-born director, including the Greta Garbo film *Ninotchka*.

Mrs. [Helen] **Lundeberg**, 1908-1999; an artist.

The **Lunts**; Alfred, 1892-1977, and his wife, Lynne Fontanne, 1887-1983; a well-known acting team, they were married for 55 years.

Helen **Lynch**, 1900-1965; actor in silent and talking films; she and Max dated while students at the University of Michigan.

George Platt **Lynes**, 1907-1955; photographer and homosexual.

Mattie **MacDonald**; possibly Mattie McDonald, @1889- ?, a Michigan native and in 1930 a resident of Macomb County, Michigan.

Alice Foote **MacDougall**, @1867-1945; owned a chain of coffee and waffle restaurants in New York; she was author of *Autobiography of a Businesswoman*.

William Eugene **MacCown** [McCown], @1899-1966; an American painter and author.

Kenneth **MacGowan**, 1888-1963; drama critic and stage producer who became story editor for RKO in Hollywood.

Aline **MacMahon**, 1899-1991; stage and film actor, best known for her character parts, she appeared in the *Grand Street Follies of 1924* and in the movie *Dragon Seed*.

Macon; this 785-foot dirigible arrived at its new hangar at Moffett Field in Los Angeles on October 16, 1933.

Maedchen in Uniform, a 1931 German film.

Lucy Cotton Thomas Ament Hahn **Magraw**, 1891-1948; see Lucy Cotton.

Everett Charles **Marcy**, 1904-1948; screenwriter.

Fania **Marinoff**, 1890-1971; Russian-born actor, married to Carl Van Vechten.

Sally/Sarah **Marsh**; see Sarah King.

Albert C. **Marshall**, @1837-1916, owner of a retail business on Main Street in Pioneer that John and Clara purchased not long after their marriage.

Maud **Massey**, Muriel Draper's maid.

Elsa **Maxwell**, 1883-1963; known for hosting parties for members of high society.

Perry D. **Maxwell**, 1879-1952; a professional golfer from Ardmore, Oklahoma.

Mayfair, a New York City hotel located in the theater district.

John **McAndrew**, 1904-1978; photographer and teacher at Vassar College in Poughkeepsie.

Henry **McBride**, 1867-1962; art critic for various periodicals.

Harold Fowler **McCormick**, 1872-1941; the son of Cyrus Hall McCormick [1809-1884], known for his development of a reaping machine; Harold's first wife was Edith Rockefeller and his second was Ganna Walska.

Charley **McDonald** [MacDonald] 1896-1980; well-known Hollywood fight promoter from 1931 to 1947.

Kenneth **McKenna**, 1899-1962; screenwriter.

Colin **McFee** [McPhee], 1900-1964; pianist, composer, and author.

Aimee Semple **McPherson**, 1890-1944; evangelist and founder of the Church of the Foursquare Gospel; she first married Robert Semple, then Harold McPherson, and, finally, David Hutton.

Nikolia **Medtner**, 1880-1951; Russian composer and pianist.

Joseph Willem **Mengelberg**, 1871-1951; a Dutch orchestra conductor.

Merlin office, New York; no information.

Edwin **Meyer**; no information.

Marcelle **Meyer**, 1897-1958, French pianist.

Roy **Meyers;** no information, but possibly the H. Meyers that Max references later.

Zion **Meyer**, 1898-1948; Hollywood movie producer, writer, and director.

Jo **Mielziner**, 1901-1976; set designer.

Marilyn **Miller**, 1898-1936; stage and film actor, born as Marilyn Reynold.

Kay **Mills** [male]; no information.

Sculptress **Mills**; no information.

Mindret Lord [Loeb]; see Mindret Loeb.

Eddie **Moeller**, 1892- ?; German-born photographer.

Phillip **Moeller**, 1880-1958; author and also associated with the Theater Guild.

Lois **Moran**, 1909-1990; silent and talking film and Broadway star, born as Lois Darlington Dowling; Timothy Moran, her mother's second husband, adopted Lois.

Marion **Morehouse**, 1906-1969; actor, model, and photographer; second wife of the poet Edward Estlin Cummings [e.e. cummings], 1894-1962].

Helen **Morris**; no information.

Lloyd R. **Morris**, 1893-1954; American-born author; his novel *This Circle of Flesh* was published in 1932.

William **Morris Agency**; "the largest and oldest talent and literary agent in the world" was established in New York City in 1898 by William Morris and was known then as William Morris, Vaudeville Agent; by 1930 William Morris Jr., had taken over management of the agency and opened an office in Los Angeles.

John **Mosher**; probably an editor at Crowell Publishing Co. in New York City, born in 1892, this John Mosher also was a playwright and author.

Jack **Moss**, 1906-1975; born as Jack Moscowitz, he was secretary and business manager to Gary Cooper early in the star's career; later he became a film producer.

Princess Violet [Violette] **Murat**, 1879- ?, a native of France; said to be a lesbian and addicted to drugs.

Pancho **Muratori** [Muraturi]; possibly Salvatore Muraturi, born in 1885.

Dudley **Murphy**, 1867-1968; director and writer.

Esther **Murphy** Strachey, 1897-1962; a "[p]olitical intellectual" [Watson, p. 188], Esther was the daughter of Patrick [@1870-1931] and Anna Murphy; Patrick was president of the Mark Cross Company; Esther was married John St. Loe Strachey [1901-1963], a British politician, from 1929 to 1933.

Noel **Murphy**; a singer and resident of France.

Music in the Air, a musical by Jerome Kern [1888-1945] and produced by Peggy Fears; it opened on Broadway on November 8, 1932 at the Alvin Theater, [New York] and ran for 342 performances.

Marguerite **Namara**, 1888-1974; opera singer and film actor who married the British actor Guy Reginald Bolton [1884-1979].

Alla **Nazimova**, 1879-1945; born Mariam Edez Adelaida Leventon in Russia, Nazimova became a well-known actor in silent films.

Robbie **Nederhoed**, 1891- ?; Dutch-born wife of William L. Nederhoed [1888-], who was also born in The Netherlands.

Pola **Negri**, 1895-1987; Polish born star of the silent screen who was unable to successfully make the move to talkies; she was married to Count Eugene Domsk [Dambski] and later to Prince Sergei Mdivani [1903-1936].

Ernest **Newman**, 1868-1959; English music critic.

[John] Kenyon **Nicholson**, 1896-1986; American playwright; his wife's name was Lucille.

[Sir] Harold George **Nicolson**, 1886-1968; born in Persia [Iran], Nicolson became a member of the British diplomatic corps; a homosexual, he married Vita Sackville-West, who also was homosexual.

Princess **Obolensky**; one-time lady-in-waiting to the Tsarina.

George **Oppenheimer**, 1900-1977; lyricist, composer, and writer for movies and television.

Paul [1901-1988] and Florence **Osborn** [@1901- ?]; Paul was a playwright and screen writer; he was a contemporary of Max's at the University of Michigan

Ignace **Paderewski**, 1860-1941; Polish-born concert pianist.

Freddy **Paine**, 1912-1999; operated a book store in New York City.

Tony **Paloni** [Poloni], 1907-1983; a prize fighter in the lightweight division.

Pantlind; a large hotel in downtown Grand Rapids, Michigan.

Austin **Parker**, 1893-1938; author and husband of Miriam Hopkins.

Douglas **Parmentier**, 1891-1967; president of a bank and a resident of Manhattan; his wife, Elsbeth, was six years younger .

Derek **Patmore**, 1908-1972; British author.

Eileen **Percy**, 1900-1973; born in Ireland, Eileen became a silent film star and also made a few talkies.

Pleyel Piano; manufacturer of keyboard instruments in Paris since 1807.

Francis **Picabia**, 1879-1953; French-born surrealist painter.

Jack **Pickford**, 1896-1933; actor, brother of Mary Pickford; born in Canada as John Smith.

Mary **Pickford**, 1893-1979; "America's Sweetheart," silent film star and wife of Douglas Fairbanks, Jr.; born in Canada as Gladys Marie Smith.

Pioneer, Williams County, Ohio; Max's hometown; a small farming community with about 900 residents, just south of Hillsdale County, Michigan, where many of his Ewing relatives resided.

Plaza Hotel; located at Fifth and Central Park Avenues in New York City, the hotel opened in 1907.

Princess Edmund de **Polignac** [Winnaretta Singer], 1865-1943; heir to the Singer Sewing Machine fortune, Winnaretta in 1893 married Prince Edward de Polignac [1834-1901], her second marriage.

Vivian **Pollock**; Jack Pollock's first wife. [Jack also mentions a Flora.]

Lily **Pons**, 1904-1976; French-born operatic soprano.

Cole **Porter**, 1891-1964; American composer and songwriter.

Seton **Porter**, 1882-1953; he formed National Distilleries in 1924 and was its President and later Chairman of the Board.

Prince George Hotel, located in New York City at the corner of Fifth Avenue and 28th Street.

Sergei **Prokofieff** [Prokofiev], 1891-1953; Russian-born composer.

Tony **Purdy**; no information.

Marion Walton **Putnam**, 1899-1996; artist and sculptor; she married Arthur J. Putnam, 1893-1966.

Nick **Putnam**, no information.

Samuel **Putnam**, 1892-1950; editor, translator, and author.

Sergei Vasilyevich **Rachmaninoff**, 1873-1943; Russian-born composer, pianist, and director.

Radio City Music Hall opened at Rockefeller Center in New York City about 1930; it was the result of the joint efforts of John D. Rockefeller, RCA, and S.L "Roxy" Rothafel.

George **Raft**, 1895-1980; film actor.

Rain, a 1932 film; in addition to Joan Crawford and Jeanne Eagles, the movie starred Walter Huston and Guy Kibbee.

Mr. **Rainey**, @1894-1964; probably William J. Rainey, program director at NBC radio in New York.

Rajne of Podakuta; possibly Podakkudi, the name of several villages in India; Rajne may have been an alternate spelling of Rani, wife of a Rajah.

Clem **Randolph**; no information.

Lady **Rathemere**, probably Lady [Lilian] Rothermere [1874-1937]; wife of Harold Harmsworth, Lord Rothermere, [1868-1940].

The **Raymonds**; no information.

Leonard 'Jack' **Renault** [Renaud], 1895-1967; Canada-born heavyweight boxer; his fights included two exhibition bouts with Jack Dempsey in Canada in July, 1922.

Gurth **Repp**, 1892-1961; a resident of Madison in Williams County, Repp purchased the Ewing store in Pioneer in May, 1934.

Jacques **Rigaut**, 1898-1929; French poet; he killed himself with a pistol shot through the heart.

Josie [Josephine/Joe] Mary **Bloyd**, 1889- ?, and Jacob Norman **Riste**, 1882-1933; residents of Battle Creek, Michigan; Josie owned and operated the Neumode Hosiery Shop in Battle Creek.

Ritz Tower Hotel, 455 Park Avenue in New York City; built in 1926.

Road #20; later referred to as U.S. 20, this major east-west highway preceded I-80 and ran through Ohio a few miles south of Pioneer.

Paul Bustill **Robeson**, 1898-1976; singer and actor.

Alice **Robinson**, @1896-1984; author [probable reference].

Carol **Robinson**, 1889-1979; pianist, piano teacher, and composer.

The **Rogers**; no information.

David **Rollins**, 1907-1997; film-actor.

Nikola **Romanoff** [Romanov] appears in Max's handwritten letter of July 1, 1926 and is identified as the Russian ambassador to England; however, the ambassador of record at that time was not a Romanoff.

Rita **Romilly** Benson, @1900-1980; stage actor.

Rosenbloom; possibly a reference to the boxer Maxie Rosenbloom, 1904-1976.

Cary **Ross**; writer, translator.

Howard **Rothschild**, 1907-1989; a member of the well-known banking family.

The **Rouses**; Harry and Sarah, residents of Williams County.

Roxy [Samuel Lionel Rothafel], 1881-1936; an impresario, Roxy was part owner of Radio City Music Hall at Rockefeller Center in New York City and he operated a chain of theaters throughout the country.

Arthur [Artur] **Rubenstein,** 1887-1982; Polish-American pianist.

Lillian **Russell**, 1861-1922; American stage actress and singer; her birth name was Helen Louise Leonard.

Ruth R.; probably Ruth Rutledge, @1914- ?; a resident of Pioneer, Ohio, Ruth was listed as a servant in the 1930 census.

Vita **Sackville-West**, 1892-1962; English novelist and poet; a lesbian, she married Harold Nicolson, who was gay.

Salome; opera, written in 1905 by Richard Strauss [1864-1949].

Frederic [Federico], 1902-1964 and Nina **Sanchez**, 1905-1990; Frederic, on the faculty of a California university in 1930, was Max's friend from their days at the University of Michigan; Nina was a librarian.

Anthony **Sansone**, 1905-1987; Italian-American body builder and model for painters, sculptors, and photographers; Max wrote that Anthony represented "the peak of physical perfection, who is the most renowned of sculptor's models. He is very anxious to come and see his likeness in my gallery!"

Marion Tiffany **Saportas**, 1895-1990; Martin Saportas [1896-1970], her former husband, who is referred to as "Jack" in Max's letters of March 6, 1933.

Sascha; probably Sascha Gorodnitzki, 1905-1986; a concert pianist.

Madame Elsa **Schiaparelli**, 1890-1973; Italian-born fashion designer.

Mrs. [Adeline] **Schulberg**, 1895-1977; owner of the Schulberg Agency in Hollywood, Adeline married B.P. Schulberg in 1913; they were divorced twenty years later; Kenneth Feldman later became her partner.

Schuler; possibly Frank Schuler, who boxed in the San Francisco area in the late 1890s.

Howard **Scott**, 1890-1970; he helped form Technical Alliance and Technocracy Incorporated.

Antonio **Scotti**, 1866-1936; Italian-born operatic basso; he retired in 1933.

Alexander **Scriabin** [Scriabine], 1872-1915; Russian-born pianist and composer.

The **Sebastians**; no information.

Gilbert Vivian **Seldes**, 1893-1970; journalist, author, and critic.

Myrtle Ewing **Shafer** [Shaffer], 1887-1976; resident of West Unity, Williams County, and a friend of the Ewings.

George Bernard **Shaw**, 1856-1950; Irish music, drama, and art critic; best known for his plays.

Norma **Shearer**, 1902-1983; movie star who was married to Irving Grant Thalberg [1899-1936] at the time of Max's letters; Thalberg was a Hollywood movie producer.

Roy, @1898 - ?, and Dorothy Butler **Sheldon**, @1900- ?; Roy was a sculptor.

Jean **Sibelius**, 1865-1957; Finnish-born composer.

Alexander **Siloti**, 1863-1945; Italian-born pianist and one of Max's keyboard tutors.

Charlie M. **Sisich,** 1898-1953; Jack Pollock's manager.

Edith [1887-1964], Osbert [1892-1969], and Sachervell [1897-1988], **Sitwell**; two British-born brothers and a sister who were recognized as poets, novelists, playwrights, and critics.

T. R. Smith, @1881- ?; editor-in-chief for the Boni & Liveright publishing company.

Snow Hill; a community that issued municipal bonds, some purchased by John and Clara Ewing; there are several towns with this name in the U.S.

Franz Emory **Solier**, 1884-1938; physician in Bryan, Williams County, Ohio; his wife's name was Louise [1886-1971], and Robert and George were their sons.

George **Solier**; @1858-1934; resident of Pioneer, Ohio, and owner of a dry goods store where John Ewing was employed early in his career. Franz Solier was George's son.

Robert H. **Solier**, 1909-1998; born in Pioneer, Ohio and the son of Franz and Louise Solier, Robert attended the Naval Academy in Annapolis, Maryland, and became an officer in the U.S. Navy. In 1932 Max and Franz drove to Annapolis for Robert's graduation.

Spitzer-Rorick Trust and Savings Bank, located in Toledo, Ohio.

Spivy's: possibly a reference to the home of Spivy Le Voe [1906-1971]; Spivy was a film actor and singer; Max wrote a song for her.

Barbara **Stanwyck**, 1907-1990; film star.

Gertrude **Stein**, 1874-1946; American writer whose salon in Paris attracted many artists and writers, including Hemingway, Picasso, and Braque; she composed the libretto for the opera *Four Saints in Three Acts*, which opened in February, 1934.

Ralph **Steiner**, 1899-1986; photographer and cinematographer.

Stephanie; an unidentified pianist.

Harold **Stern**, 1902-1983; orchestra leader.

Leonie **Sterner**, 1897-1985; a photographer, she was married to Harold Sterner [@1895- ?], who was an architect.

The **Stettheimers**; sisters Florine [1871-1944], Ettie [Henrietta], 1875-1955, and Carrie [@1878-?] and their mother Rosetta [@1850-1935] entertained artists and others at their Upper West Side apartment in New York City; Florine was an artist and one of Max's close friends; Ettie published two novels, and Carrie created a dollhouse complete with miniature furnishings and art works done by established artists; the dollhouse is on display at the Museum of the City of New York.

Emily **Stevens**, 1882-1928; a stage and screen actor, Emily committed suicide on January 3, 1928.

Wallace **Stevens**, 1879-1955; American attorney and poet.

Rosalie **Stewart**, 1800-1971; theatrical producer, she was born Rosalie Stewart Muckenfuss.

Lewis H. **Stoneham**, 1903-1945; one of Max's fellow students at the University of Michigan; Lewis graduated in 1923.

Hubert Julian **Stowitts**, 1892-1953; started as a dancer, later turned to painting and design, with special emphasis on India; generally went by his last name only.

Igor Fedorovich **Stravinsky**, 1882-1971; Russian-born composer whose works include "The Rite of Spring" and "Firebird."

The **Stumps**; John [1883-1960] and Mary Wortley Stump; see Mary Wortley for more information.

Tade [Tadeusz] **Styka**, 1889-1954; Polish-born artist.

Noel **Sullivan**, 1890-1956; his father, Francis J. Sullivan [1852-1930], was a successful attorney in San Francisco around 1900.

Margaret **Sullivan**, 1911-1960; film actor.

Gloria **Swanson**, 1897-1983; actor best known for her parts in silent films, but also for the portrayal of herself in *Sunset Boulevard*.

Clara H. **Sweet**, 1876-1947; a friend of John Ewing's family; born and died in Pioneer, but lived in Toledo many years; named administrator of the Ewing estate after Max's death.

Helen **Tag**, @1908-?; a resident of Adrian, Michigan.

Mrs. [Margaret L.] **Talmadge**, 1870-1933; mother of Norma Talmadge, who became a successful Hollywood figure.

Lilyan **Tashman**, 1899-1934; actor who made the transition from silent films to talkies; married twice, first to Al Lee and then Edmund Lowe; considered a "social leader" in Hollywood during the 1920s and early 1930s.

Dwight Bixby **Taylor**, 1902-1986; screen writer.

Pavel **Tchelietchoff** [Tchelitchew], 1898-1957; Russian surrealist painter.

Lou [Louis] **Tellegen**, 1881-1934; born as Isadore Louis Bernard Van Dommelem; early actor on the silent screen who appeared in the 1912 film *Queen Elizabeth* with Sarah Bernhardt [1844-1923]; Geraldine Farrar, the operatic soprano from whom he was divorced, was one of his five wives [1916-1920] Eva Casanova was another, Tellegen committed suicide.

Mary Louise Cecilia **Texas Guinan**, 1884-1933; film actor and owner of a popular speakeasy/night club in Manhattan

Virgie [Virgil] **Thompson**, 1896-1989; composer; he wrote the music for Four Saints in Three Acts, which opened in Hartford, Connecticut in February, 1934.

Lawrence **Tibbett**, 1896-1960; a baritone who appeared in many operas, starred in several movies, and sang at the Metropolitan Opera House in New York City, as well as other major American and European cities.

Princess **Toubetskoy;** apparently Max misspelled the name; see Princess Troubetzkoy, below.

George F. **Towne**, [Town] 1878-1954; resident of Camden, Hillsdale County, Michigan.

Iris **Tree**, 1897-1968; British poet.

Princess **Troubetzkoy**, 1863-1945; born in Virginia as Amelia Rives; married John Armstrong Chanler [@1863-?], from whom she was divorced and then in 1896 married Prince Pierre Troubetzkoy of Russia [1864-1936]; Princess Troubetzkoy was a writer.

Virginia **Tryon**, @1902- ?; Virginia graduated from the University of Michigan in 1923; although a year ahead of Max, they knew each other

Lenore **Ulric**, 1892-1970; star of stage and both silent and talking films.

Vadim **Uraneff**, 1895-1952; a native of Russia, who moved to California and was known primarily for his roles in horror films.

Lewis **Valentine**, @1881- ?; resident of Hillsdale County, Michigan.

Emily Davies **Vanderbilt**, 1903-1935; born the same year as Max, in 1923 she married William Henry Vanderbilt.

Mrs. [Schuyler] **Van Rensselaer**, 1851-1934; American-born Mariana Griswold married Schuyler Van Rensselaer [1845-1884]; she was an author and art and architectural critic.

Carl **Van Vechten**, 1880-1964; novelist and photographer, dance and music critic; known as a homosexual, he maintained a marriage of nearly 50 years to Russian-born actor Fania Marinoff [1890-1971].

Douane [Duane] **Van Vechten**, 1899-1977; Carl Van Vechten's niece, she was a noted artist in her own right and a patron of the arts.

Lupe **Velez**, 1908-1944; Mexican-born Hollywood movie star.

Vincent and Edington; a large and successful Hollywood talent agency, formed by Frank W. Vincent [1877-1946], and Harry E. Edington, [1888-1949].

Hans **Von Herwarth** [Hans Heinrich Herwarth von Bittenfeld], 1904-1999.

Prince **Von Lichtenein**, 1853-1938; Prince of Lichtenstein from 1929 to his death.

Waldorf Astoria Hotel was moved to 301 Park Avenue, New York City in 1931, after vacating its original building near 350 Fifth Avenue to make room for the Empire State Building.

A'lelia **Walker**, 1885-1931; only daughter of Madame C.J. Walker, [1867-1919; her full name was Sarah Breedlove McWilliams Walker]; A'lelia hosted a salon in Harlem during the Harlem Renaissance; she helped her build the Madame C.J. Walker Mfg. Co., founded in 1905; the company manufactured and marketed hair and beauty products to African-American women; Madame Walker became the first black millionaire in the United States and left her fortune to A'lelia, whose birth name was Lelia Robinson McWilliams; A'lelia married, in sequence, John Robinson, Wiley Wilson, and Dr. James Kennedy; she had an adopted daughter, Mae.

Jimmy [James John] **Walker**, 1881-1946; Mayor of New York City from 1926 to 1932.

Mina [Minna] **Wallis**, 1893-1986; one of the principals of the firm Curtiss & Wallis that handled such movie stars as Myrna Loy.

Phyllis **Walsh**; no information.

Ganna **Walska**, @1887-1984; Alexander Smith Cochran was her third husband and Harold McCormick her second; she was married six times in all; born as Hanna Puacz, Ganna became famous for her 37-acre gardens in Santa Barbara, California, which she named Lotusland.

Mrs. **Walton**; no information.

Fannie **Ward**, 1871-1952; star of the silent screen beginning in 1915.

Eddie **Wassermann** [Wasserman/Waterman], 1896- ?; possibly a New York stock broker.

Ruth **Waterbury**, 1896-1982; editor of *Movie Mirror*, a magazine for film enthusiasts.

Wauseon; a community of about 2,000 people in Fulton County, just east of Williams County, Ohio.

Mr. Alvine **Weber**, 1898-1978; teller with Spitzer-Rorick Bank in Toledo, Ohio.

Johnny **Weissmuller**, 1904-1984; Olympic swimming champion and movie star, best remembered for his role as Tarzan.

Rita **Wellman**, 1890-1965; playwright and author; she was married to Edgar Leo.

Mae **West**, 1893-1980; film star born as Mary Jane West.

Glenway **Westcott**, 1901-1987; American-born novelist.

Lloyd **Westcott**, 1907-1990; he was associated with a publishing firm in the early 1930s; later he became a dairy farmer in New Jersey.

Helen **Westley**, 1875-1942; stage and film star.

Ann Arbor **Wheelers**; William and Elizabeth Wheeler, both born about 1880; in 1920 William was Director of Music Department at the University of Michigan.

The **Whitalls**; James Whitall, 1888-1954, and his wife Mildred, 1888-1973.

Mrs. Paul **Whiteman** [Mildred Vanderhoff]; third wife of Paul Whiteman [1890-1967]; Paul organized and directed a popular orchestra.

Mrs. Harry Payne **Whitney** [Gertrude Vanderbilt], 1875-1942; patron of the arts and founder of the Whitney Museum.

Dorothy **Wilde**, 1895-1941; a niece of Oscar Wilde [1854-1900], Dolly was known for her lesbian leanings and as a 'woman about town."

President Woodrow **Wilson**; 1856-1924; President of the United States from 1913 to 1921.

The **Winslows**: Annadella [Anna Della], @1885- ?, an interior decorator; Annadella's father, Edward, 1859-1941; her mother, Elizabeth, 1862-1931; and sister, Martha, @1893- ?; the family resided in Fieldston, Bronx, New York.

J. [Joseph] Riford **Worth**, 1901-1951; a friend of the Ewings and the son of Sarah Riford Worth, who often was referred to as "Aunty Bird," though in fact she was not related to the Ewings; the Worths were from Benton Harbor and Grand Rapids, Michigan and later Minneapolis, Minnesota.

Mrs. Sarah Riford **Worth**, 1867-1934; see J. Riford Worth.

Mary **Wortley**, @1886- ?; a milliner, she worked as a clerk at the Ewing store and lived with John and Clara between 1910 and 1920; she married John Stump in 1921.

The **Wrightners**; husband and wife; no additional information.

Cobina **Wright** I, 1887-1976; newspaper columnist.

Anthony **Wrynn**, 1903- ?; American-born author and poet.

Elinor Morton Hoyt **Wylie**, 1883-1928; poet and novelist; married to Phillip Hichborn, then Horace Wylie, and finally William Rose Benet [1886-1950].

Princess **Xenia** [Zenia], 1875-1960; sister of Nicholas II and member of the Russian aristocracy; born as Princess Xenia Alexandrovna Scherbatova-Stroganova.

Wylie Ross Clark **Youmans**, 1898-1969; he was Assistant Cashier at a bank in Burley, Idaho; his wife, Bernice, lived from 1899 to 1984.

Giuseppe **Zangara**, 1900-1933; born in Italy, Zangara attempted to assassinate President Roosevelt on February 13, 1933, but missed and instead wounded the Mayor of Chicago, Anton Cermak, who later died from peritonitis; Zangara was executed on March 20, 1933.

Flo **Ziegfield**, 1867-1932; best known for his long-running series of revues, Ziegfield's Follies.

Appendix C: Yale University Max Ewing Collection

YALE UNIVERSITY

BEINECKE RARE BOOK AND MANUSCRIPT LIBRARY

PRELIMINARY SURVEY

MAX EWING [A.K.A. IMLAC?] MSS SURVEY

This is a survey done of materials in the Yale Collection of American Literature. Not all materials have been processed or itemized, but may be requested for the Public Services Desk.

Call number: Za Ewing [Unless otherwise specified in bracket]

(Note: * = See manuscripts card catalog for more information)

Principal Correspondents:

> Correspondence regarding Going Somewhere.
> Correspondence regarding On Looking At A Stained Glass Window.
> Family correspondence. 4 boxes. Note: There is a catalog of the family correspondence prepared by Mark Lutz stored with the correspondence.
>
> Ailes, Edgar H.
> Bishop, Frank
> Conrad, Lawrence and Roberta
> De la Mar, Alice
> Draper, Muriel
> Ewing, Doris
> Gordon, Taylor
> Henry, Mildred
> Larsson, Ellery
> Lynes, George P.
> McAfee, William John III

Osborn, Paul
Ross, Cary
Sheldon, Dorothy Butler
*Stein, Gertrude [Za Stein]
Stettheimer, Florine
Van Vechten, Carl
Waterman, Edward

Manuscripts:

Addressbook
The Americans Come. TS.
Caprioles In An Opera House. MS.
The Career Of Passionate Nalda
Carl Van Vechten—His Life And Works. TS.
Catalogue [Of Photographs Owned By Max Ewing]. TS.
Christening Service. MS.
Concerning The Eccentricity Of Thamar Tooting. TS.
Decadency In A Sacristan. MS.
Diary, 1916
Diary, 1917
Diary, 1918
Diary, 1933
Diary, 1934
Double Dealer. TS.
Elysium In Hell. MS.
Etes-Vous Polygame? Recording.
The Falling Star. TS.
Fifteen Impressions Or Reactions. MS/TS.
A Film Phenomenon. TS.
Food Of Love. TS.
For The Benefit. TS.

Gertrude Stein On Donald Angus. TS.
Going Somewhere. TS.
The Golden Girls. TS.
The Greatest Good. TS.
Grimalkin In An Aperture. MS.
Guest List. TS.
Imlac In America. TS.
Indipohdi. TS. [Max Ewing And Others]
An Intelligence Test. Recording.
Intelligence Test. TS.
Isn't It Awful? Recording.
James Caleb Ewing. TS.
Just A Little Love Song. MS.
The Kalsinjammers [?]. MS.
A Life Behind. TS.
List Of Books Read. Oct. 1920-1925. TS.
List Of Books Read. [N.D.]
List. Miscellaneous. MS/TS.
Me An Puppo. MS.
Midwinter. MS.
Much Ado About Baby. TS.
No One In Town. MS
Notebooks. (2)
Notes. ["Crickett-Wickett-Pick It…"] MS.
Notes. [First Lines Of Poems?] MS.
Notes. [Miscellaneous] MS.
On And Off The Isle Of Youe. MS.
On Looking At A Stained Glass Window In The U. Of M. Reading Room. MS.
[One Cannot] See The Technique For The Tears (?)]. MS.

One Through Two Springs. TS.
Out Of My Mind. TS.
Out Of My Mind, Book Ii: New York And Other Leopards. TS.
Picayunes: Nineteen Studies In Subtlety By Imlac. TS [Printed?]
The Poetry And Prose Of Glenway Wescott. TS.
Queen In Nictitation. TS.
Reminicsences And Hysterias. Recording.
Return Ticket. TS.
Salome In Spats. TS.
[Shakespeare. Dialogue For A Play Containing Various Shakespearian Characters.] MS.
[Songs.] TS.
Sonnets From Paranomasian. TS.
Sound Stuff And Nonsense In Schopenhauer's Aesthetics Of Music. TS.
Ten Cents A Block. TS.
Toodles And Old Puppo's Fight. MS.
Topaz In A Trance. TS.
Unicorn In Grammercy Park. Ts.
Trying To Get Along. TS
Vaudeville In The High Place. TS.
Wandering In A Phantasy. TS.
What Am I Worth? TS.
Where Nature Charms. [By Theo Ferris?] MS.
With Erato. MS.
Xanadunaian In Bas Relief. TS.

Other:

Conrad, Lawrence H. 3 TLS to Carl Van Vechten regarding Indipohdi
Contract: Going Somewhere. Alfred a Knopf, Inc.

*McAfee, William John III. Going Nowhere: A Study of Max Anderson Ewing. TS.

Supplement to catalog of extraordinary portraits.

Tucker, Jean. [Comments on Max Ewing's handwriting and the personality traits it reveals?] TS.

Wier, Marion Clyde. The Agamemnon of Aeschylus. Annotated by Max Ewing.

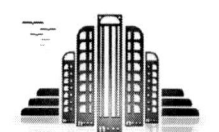

Other books by Dr. Ewing

Directory of People Northwest Ottawa County
Directory of Places Northwest Ottawa County
Directory of Businesses Northwest Ottawa County
Directory of Topics Northwest Ottawa County
Grand Haven Area 1860-1960 in Photographs
Grand Haven Area 1905-1975 in Vintage Postcards
Maritime Grand Haven
Then & Now Grand Haven Area
Slaves Soldiers Citizens African Americans in Northwest Ottawa County
From Home to Trench The Civil War Letters of Mack and Nan Ewing
Our People Their Stories Grand Haven Area
Ace in Spoken English (a textbook for Chinese university students)